Stars in Our Eyes

Stars in Our Eyes

The Star Phenomenon in the Contemporary Era

Edited by
Angela Ndalianis and Charlotte Henry

PRAEGER

Westport, Connecticut
London

Library of Congress Cataloging-in-Publication Data

Stars in our eyes: the star phenomenon in the contemporary era / edited by Angela
   Ndalianis and Charlotte Henry.
      p. cm.
   Includes bibliographical references and index.
   ISBN 0–275–97480–4 (alk. paper)
      1. Motion picture actors and actresses.   2. Celebrities.   I. Ndalianis, Angela, 1960–   II.
   Henry, Charlotte, 1970–
   PN1998.2.S695   2002
   791.43′028′0922—dc21   2001053081

British Library Cataloguing in Publication Data is available.

Library of Congress Catalog Card Number: 2001053081
ISBN: 0–275–97480–4

First published in 2002

Praeger Publishers, 88 Post Road West, Westport, CT 06881
An imprint of Greenwood Publishing Group, Inc.
www.praeger.com

Printed in the United States of America

∞™

The paper used in this book complies with the
Permanent Paper Standard issued by the National
Information Standards Organization (Z39.48–1984).

10 9 8 7 6 5 4 3 2 1

Acknowledgment

Publication of this work was assisted by a publication grant from the University of Melbourne.

Contents

Introduction

Angela Ndalianis

In an article that explores the cultural changes of our era, Francesco Guardini suggests that "a new form of 'monarchy' " has emerged in our time. The new kings and queens are "sports stars, music stars, models and supermodels" and they operate like a new aristocracy. The latter part of the twentieth century not only witnessed the birth of " 'true' Hollywood stars" but also royal stars like Princess Diana, supermodels like Linda Evangelista, sports stars like Magic Johnson, and computer game stars like Lara Croft. In our current times, even candidates to the American presidency seek legitimacy from the stars: Arnold Schwarzenegger, Barbra Streisand, Bruce Willis, and Madonna have been used by Republicans and Democrats alike to authenticate their political belief systems.

So obsessed is our culture with the media star, that new terms like "super-star" and "mega-star" have been coined in order to put in place a new and expanding hierarchy: those who are truly and specially "gifted" (the super and mega) now exist on a plane above the semi-gifted who continue to enter the ranks of stardom at an exponential (and, some would say, indiscriminate) rate. Contemporary society is saturated by media signs and representations that seek to glorify—and thus make economically viable—a diverse range of media personae.

Expanding on the pioneering work of writers like Richard Dyer (*Stars*) and the edited anthologies by Christine Gledhill (*Stardom: Industry of Desire*) and Jeremy Butler (*Star Texts: Image and Performance in Film and Television*), the chapters in this book focus on the star phenomenon of the post-1960s era. Whereas those texts placed heavy emphasis on pre-1960s cinematic

Lance Henriksen as Frank Black in the television series *Millennium*. ©
10-13/Fox TV/Jack Rowland (Kobal Collection).

celebrities, this anthology directs itself to ways in which the star system has become a more invasive and complex phenomenon within contemporary society, extending its impact beyond the cinema and disseminating multiple star signs through powerful new media forms such as the Internet. Dyer (1986), among others, has suggested that the star has, throughout the twentieth century, been primarily a phenomenon of the cinema (p. 70). Yet, in light of changes witnessed in the last four decades, this statement requires reconsideration. While acknowledging the continued dominance of the film star—and drawing on a variety of theoretical and critical models including semiotics, ideology, cultural studies, and ethnography—this anthology widens the parameters of the star system to include new celebrities who have captured the media's and the public's fascination.

The historical conditions allowing for the emergence of the star system have been well documented elsewhere by writers such as Richard de Cordova, Dyer, Gledhill, and Brian Gallagher; what follows, therefore, is a sketch of some of the key features that lay the foundations for the star system. Having its origins in nineteenth-century theater (Dyer, 1986, p. 102), it was the nickelodeon boom of around 1912 and, in particular, Carl Laemmle's now mythic promotion of Florence Lawrence as star that initiated the transformation of anonymous film personalities to named actor and star (Staiger, 1991, p. 3; de Cordova, 1991, p. 24). From this early period the dissemination of the image of the film star was the result not only of the film product but also the publicity and promotion that circulated around the celebrity, which included other media texts like film promotions, posters, and fan magazines.

Since its early cinema origins, and supported especially by the Hollywood studio structure that was to follow, the star system blossomed, becoming—along with genre—one of the major marketing tools of the industry. While star images were "made," disseminated, and controlled by the studios during the classical Hollywood period, the 1950s saw further transformations. This metamorphosis, which was epitomized by celebrities like Jimmy Stewart, marked a shift toward the "freelance film star" who was no longer attached to a single studio. Accompanied by increased individual control of their images by the actors themselves (Gallagher, n.p.), film stars had greater control over the films they chose to appear in, the studios they opted to work with, and the publicity that was distributed to audiences. As time passed, the star system underwent further changes that paralleled the cultural changes that accompanied the arrival of the 1960s.

Dyer (1986) has suggested, for example, that during the classical Hollywood period "stars were gods, heroes, models" who stood as "embodiments of ideal ways of behaving." More recently, however, they are less ideal and godlike and marked more by their ordinariness, having become "embodiments of typical ways of behaving" (p. 24). Indeed, in the 1990s and the first decade of this century this phenomenon has made itself felt quite dramatically in television shows like *E!* and *Entertainment Tonight* that highlight details—from the mundane to the outrageous—that inform the routine private and public lives of media personalities. In addition to relating the everyday experiences of these personalities (the marriage of Michael Douglas and Catherine Zeta-Jones; the risqué adventures of Hugh Grant; the tragic drug ordeals of Robert Downey Jr.), such shows expand the strata of stardom. The cult of personality is also included in the star model, with the result that a new hierarchy is set into place: the bottom of the scale is occupied by the personality who may (if worthy) rise to the level of star or, perhaps, even superstar. In addition, it is not the film actor alone who is the subject of such shows. Shows like *Entertainment Tonight* are indicative of the transformations that the star system has undergone: the parameters of stardom now also embrace the pop star, television star, sports star, and supermodel.

The star system was, and is, a pivotal device that drives the success of Hollywood cinema. In the last four decades, however, the star phenomenon has made its presence felt in multiple media areas. Gledhill has noted the "hegemony of Hollywood" with regard to its monopoly on stars, while also recognizing the extension of stardom, since the 1950s, away from the cinema and into areas such as the music industry and the sports world (p. xiii). Since 1991, however (the year Gledhill's anthology was published), the impact of this expansion has made itself felt all the more dramatically.

The restructuring of the Hollywood film industry along conglomerate lines since the 1960s has resulted in an underlying rationale that operates differently to the system of the pre-1960s era.[1] The industry is greatly, and economically, reliant on cross-media concerns and the image of the star follows a similar cross-media logic. With emphasis now being placed on horizontal rather than vertical integration, the entertainment industry's vested interest in computer game companies and television networks, in addition to the cinema, has resulted in an extension of the star system into these other areas of entertainment media. Likewise, conglomerate interest in the realm of the music industry, sports (ranging from football to World Championship Wrestling), and the fashion world has also learned a lesson or two from the marketing potential of the star system—a system that has always relied on expanding fascination with its products by developing public interest in individuals who magestically encapsulate the media form they represent.

Time Warner, for example, draws on numerous film stars as one publicity drawing card in order to attract audiences to film products that are released through its numerous film company ventures, including Warner Brothers, Orion Pictures, New Line Cinema, Castle Rock Entertainment, and Telepictures Productions. However, in the last two decades, Time Warner has radically diversified its commercial interests. Not only does Time Warner have stakes in television productions and companies like the WB television network but it also has financial investments in sports teams such as the Atlanta Braves (Major League baseball), the Atlanta Hawks (National Basketball Association), the Atlanta Thrashers (National Hockey League), and World Championship Wrestling.[2] Such diversification has resulted in the application and extension of the marketing principles of the film star system to other media concerns. The film, television, and sports icons have become one of the methods of attracting audiences to the Time Warner media spectrum. In addition, the $180 billion merger of America Online and Time Warner in January 2000 served to amplify the role of the Internet as a powerful tool for disseminating the Warner product—and the stars who appear in these products.[3]

Likewise, the rise in popularity of the "auteur theory," as elaborated in the French *politique des auteurs* and popularized by Andrew Sarris in the 1960s, highlights yet another development of the star system in the contemporary era. Riding on the success of auteurism, the film industry—in particular, in the wake of the "movie brat" film school generation of directors like Steven Spielberg, Francis Ford Coppola, Martin Scorsese, and George Lucas—recognized the marketing possibilities of elevating the more popular and successful Hollywood directors to the level of star. "A film directed by James Cameron" has become as big a drawing card as "a film starring Harrison Ford."[4]

In addition, the 1980s witnessed the advent of digital special effects technologies, which, as showcased in films like *The Abyss, Jurassic Park,* and *Star Wars: The Special Edition,* have resulted in the audience's obsession and fascination with special effects as stars of current cinema—a fascination echoed in the 2000 Academy Awards, which included Buzz Lightyear and Woody from the digital effects films *Toy Story* and *Toy Story 2* presenting one of the awards. Indeed, the increasing cross-media and more enveloping developments in the star system are highlighted and supported by a rise in the cross-disciplinary nature of stardom, a feature that has always been inherent to the star system (Gledhill, p. xiii). Since the 1980s, however, in addition to fan magazines and studio publicity, star icons have found their most potent form of dissemination on the Internet.

In the midst of all these considerations we are confronted with the fan. What makes a star a star for the fan? Dyer has highlighted the significant role played by charisma. Extending on Max Weber's definition of charisma for the purposes of political theory, he states that the term is defined as "a certain quality of an individual personality by virtue of which he [*sic*] is set apart from ordinary men and treated as [if] endowed with supernatural, superhuman or at least superficially exceptional qualities" (quoted in Gledhill, p. 57). A variety of factors—ranging from the performance skills of a particular actor, to industrial and marketing issues that can give rise to a star's meaning-production and public acceptance—come into play to generate this charisma.

Arnold Schwarzenegger is a star who is the recipient (although he does not know it) of my adoration. For me, he is a star. Yet the "meaning" that surrounds and is circulated around the persona of a star like Schwarzenegger is a culturally agreed upon meaning. Schwarzenegger is a star. As a product of the entertainment industry and his own scrupulous self-promotion, his image has been circulated widely through his films, entertainment magazines, the

Internet, bodybuilding magazines and competitions, and television. He is a box-office legend. The fact is, whether an individual does or does not want to embrace Schwarzenegger as star, he remains one because of cultural consensus.

But stars can also be very personal things. No matter how we try to theorize and understand the characteristics that lead to their production of meaning—historical, ideological, and cultural factors—they retain a mysterious quality that is difficult to articulate and quantify. And sometimes stars can "shine" and rise above the rest because of the way they interact and merge with an individual's subjectivity, producing meaning that is personal to him or her. Lying somewhere in the amorphous realm beyond cultural consensus, Lance Henriksen is such a star for me. That craggy, ragged face signals—for me—a complex human depth. This is a face that functions like a palimpsest, being layered with multiple meanings that speak of the range of contradictory states inherent in the human soul: from an actor who is capable of harsh brutality (as witnessed in his performances in *Hard Target* and *Near Dark*), to a fragile life form who searches for the meaning of humanity (*Aliens*), to a man of few words who literally carries humanity's fate and sins on his shoulders (*Millennium*). Henriksen's star status lies somewhere on the margins. His charisma and "specialness" are qualities that shine and emit an aura that remains personal to me.

In *Stars* Dyer posed a number of questions that centered on the meaning-production of stars, questions that dealt with the signification of stars, why they exist, their relationship to the social structure, and the ideological impact of their consumption. This anthology extends many of these questions, while also focusing on specific meanings that circulate around particular stars in our contemporary era. The book is separated into three sections: Individual Case Studies, The Cultural Impact of Star Images, and Directors and Characters as Stars. In Part I—Individual Case Studies—the chapters will explore issues of the star's appeal. How do they produce meaning? What is the relationship between stars and acting? What is the relationship between celebrities and society? Stars, it may be argued, often transcend their acting or character roles. Their persona explodes beyond the limits of a film, closely intersecting with their acting style while, in turn, also impacting on the broader social milieu. Through a series of case studies of film stars, the chapters in this first section examine—through diverse means—how stars acquire particular meaning within the context of specific historical moments.

In the chapter "The Misleading Man: Dennis Hopper," Adrian Martin investigates the complex network of signification that produces the persona that is Dennis Hopper. Basing his analysis on a range of theoretical and critical positions—including performance studies, cultural studies, and "star" studies—Martin considers Hopper the actor as a "sign": he may be a mass media construction, but more specifically, the star Dennis Hopper is also a product of his talents as actor and performer. Arguing that Hopper as star is the result of an "alchemical" mix that includes images produced by the film industry, film successes, issues of gender, and the cultural meaning of this actor as a sign of his times, Martin explores how Hopper's image has changed over time. Despite these transformations, enmeshed within Hopper's ability as an actor is his capacity to embody a cultural history that is reenacted in most of his roles: his work presents contemporary audiences with a retrospective of varied facets of the 1960s era. In Martin's words, Hopper is "less an emblem of the 1960s, frozen in time, than an embodiment of the continuing *legacy* of that era."

Focusing on Arnold Schwarzenegger, in "The Replicator: Starring Arnold Schwarzenegger as the Great Meme-Machine," Louise Krasniewicz and Michael Blitz examine the ways in which popular stars have an immediate impact on our lives. Not only can they "become reference points for our actions, our decision making, our thoughts" but they can even invade the space of our dreams. In an attempt to understand the cultural process by which the Schwarzenegger cultural icon is disseminated within the public and private sphere, Krasniewicz and Blitz employ the theoretical model of memetics, an interdisciplinary model that investigates how ideas that may seem trivial can develop and infiltrate many facets of our lives. The chapter argues that, relying on replication, memetics operates through imitation, reflecting a "human need to connect, communicate, share narratives, and make meanings" in order to "confirm our own humanity." In the last few decades, Schwarzenegger has played a significant role in this form of replication.

Greg M. Smith's chapter, "Choosing Silence: Robert De Niro and the Celebrity Interview," provides a study of the actor. The celebrity interview appears to offer the fan fairly unproblematic access to the real person behind the film star's image. Yet when Robert De Niro refuses to answer questions or even to give interviews at all, the assumptions regarding access to the "real" De Niro are called into question. Investigating the numerous articles in the popular press that feature De Niro avoiding interviews, Smith seeks to explain the discursive significance of this foregrounded silence. This silence has bearing on the nature of the film star, the American Method of film acting, and the literature concerning Western conceptions of the self. Searching between the gaps of silence, Smith concludes that, while refusing to talk about the psychological preparation that informs his roles, De Niro instead freely discusses the preparation his body undergoes, offering his body freely into the discourse. In addition, the verbal silence that reverberates through his interviews places De Niro in a powerful position that allows him relative control over his star persona, not only calling into play issues of the artifice of the Hollywood publicity machine in its fascination with (and economic reliance on) star production, but issues also of identity itself as a social construct.

The cultural and ideological ramifications of the star system have been studied in depth by Richard Dyer, Christine Gledhill, and Jackie Stacey. Developing on the research of these film academics, the chapters in the second part of this anthology—The Cultural Impact of Star Images—follow new avenues with regard to the cultural function served by stars. Focusing on Keanu

Reeves, in "The Keanu Effect—Stardom and the Landscape of the Acting Body: Los Angeles/Hollywood as Sight/Site" Carmel Giarratana asks why, despite consistently bad performances (or, at least, bad critical reviews), Keanu Reeves continues to be a star. Rather than investigating stardom from the perspective of fandom and economics, the chapter explores the actor's body as a site or discursive space that is akin to a landscape across which are imposed many discourses. Viewing Reeves's body as an empty landscape, Giarratana suggests that this allows directors, cinematographers, and viewers "to construct upon his 'star' features the richest of human geographies." Through a close analysis of Keanu Reeves's performance in *Speed*, it is argued that the film collapses the spectacle that is Los Angeles/Hollywood through and across the body of its star, providing the viewer with a complex array of dystopian, utopian, and heterotopian cultural spaces.

Moving away from the realm of film star, through an examination of Diana, Princess of Wales—and the efficiency of the media that made her a truly popular figure—in "More Sign Than Star: Diana, Death, and the Internet" Michael Punt examines the way many people used the occasion of her death to express a deeply felt grief. Like all stars Diana embodied the "rise to fame" mythos associated with film stardom, rising from ordinary person to princess, and inheriting the public scrutiny of the media as a result. Following an alternate path, Punt argues that, in the aftermath of Diana's death, it was the grieving public that was revealed as being the true star, transforming and shaping the "meaning" of Diana to its own cultural ends as critiques against dominant power structures. The chapter examines how ordinary people used the funeral for other, tangentially related purposes. Some of these uses meshed with a number of other recent trends that were evident in the popular success of the *X-Files*, conspiracy-theory bulletin boards, and slash fan fiction. Punt suggests that an understanding of the extraordinary intersection of determinants of the public grieving may lie with a perceived loss of intellectual and psychological control that is induced by the centralization of power and the efficiency of the media in gathering news.

Leonie Cooper's chapter, "Virtually Touching the Stars—from the Moon to Heaven's Gate and Beyond," shifts the focus of the star icon yet again, investigating the modern phenomenon of the astronaut as star. Exploring the parallels between celestial and media stars, Cooper maintains that, in conquering the celestial stars and opening the way for humanity to reach the previously unattainable, the astronaut of the 1960s (along with the NASA institution he represented) entered the constellation of media stars, thus attaining a public and cultural status not witnessed before. Through a close analysis of the Space Mirror Memorial at the Kennedy Center at Cape Canaveral (which frames itself in the context of the star figuration of the 1960s astronaut), the chapter examines how celestial bodies such as the moon functioned, and continue to function, as imaginary landscapes upon which the human desires and cultural visions of a virtual cosmology are being projected. From within the virtual realities of our terrestrial culture, the stars are the patterns of light that enact the contemporary human struggle to both transcend and affirm our limited, material point of view.

The focus of the final section of this anthology—Directors and Characters as Stars—follows two avenues. The first, through a close analysis of the director Sam Peckinpah, investigates the way the "auteur as star" complicates considerations of the cult of the star in contemporary cinema, functioning both in relation to, and in excess of, the star image of the actor. In "The Auteur as Star: Violence and Utopia in the Films of Sam Peckinpah," Gabrielle Murray focuses on the relationship of the director to the star system and the effects of the cult of the auteur on star studies. Peckinpah is a director who surrounded himself with stars like James Coburn, Jason Robards, and Steve McQueen and a loyal group of supporting actors that included Ernest Borgnine, Strother Martin, and Warren Oates. However, most discussions around his films fixate on Peckinpah's mastery of cinematic violence. It is as if these actors' individual personae are repressed, lost, or outshone by Peckinpah's directorial vision. Murray rebalances the focus on Peckinpah as auteur-star of violent aesthetics by analyzing the thematic and stylistic consistencies in his works. In particular, Murray explores Peckinpah's concerns with the human condition, finding a utopian impulse underlying his images of apocalyptic violence.

The final two chapters in this section explore the relationship between character and star. Gerald Mast has stated that "movie stars do not so much play characters (as stage actors do); they are the characters. The movie star capitalizes on an essential paradox of the movies—that they are fictional truths" (in Gallagher, n.p.). This relationship between character and star is explored via an alternative path: what happens when the character gives rise to the star rather than visa versa? In "Birth of a Hero: Rocky, Stallone, and Mythical Creation" Rikke Schubart analyzes the relationship that exists between the star and character roles. The fairy tale of Rocky, a down-and-out boxer who gets his once-in-a-lifetime shot at a title, has always been synonymous with the success of Sylvester Stallone, a broke, unemployed, ridiculed actor who wrote an Oscar-winning movie in three days, in the process creating a mythological superhero and becoming a worldwide box-office star in his first leading role. The public would forever confuse Rocky (and later Rambo) with Stallone, uniting fiction and actor into one persona. The character of Rocky was closely entangled in the myth of the American Dream, a myth Stallone himself believed in and one that inspired him when creating this character. Drawing on the writings of Northrop Frye, Schubart suggests that the mythic function that fused the character Rocky with the star persona of Stallone reached audiences on a cultural level, keeping the dream alive and connecting myth with social reality. Combining biographical research with textual analysis, this chapter analyzes the stardom of Stallone as one of those "pure" Hollywood moments where reality and fiction make a perfect fit, generating a star that influenced an entire generation.

Dyer has suggested that stars are like characters in stories but unlike characters they are also real people (p. 22). The final chapter argues that new effects
technologies and the entertainment media have transformed this assumption,
creating characters who are stars but not necessarily real people. The effects illusions that dominate much of contemporary entertainment media are indicative of the accelerated pace in which entertainment industries are transforming
as a result of new computer technologies. In the last decade this trait has
changed dramatically. In the chapter "Digital Stars in Our Eyes" Ndalianis argues that the human star has found a worthy opponent in the digital realm.
Digital effects such as the liquid-morphing terminator in *Terminator 2: Judgment Day*, the computer-generated dinosaurs of *Jurassic Park*, and the multiple digital characters in *Star Wars: The Phantom Menace* adopted starlike
qualities, sharing the screen space with human celebrities. In addition, we have
witnessed the emergence of digital characters such as Lara Croft of the *Tomb
Raider* series and the figures of the *Creatures* trilogy who populate computer
game spaces. While having their origins in a synthetic world, and while their
claim to fame is character based, these digital actors have had a dramatic cultural impact beyond their game narratives. These new media transformations
require a reconsideration and expansion of the parameters we establish to deliberate on what precisely constitutes a star. These digital creatures introduce a
new mystery to the star phenomenon: technological mystery.

NOTES

1. For an in-depth overview and analysis of the changes that affected the Hollywood system in the 1960s and beyond, see Wasko; Hillier; and Wyatt.

2. Other examples of Time Warner's diversification include the acquisition of the
broadcasting systems: Turner Broadcasting System, the WB Television Network and
WB Television Animation, Time Warner Cable, the CNN Networks, and Home Box
Office; the publications: *Time, Sports Illustrated, Fortune, Life, Entertainment
Weekly*, Warner Books, DC Comics, *Mad* magazine, and Time Life Inc.; the music
companies: Elektra Entertainment Group, WB Records, WEA Inc., and Maverick; re-
tail interests in: WB International Theaters, WB Studio Stores, WB Recreation Services, and WB Worldwide Licensing; and the theme parks: Six Flags and WB theme
parks. For detailed accounts of the Time Warner conglomerate and investments, see
Albuniak, D'Alessandro, Goldsmith, and "The Daly-Semel Years."

3. On the Time Warner/America Online merger, see Goldsmith, "America Online
and Time Warner Announce Framework for Agreements," and "America Online and
Time Warner Merge."

4. See Corrigan's excellent account of the contemporary period's fascination with
auteur as star.

REFERENCES

Albuniak, Paige. "New Media Moguls." *Broadcasting & Cable*. September (2000).

"America Online and Time Warner Announce Framework for Agreements." *PR Newswire*. April 7 (2000).

"America Online and Time Warner Merge to Create World's First Internet-age Media and Communications Company." *Business Wire*. January 10 (2000).

Butler, Jeremy G., ed. *Star Texts: Image and Performance in Film and Television*. Detroit: Wayne State University Press, 1991.

Corrigan, Timothy. *A Cinema without Walls: Movies and Culture after Vietnam*. London: Routledge, 1991.

D'Alessandro, Anthony. "The Urge to Merge." *Varity*. May 15 (2000).

"The Daly-Semel Years." *Variety*. July 19 (1999).

de Cordova, Richard. "The Emergence of the Star System in America." In Gledhill, Christine, ed., *Stardom: Industry of Desire*. London: Routledge, 1991: 30–39.

Dyer, Richard. *Stars*. London: British Film Institute, 1986.

Gallagher, Brian. "Some Historical Reflections on the Paradoxes of Stardom in the American Film Industry, 1910–1960." *Images: Journal of Film and Popular Culture*. March 3 (1997).

Gledhill, Christine. "Introduction." In Gledhill, Christine, ed., *Stardom: Industry of Desire*. London: Routledge, 1991.

Goldsmith, Jill. "Land of the Giants." *Variety*. May 15 (2000).

Guardini, Francesco. "Old and New, Modern and Postmodern: Baroque and Neobaroque." *McLuhan Studies* 4 (1996). Available at http://www.chass. utoronto.ca/mcluhan-studies/v1_iss4/1_4index.htm.

Hillier, Jim. *The New Hollywood*. London: Studio Vista, 1992.

Sarris, Andrew. *The American Cinema: Directors and Directions, 1929–1968*. New York: Dutton, 1968.

Stacey, Jackie. "Feminine Fascinations: Forms of Identification in Star-Audience Relations." In Gledhill, Christine, ed., *Stardom: Industry of Desire*. London: Routledge, 1991: 141–63.

Staiger, Janet. "Seeing Stars." In Gledhill, Christine, ed., *Stardom: Industry of Desire*. London: Routledge, 1991: 3–16.

Wasko, Janet. *Hollywood in the Information Age: Beyond the Silver Screen*. Oxford: Polity Press, 1994.

Wyatt, Justin. *High Concept: Movies and Marketing in Hollywood*. Austin: University of Texas Press, 1994.

Part I

Individual Case Studies

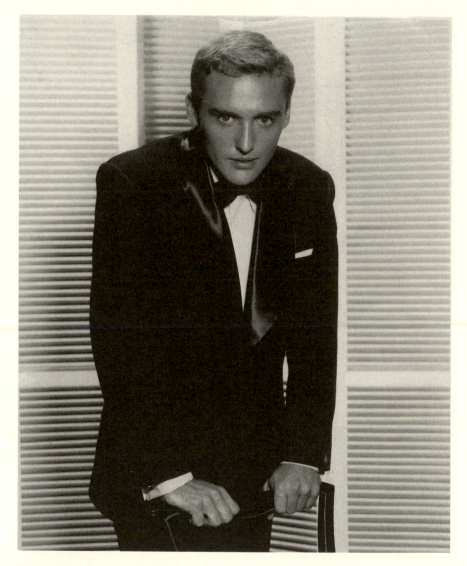

Dennis Hopper. © Kobal Collection.

———— Chapter 1 ————

The Misleading Man:
Dennis Hopper

Adrian Martin

As the new century begins, the man is almost 65 years old, with 50 years in the film business behind him. He is short, no neck, square, and solid, a little beefy, but still quite handsome, "well preserved" as the saying goes—so much so that a contemporary, who began as a teen actor in Hollywood only a few years before him, is now cast as his mother and, in another film, the futuristic plot contrives to pair him with a woman his own age but cryogenically suspended in her youthful beauty.[1]

What determines the parts that this actor gets to play on screen these days? It is an intricate, sometimes barely fathomable alchemy of factors: his potentialities and limitations—or at least how these are perceived and construed by the film industry; specific movie successes that suddenly give the actor a bankable association and create for him an "image"; the fact that any durable screen persona is usually a dynamic amalgam of various, even contradictory, facets that can be used and combined differently in film; how the actor's age and physique, at any given stage, mesh (or fail to mesh) with a certain repertoire of standardized, narrative movie "types"; the very particular relation he entertains in relation to his own gender—maybe at once the most obvious and most difficult "given" that any actor has to work with, in terms of what it both determines and allows; and, hovering over all of this, a certain hard-to-define, forever shifting, never completely articulated, but always powerfully influential force of the felt cultural meaning of this actor as some kind of vague icon, some sign of his times.

Dennis Hopper, a prolific, energetic, charismatic performer in A-grade and B-grade films alike, in popular cinema and in art cinema, and a ubiquitous, if "B-list" media celebrity, also comes loaded (more than most current actors) with a past—out of the 1950s: James Dean and *Giant* (1956); out of the 1960s: *Easy Rider* (1969), which he also directed, and then everything that follows these brilliant origins: the 1970s burnout (when, in fact, he never stopped working around the world) and the mid 1980s comeback, heralded by his role as Frank Booth in *Blue Velvet* (1986). As the years and decades roll by, the names, creators, and iconic figures with which Hopper is associated either on or off screen also shift and change in a dizzying procession: from Dean, Natalie Wood, Henry Hathaway, Curtis Harrington (*Night Tide*, 1961), and Roger Corman to Wim Wenders, Francis Ford Coppola, Alex Cox, Charles Bukowski, and William Burroughs; from David Lynch, Dean Stockwell, Neil Young, Christopher Walken, Quentin Tarantino, and Barbara Hershey to Sean Penn, Keanu Reeves, John Dahl, Jan DeBont, Abel Ferrara, Gary Oldman, and Kevin Costner.

His image changes too—most notably, of late, from the gothic, noir, and Tarantino associations of the 1980s and 1990s (*Blue Velvet; Red Rock West*, 1992; *True Romance*, 1993; and his own *The Hot Spot*, 1990), what he himself enthusiastically dubbed the "Blood Lust Snicker in Wide Screen" phenomenon, or the "new wave of violence in movies" (Hopper and Tarantino, pp. 13–14), to a closer identification in the general mediasphere with a role he had long played in real life. This is Hopper, the connoisseur and collector of modern art since his friendship with Dean; art photographer and painter; fixture of *Interview* magazine; distinguished (if quirky and sometimes deliberately self-mocking) talking head in numerous TV documentaries (on Duchamp, Warhol, and the UK series *This Is Modern Art*); and virtually second-degree "performance artist" in films of a much-touted wave of narrative features by celebrated New York artists (Julian Schnabel's *Basquiat*, 1996; and David Salle's *Search and Destroy*, aka *The Four Rules*, 1995).

His own work as director anticipated this trend: in *Backtrack* (1989, which also circulates in a butchered form as *Catchfire*), Jodie Foster plays an artist modeled on Jenny Holzer, whose "wall socket art" is decried and upstaged by Dennis, a sleek hit man. At the end of the 1990s, the disquieting B-movie *Michael Angel* (1999) brings together the psychosis of Booth with this carefully nurtured art world association: Hopper plays a serial killer whose artfully gruesome blood splatterings at the scenes of his crimes bring him perverse recognition as "a brilliant abstract expressionist." Tailored elegance—a far cry from the earlier, op-shop, cowboy-hippie look—comes to the forefront in the Hopper incarnation of the 1990s (it is a prime element in Schrader's *Witch Hunt*, 1995). Here his characters' costumes are increasingly supplied by Armani or Hugo Boss, and his haircuts are invariably short and sharp.

Bringing along these various associations to each new role of the 1980s and 1990s—and cast in part because of them—Hopper has faced the risk of becoming merely a "convocation of all that he had previously done . . . an emblem, a citation, a monument—to the point of becoming a museum piece." But, as Jean-Marc Lalanne goes on to comment in his analysis of the career of

Jean-Pierre Léaud, what such a process can overlook, obscure, and constrain is the emblematic figure's "extraordinary possibilities as an actor" (p. 55).

It is the aim of this chapter to speculate on the logic underpinning Hopper's career moves as an actor over the past two decades. Attempting to get the measure of who Hopper "is," to circumscribe his screen persona, will involve numerous sidelong comparisons with many contemporaneous male actors whom he most definitely is not. Of course, a critic is prone to find logic where, in the flow of an actor's life, there is only a volatile mixture of opportunity, advice, luck (good and bad), timetabling clashes, hunches, deals, projects honoring friendships, roles that establish working relationships and potentially allow future films to come to fruition, and maybe—somewhere, somehow through all of that—the fragile thread of a "vision."

Nonetheless, this chapter places its bets on the striking coherence of Hopper's films, when viewed from a particular angle. My study is placed at an improvised intersection of performance studies (James Naremore, Luc Moullet, John Flaus), cultural studies, "star" studies (Richard Dyer, Edgar Morin), textual studies of a "body too much" and its unsettling of the given relations between actor, star, and character (Jean-Louis Comolli, Lesley Stern, George Kouvaros), and the complex, synthetic work most recently undertaken by Nicole Brenez in her "figural" analyses of performers including Christopher Walken and Lon Chaney.[2] Biographical and journalistic material could also count for a lot in this attempt, but on this occasion, for the most part, I am placing such sources to one side.[3] And only fleeting allusions will be made to Hopper's fascinating directorial career, so far covering seven films from *Easy Rider* to *Chasers* (1994).

The chief impulse animating this chapter is that the consideration of an actor as a "sign"—within specific filmic texts or as a mass media construction—should never stray too far from the material particularities of what it is the actor actually does, on a set in the practice of a craft, or within the demanding framework of an ongoing career. All the same, there is an elaborate, "abstract" side to the public life and circulation of any screen star—a process usually spinning far beyond the actor's control—one that is as real in its effects as the material work of performing in front of a camera. This chapter will strive to keep a handle on both the abstract and concrete aspects of Dennis Hopper—to see him as he is, and for what he has achieved; and at the same time to think creatively about what kind of larger "system" he has served to generate.

Dennis Hopper is a creature, a product, of the 1960s—indelibly associated with that decade in the form in which it has been so relentlessly mythologized, de-mythologized, and re-mythologized by the mass media ever since (Martin, pp. 28–33).[4] Part of Hopper's appeal—in career terms, probably both a fortune and a curse—lies in the fact that he not only embodies a certain cultural history, but also must perpetually reenact it (in various explicit or implicit ways) in most of his roles. His work offers a way of remembering and negotiating the 1960s—or not remembering it at all, censoring it (memory and psychic

censorship being the key, twin themes of Abel Ferrara's *The Blackout*, 1997).
The shape of Hopper's recent career—1970s burnout, 1980s comeback,
1990s success—easily bolsters many different or contradictory versions of
what the 1960s might mean to us today, depending on which part of that narrative is stressed, how it is alluded to and reflected upon in any one of his films.
Hopper is, willy-nilly, the 1960s "without apology" or smothered in regret, a
post-Beat relic or a pre-punk role model, the living spirit of an era or its
haunted ghost. Through him, different social interest groups can work
out—in that strange, imaginative space provided by cinema—something of
their relation to the 1960s.

Other actors are similarly emblematic, like Hopper's *Easy Rider* confreres
Peter Fonda and Jack Nicholson, or the national stars created by the various
New Waves of the 1960s all around the world (Léaud, Lou Castel, Zbigniew
Cybulski, David Warner). But to none of these actors has the 1960s identification stuck so persistently or tenaciously. This has to do not only with the parts
that Hopper gets, but also the kind of vibe or sensibility he embodies and projects on screen. Hopper's abundant energy as a presence is an identifiably
1960s energy within standard pop culture lore: he is the rebel, the anarchist,
the good-hearted doper and drinker, the wild and crazy guy with a brimming
libido and a manic, instantly recognizable laugh.

Hopper's "countercultural" 1960s persona is nostalgically indulged in the
teen comedy *My Science Project* (1985) and the "trading places" plot of *Flashback* (1990)—not forgetting Altman's little-seen *O. C. & Stiggs* (1987), an
odd and chaotic homage to the juvenile anarchism of *Mad* magazine, Afro music, and Hopper's role in *Apocalypse Now* (1979). On another level, his persona
receives an upbeat, "back to the future" workout when projected into the radical, utopian, or dystopian worlds of *The American Way* (a.k.a. *Riders of the
Storm*, 1986) and *Space Truckers* (1996). These films, like *Waterworld* (1995),
deftly marry Hopper's trademark 1960s look with the punk "bricolage" or
"scavenger" mode of costume popularized by the *Mad Max* films.

But if Hopper sometimes carries with him the dream of the 1960s, he does
not ultimately embody a utopian yearning or aspiration. Failure, death-drives,
and burnout shadowed him from the start, from the James Dean association to
the inaugural moment of generational error—"we blew it"—in *Easy Rider*.
So, those Hopper dramas that involve explicit, sometimes elaborate references
to the 1960s—from his own *The Last Movie* (1971) and *Tracks* (1976) to
Apocalypse Now, *River's Edge* (1986), *The Indian Runner* (1991), and *Jesus'
Son* (1999)—are usually sad, ugly affairs, tales of genocide, cultural devasta-
tion, suicide, and betrayal. Hopper, in the long run, is less an emblem of the
1960s, frozen in time, than an embodiment of the continuing *legacy* of that
era, of the wear and tear visited by the vicissitudes of personal and public history upon its dreams and ideals, a living "test" of its ability to either survive as
inspiration, or die pathetically, as if to reveal its originary bankruptcy.

A project to which Hopper is reportedly currently attached as director, an adaptation of the novel *The Monkey Wrench Gang*, tackles a subject that has become popular since Lumet's *Running on Empty* (1988): What happened to the 1960s activists (here, a jolly, multicultural gang of nonviolent "eco-terrorists") who, 30 years later, are still dodging the law and hiding their identities, meanwhile trying to raise their own families and live like normal people? In such stories (*Flashback* provides another, low-key example), the 1960s figure is a form of "original sin" that is difficult to wash from one's soul.

The tele-film *Doublecrossed* (1991) elegantly offers, in the course of its true-life story of Barry Seal, the full melange of Hopper's 1960s-related images. He is "wild and crazy," lawless, reckless Dennis—a devil-may-care dope smuggler bonding with his best male friend as he pilots his plane into Latin American and Third World hot spots with abandon. He is manic, but not willfully self-destructive—fondly remembering how, in the "peace and love" days, drugs were merely used for pleasant "recreation."[5] Likewise, while he is a naturally anarchic soul, he is not deceitful or manipulative. "This may come as a surprise to you," he says to the government agents who eventually nab him, "but I'm an honest man." Finally, when government bureaucracies have left Seal out to dry, and even his best friend has gone down in a "last run," he drives ritually, stoically, to the place where he knows a rendezvous with death awaits him.

The 1960s "countercultural" legacy has had another, paradoxical outcome for Hopper as an actor. Like Rip Torn or Donald Sutherland, he has ended up often playing exactly the reverse of what his mythological association would decree: law enforcers (*Nails*, 1992; *Road Ends*, 1997), corporate "suits" (*Black Widow*, 1987), money men (the wealthy art buyer and Warhol patron Bruno Bischofberger in *Basquiat*). A certain mode of agitprop satire is clearly brought into play by such casting—although, by the 1990s, Hopper (like Sutherland) has "grown into" such roles so well, and on such a grand scale thanks to the success of *Speed* (1994), that the political irony may have altogether disappeared.[6]

Now, in popular perception, Hopper has probably become a standby "heavy" or villain, in either the cartoonish, highly artificial, and generic mode of *Waterworld* and *Super Mario Bros.* (1993), or the more naturalistic dramatic mode of *Paris Trout* (1991), where the actor (like James Woods in *Citizen Cohn*, 1992, and *Ghosts of Mississippi*, 1996), in one sense brings his countercultural days to a close by playing a full-out, viciously right-wing, murdering racist. What kind of satisfaction is involved for viewers in this paradoxical spectacle? A clue is provided by a video cover for *Paris Trout*, which bluntly advises its rental consumer: "If ever you wanted to hate someone, this is your man!"

Hopper comes to us these days as a figure of evil. But what complexion of evil is this, exactly? Although Hopper's villains can be shady and even omnipotent, it is hard to imagine him as the sort of cold, steely, Nietzschean intellectual portrayed (for example) by Jeremy Irons in *Die Hard with a Vengeance* (1995). The reason for this is simple: Hopper always plays men of impulse, driven beings. (Anti-intellectualism comes naturally to him: in *Search and Destroy* he rails against the "intellectuals" and "guardians of our culture" who trashed his last book; in *The Last Days of Frankie the Fly*, 1996, he sneers at an amateur filmmaker as "Mr. NYU"; in *Carried Away*, 1996, he upsets the "pompous assholes" of education administration; and in *Michael Angel* he advises: "Never hire a model who thinks she's an art critic.") His characters do not merely feel or express emotions—they are gripped, possessed by them.

The is reflected in the trancelike quality of many Hopper performances. His characters trust their feelings and are spurred into action by them; their only imaginable "program" is one powered by lust, greed or revenge, not by abstract principle. Even when Hopper mouths statements of "ideology" (as in *Paris Trout*), he delivers them in a glazed, robotic way, as if such rationalizations of pure emotion were simply for the benefit of the world, not the key to an animating, inner will. In *Blue Velvet*, Booth's extravagantly histrionic psychosis (manifested in bursts of violence, fabric fetishism, and ceaseless, bizarre verbal obscenities) resembles the exhibited symptoms of Tourette's Syndrome; it serves implicitly to "absolve him from guilt somewhat" (Routt and Routt, p. 51). We cannot exactly feel sorry or sympathetic for Booth or Trout, but at least we can intuit the pit of dark, twisted humanity that pushes them to the most extreme acts. In this sense, Hopper's persona, even at its sickest, is nonetheless "transparent" (a concept to which I shall return).

Is Dennis Hopper a good actor? This is the kind of question that film theory never asks—often because the texts it picks over are already canonized exemplars (from *Battleship Potemkin*, 1925, to *The Piano*, 1993); it is seemingly "beyond" such trivial nit-picking. Film reviewing, on the other hand, both asks and answers it all the time—but usually only to assert, in a sentence or two, that a given performer is great or lousy, charismatic or underwhelming, perfectly cast or miscast. The wide Sargasso Sea of film criticism in between seems most often afraid to attend to the particularities of the craft of acting, although those critics who do attempt it (from Manny Farber and Pauline Kael to Kathleen Murphy and Kent Jones) benefit from boldly walking this edge.

In the case of Hopper, there is an unfortunate, dimly understood myth or cliché that needs to be hurdled before any real study can begin. Hopper is caricatured in many places as a typical Method actor. In the annals of received, popular, media-fed wisdom, Method performers are in some sense not reflective, craft-based actors at all: they are unable to create any distance between themselves and their role; they immerse themselves in pure emotion; they "become" their parts through various rituals that are regularly the butt of lampooning, satirical jibes. A capsule entry in the *Time Out Film Guide* on *Tracks* summarizes this easy line on Hopper as an actor, calling his performance a "terminal piece of Method acting" (Pym, p. 840).

The image of Hopper as a Method-induced "raver" slides easily into the judgment that he is a bad actor—or, at the very least, an over-actor. Leonard Maltin's entry on *King of the Mountain* (1981) in his *Movie & Video Guide* determines that Hopper "overacts outrageously" (p. 739). Cult fans invert such a verdict, but tacitly agree with the terms of its evaluation, when they praise the actor's "excess," his spectacular circus turns that leap out of the narratives containing them. Tarantino's appreciation is typical:

One of your performances that's one of my favourites—it's a wacky, kooky performance—is in *The Glory Stompers* [1967]. I *loved* you in that. You know, that *is* the beginning of you as Frank Booth in *Blue Velvet* right there. . . . *The Glory Stompers* is really cool, because it looks like you're improvising it throughout the whole thing. . . . You have this one line which is *so* fucking funny in it: when you're fighting this guy, you beat him up, and then you look around and say: "Anybody got anything else to say? Turn it on, man, just turn it on." (Hopper and Tarantino, pp. 21–22)

Intimately related to the prevailing perception of Hopper as (whether gloriously or ingloriously) an out-of-control Method actor is the assumption that he only ever really plays "himself"—and that such a mode of performance constitutes his evident limit, his lack of "range" as an actor. There can be no doubt that Hopper is in the company of many American actors since the 1960s—including Warren Oates, Harry Dean Stanton and Harvey Keitel—who are cast as more or less singular, immediately recognizable screen "entities," used by filmmakers for their particular *schtick*, their familiar physical presence, mannerisms and intensity.

What are the limits of Hopper's acting range? It is true that, for instance—unlike Al Pacino, say—accents are not his bag. His adoption of different American idioms (as in *Frankie the Fly*) or a European lilt (*Basquiat*) sounds somewhat tentative. There is also the intriguing fact that Hopper is rarely cast in period pieces—when he is, the period is not very far away in time (*Paris Trout*) and is thus minimized as a constraining framework; or there is virtually no attempt to constrain or integrate the star's performance into the period (most spectacularly the case in the Australian bushranger Western *Mad Dog Morgan*, 1976). It is as if (like Léaud) Hopper is too much, too extravagantly "himself"—and also too much an emblem or mirror of present-day associations and idioms—to be accepted within the dramatic illusion of the historical film. (It is in this light that one can appreciate Scorsese's daring in casting Stanton, Keitel, Hershey, and Willem Dafoe in his quasi-experimental biblical project, *The Last Temptation of Christ*, 1988.)

Being perceived as always playing "oneself" in cinema means, essentially, being identified by a repertoire of mannerisms. No matter what the role, these mannerisms are going to tumble out and constitute some kind of show in itself, above and beyond the plot, style, and themes of any given film. Hopper's mannerisms (like those of Jeff Goldblum, Vincent Gallo, or Crispin Glover) are, without a doubt, prodigious. Physically, these include the following: his way of using hands (either fingers pointing or wielded as outstretched palms) and arms in broad, extravagant, punchy movements that underline key words and points that he speaks; his manic, nervy way of nodding, often with the entire top half of his body, and of shuffling from side to side, from foot to foot; his full-out register, involving bulging, wide-open eyes and shouting—usually reached via the vocal intermediary of an exasperated question asked in a raised pitch.

Verbally, Hopper's inventions (and clearly he has a creative hand in writing or rewriting a good number of them) could fill a large book. A degree of improvisation, stream-of-consciousness, or free association seems to govern the wildest linguistic flights in Hopper's *oeuvre* (and one must admit that, in the darkest late 1970s–early 1980s days of his career, there are flashes of utter dissociation and incomprehensibility on screen). Beyond the inescapable 1960s-era markers (the ubiquitous use of "man" as verbal punctuation), Hopper uses a Beat poetry– or jazz music–inspired way of breaking down and repeating the parts of a line in several phrases or sentences—"Get some money, man. Go! Get money!" (*Search and Destroy*); "New York actresses go there. That's the place actresses go" (*Frankie the Fly*)—and a wholly individual way of stressing or stretching out certain words or syllables in a phrase ("*home* is *where* you *haaang* yourself," *Eye of the Storm*, 1991).

Fanciful obscenity is an integral part of this verbal facility, as are the pithy catch phrases so beloved of contemporary American cinema ("do it for Van Gogh," "choose life," "learn to live with it"). The soliloquy in *The Blackout*—where his performance as the director of an audio-visual "happening" is based on personal memories of Nicholas Ray making *We Can't Go Home Again* (1973)—is classic Hopper at his most free-form, mannered, and exhibitionistic: "Since film, since film was too expensive for us, and we *video artists*, as we like to call ourselves, who're gonna regenerate the world, and pay for our own *film videos*, you know what I mean, *vidiots* that we are, *freaks* to the light, freaks to the light, freaks, freaks that record our own image, freaks that record our own image, man, whoa, alright, alright." But can all this pointing, yelling, and free-associative raving mean that Hopper is (like Timothy Carey) "undirectable," a personality that is just "let go" in front of a camera?

Every individual acting style—and, in extreme cases, specific acting performances—implies, allows, or encourages a certain *mise en scène* that will best render it. In practice, directors whose own personal styles are already strong and established either adapt their *mise en scène* to accommodate an actor, adapt that actor to accommodate the *mise en scène*, or deliberately set the two elements into a dialogical or conflictual relationship. (And this schematic, conceptual sketch of the directing process does not even begin to address the craft problems of blending diverse actors of different styles together.) Some filmmakers (Tony Scott in *True Romance* and Bigas Luna in *Reborn*, 1984) take a recognizably Godardian approach to capturing Hopper's physical mannerisms: they deliberately place bits of his body language (like his gesticulating hands) just beyond the boundaries of the frame, as if his energy can scarcely be contained there; or they shove him off-center or into zones of blur; or they film him from the back—strategies that fuel the image of Hopper as an actor of excess. Others (like Stephen Gyllenhaal in *Paris Trout*) carefully contain the familiar gestures and isolate them, using the pointing fingers and raised voice as "steps" or vectors within the dramaturgy of the scene. Many others clearly encourage a margin of improvisation from Hopper and simply (whether through aesthetic design, as in Ferrara's case, or a lack of it) "go wide" with their coverage.

The obvious fact that Hopper learns his lines and hits his marks in so many films (and that he ably guides others to do so in his own films) testifies beyond doubt to his professionalism and his ability to take direction.[7] More spectacularly, *Carried Away*, because of its vast difference from every other Hopper film, provides ample evidence of how "actorly," in a conventional sense, he can be, when cast boldly. Bruno Barreto's film is a melancholic, reflective portrait of a precarious rural community. It exhibits a sense of pacing and imagery that recalls the work of Terrence Malick (*Days of Heaven*, 1978) and Gary Sinise (*Miles from Home*, 1988). Hopper is cast "against type" here, as "a mediocre teacher and a worse farmer," visibly showing the strain of age. All of the actor's mannerisms have been pared back and his typical look (for the 1960s or for the 1990s) has been radically altered, via old-fashioned glasses, a pipe, and baggy, unglamorous costume. Instead, the role comes decked out with some classic signs of acting dexterity—such as the walking stick that Hopper uses to limp around on.

Hopper is a far more controlled and focused performer than he is sometimes taken to be—often, the excess and mania of the characters he plays are mistakenly assumed to be the excess and mania of the actor. One endlessly enthralling sign of Hopper's skill is his ability to listen to other actors who share a scene with him, how he registers this in silent reaction shots. This is a significant test of any actor: the famous encounter between Hopper and Walken in *True Romance*, for instance, is a model demonstration of different modes of listening. Walken (like Meryl Streep) is a histrionic listener; in every shot where he does not speak, he rolls his shoulders, widens and narrows his eyes, and looks ostentatiously around the room for reactions from his gang. Hopper, by contrast, is a supportive, ensemble player, intensely fixed (without freezing, as Robert De Niro or Herbert Marshall do) on the utterances, facial expressions, and overall body language of the other players. He performs listening with a director's instinct: his gaze, his gestures of touch, his relay of other actors' energy are all ways of aiding and guiding the essential dramaturgical "lines" of a scene.

From out of the 1960s, Hopper brought a brooding air of violence, often psychotically tinged (*Eye of the Storm* pivots on the unpredictable nature of his character's aggressive explosions), and also a difficult-to-manage kind of sexuality—latent qualities that David Lynch cannily made manifest in *Blue Velvet*. Not for Hopper was the middle-age career as "cheeky devil" or sly romantic that Nicholson has so fulsomely enjoyed and cannily guided from film to film. Hopper is often a solitary figure in his movies—no partner, no family, no "tribe." Sex scenes are strikingly rare in his filmography, and tend to be deliberately perverse or shocking when they do appear (as in *Blue Velvet*, *Backtrack*, *Carried Away*, and *Lured Innocence*, 1998). Kinky foreplay with Hopper, completely clothed, "directing" the action like an elegant, elder libertine, displaces sex scenes in *The Blackout* and *Michael Angel*. "Feel good" specials (like *Hoosiers*, 1986, and *Chattahoochee*, 1990)—in which Hopper reforms his self-destructive ways, overcomes his demons, integrates himself into a community, and succeeds or enables others to succeed—are rarer still.

All this implies that Hopper, although he is some kind of star, and regardless at times of his top billing in the credits, is rarely a "leading man," and almost never a hero (certainly not a romantic hero). By the same token, it still appears impossible for movies to slot him successfully into the standard roles available for older actors. As a prime example, Hopper never cuts it as a "straight" father figure. Logically or abstractly, as cultural symbol or emblem, he figures as a patriarch of a particularly dark, diseased sort—in the sense that his world of the 1960s begat the world with which younger characters underneath him now struggle (this sense is especially strong in *River's Edge*). But, specifically and concretely, once cast as an actual father, Hopper is either entirely dysfunctional, uncontrolled, and troublesome in this familial role (*Out of the Blue*, 1980; *The Pick-Up Artist*, 1987), or he is more like a strange brother, friend, or even double to his son (in *True Romance* he paternally kisses his son's fiancée and then muses to himself as they drive off that she "tastes like a peach"). Either way, he is rather "uncivilized" and uncivilizable, however lovably so—and that sets him apart from male stars ranging from Cary Grant to Harrison Ford. Many of the fascinations, contradictions, and complexities contained in Hopper's aggregate screen persona arise from the consequences of the simple fact that his very specific "maleness" is hard to place, or tame.

Blue Velvet is unquestionably the central event of Hopper's later career. The film gave him, simultaneously, an association with a burgeoning genre—the neo-*noir* erotic thriller—and an ambiguous, troubling, multiple role inside the genre's model scenario. On the one hand, *Blue Velvet* placed Hopper squarely into the "symbolic father" role of many a film noir: powerful, controlling, violent, the leader of a criminal mob or system, and, most importantly, intensely possessive of a younger woman. Invariably, his "claim" over that woman will be challenged by a younger man who enters this world and brings about its downfall—the classic, Oedipal triangle of father, mother, and son, with its in-built clash of generations and anxious inquiry into the brutal legacy of patriarchy.

It is a male-centred scenario, naturally—less unconscious, primal myth than easy, generic formula these days—and one that allows a standard dramatic ambiguity: Will the son overthrow the values of the father, or merely perpetuate them? Such a "family romance" triangle plays itself out, post–*Blue Velvet*, in

Eye of the Storm, *Midnight Heat* (1991), *Top of the World* (1997), *Paris Trout*, in the "subtext" of *Michael Angel* (where Hopper's nemesis is a sexually repressed priest), and as sci-comedy in *Space Truckers*. Even within this triangle, Hopper's position can shift: in *Backtrack* and *Freddie the Fly* he is the one who transgresses the "boss" and goes for the girl, either out of desire or an urge to save her (but in neither, interestingly, does he end up with this woman).

By the same token, Booth in *Blue Velvet* has a decidedly peculiar and unstable relation to his own sexual identity. In his famous, inaugural scene with Dorothy (Isabella Rossellini), he is both the "daddy" who barks commands and brutally beats his female slave, and the "baby" who "wants to fuck." In other words, he is both father and child, and whenever he switches roles he re-casts Dorothy as either daughter or mother.[8] However, Booth hardly seems to master (except through sudden violence) this circuit of identity-switching and sadistic-masochistic polarities. His apparent dominance in this perverse relationship is contradicted or complicated by his massive insecurity (he cannot bear to be looked at), his dependence on external stimulants (the blackly comic "reveal" of his oxygen mask), and his suggested impotence—as well as, in a later scene, a strong dose of homoerotic or polysexual desire.

Homosexuality (repressed or otherwise) will rarely pop up again in Hopper's subsequent screen persona. But childishness of various sorts will be everpresent. In *Black Widow*, his cameo as a rich magnate has him hovering over a child's toy whose controls he cannot comprehend, yelling: "I'm five fucking years old!" In *Doublecrossed* he is so childlike that the film cannot see its way clear to actually show a scene of Seal as an apparently devoted father interacting with his own children (and also so male centered that the film cannot successfully evoke his apparently happy marriage). *Paris Trout* is structured around short, intense, mysterious scenes of Hopper standing over his senile, comatose mother, anxiously asking, "Are you there?"—and finally deciding to kill her so as to "end all my connections with everything that came before" (an epitaph that would fit many Hopper characters). Retapping the gothic vein, Hopper as artist in *Michael Angel* howls like a vampire before a grotesque, self-made altar to his dead mother: "Why did you do this to me? You know I'm anemic again, Mother!" Only *Carried Away* shows Hopper in a tender, caring relationship with an aging mother.

Is there pathos in Hopper's aging screen persona? Yes, but not exactly the kind of raging, teary, tragic male pathos available to Nicholson in his riskiest dramatic parts (from *The King of Marvin Gardens*, 1972, to *The Crossing Guard*, 1995), De Niro (*Once Upon a Time in America*, 1984), or Nick Nolte (*The Prince of Tides*, 1991; *Affliction*, 1998; *The Thin Red Line*, 1998). Many of Hopper's roles in the 1980s and 1990s hark back to the sorts of parts Robert Mitchum took in his later years on screen: the once-glorious guy on a "last run," taking a last chance on a last job, as he reflects on passing time and the waning of his energies (*El Dorado*, 1967; *The Friends of Eddie Coyle*, 1973; *The Yakuza*, 1975; *Farewell, My Lovely*, 1975). The crime genre is a natural locus for such character-types, and Hopper has specialized in playing the small-time, low-life crook or operator—the "little man," the loser—in such films as *Boiling Point* (1993) and *Freddie the Fly* (the former gives him an immortal exit line, as he throws up his hands before a flank of cops and whines: "You never win!").

Male pathos slides easily into male comedy in Hopper's screen career. This gives him, especially for his age and given his tortuous personal and professional history, a lightness that we do not associate with, for instance, the "old age" roles of Jason Robards (*Magnolia*, 1999) or James Coburn (*Affliction*). There is one striking index of the comic dimension of Hopper's roles in the 1990s: it is hard to think of another actor of his vintage who is today glimpsed so often, and with so little glamour, in his underwear—*Frankie the Fly*, *Carried Away*, *Eye of the Storm*, and, in *Chasers*, a cameo as what Maltin calls a "perverted underwear salesman" (p. 233). Hopper's size serves the comic side of his acting well: the quick, agile movements he executes when walking, bending, nodding, ducking, or weaving build a quietly humorous and utterly infectious aura around his tough, little body (see the splendid set piece in *Doublecrossed* where Hopper "works a room" of stiff, static government agents, taking possession of all the theatrical possibilities of the crowded office space). It is through such lightness that Hopper connects, even in the midst of otherwise dramatic roles, with that hovering quality of childishness. A line from a brief, autobiographical memoir by Hopper is resonant: "I was Errol Flynn and Abbott and Costello" (Hopper, "Personal Bio").

There is a moment in *Blue Velvet* that is so odd (in itself, and within the system of the entire film) that few commentators seem to have processed it sufficiently to even mention it. It is at the end of the highly theatricalized scene in which Booth mingles with Ben (Dean Stockwell) and his weird hangers-on, stopping now and then to menace the captive Jeffrey (Kyle MacLachlan). Like many domestic settings in Lynch's cinema, the room in which all this takes place is disquietingly like a stage, with its curtains, its spectators, its various zones of action. Theatricality informs the fine detail of Lynch's *mise en scène*, too—especially the way he brings characters in and gets them out of such settings. So Booth, for instance, makes a dramatic "stage entrance" in the opening shot of this scene, walking determinedly into the frame and occupying its center. Many filmmakers use such subtly theatrical or histrionic inflections of an essentially naturalistic mode of staging. But Booth's exit, as rendered by Lynch, is truly strange and not in the least bit naturalistic: after yelling to no one in particular the conclusion of his obscene speech ("Let's fuck! I'll fuck anything that moooves!") as the camera moves in closer to him, he simply disappears, pops out of the scene like a cartoon character while the decor stays on screen, exactly as it was, for a second.

This violation of realistic norms is perhaps not so unusual if we consider Lynch as an artist who takes great care to give the screen presences of his actor-characters a "figural" dimension—that is, he is fascinated with the appearance and disappearance, the coming into being, of the people in his work—beings of shape, line, weight, volume, mass, reflections of light or darkness, absorbed to greater or lesser degrees into the phenomenal world around them. Hence we find the imagery in both *Blue Velvet* and *Lost Highway* (1997) of characters emerging from or blending into deep darkness—and their overall existence as veritable "machines," electrified, transmittable, sputtering into life and winding down as the cinematic apparatus itself does. In contemporary American cinema, only Abel Ferrara's work matches the intensity of Lynch's figural preoccupations. And both directors favor actors who lend themselves to, or seem to suggest, such figural distortions and transformations—see, for a magisterial example, the successive apparitions of Christopher Walken as a phantom for Ferrara, whether he is playing a gangster (*King of New York*, 1990; *The Funeral*, 1996) or literally a vampire (*The Addiction*, 1995).

Hopper (like Dafoe) serves both Lynch and Ferrara well because he is a *transparent* actor, a performer who is always solidly *there* in the moment, in the scene. That quality satisfies Lynch's taste for the excessive and the grotesque, as well as Ferrara's desire to emulate the Cassavetes tradition of seemingly "raw" performance. Transparency, however, is a dual quality, both in everyday language and in cinematic performance: it refers to a directness or one-dimensionality, as well as an opacity, a fading-away that allows a seeing-through. The transparent actor is fully present, and yet he is always on the verge of fading out, disappearing. This is, at least, how directors such as Lynch and Ferrara seize upon the screen possibilities of Hopper and Walken: their dual transparency allows them to be transformed into cinematic figures.

In the entire gamut of screen acting, we could compare the quality of transparency to something like irony or dissimulation—an actor's capacity to project, in the same moment, a multilayered complexity of masks, motives, and characteristics, a game in which something is shown on the surface and something else is hidden, revealed or suggested only fleetingly and subtly. In the case of predominantly naturalistic actors like Jeremy Irons (in films such as *Reversal of Fortune*, 1990, or *Dead Ringers*, 1988), this capacity to simultaneously show and suggest different traits affords a psychological depth that is meticulously crafted and lock-stepped with the overall thematic complexities, dramatic moves, and stylistic textures of the film. In a more pop tradition, the inherent attributes and box-office successes of certain actors lead them inexorably toward roles, in either action-drama or comedy modes, that exploit disguise, mimicry, and ceaseless outward transformation (Val Kilmer in *The Saint*, 1997; Robin Williams in *Mrs. Doubtfire*, 1993, and *Bicentennial Man*, 1999).

Hopper is good at what he calls "the switches" in a scene (Hopper and Tarantino, p. 20)—see, for instance, the wonderful split-second in *True Romance* when the mask of bravado on his face falls and then recomposes itself as Walken's back is momentarily turned. But he is an actor given, for the most part, neither to irony nor disguise. As a cinematic figure, however, his action is prodigious. How Lynch pictures Hopper in *Blue Velvet*—seizing the frame and then literally disappearing from it—sets the pattern for his presentation in many, far less ambitious films that come in its wake. Why exactly this should occur, consistently, from movie to movie is likely to remain a mystery, but the evidence on screen suggests that Hopper imports into a film, and prompts in its makers, not only certain *mise en scène* predilections but also a whole way of figuring and imagining his character.

Take, for instance, his manner of entering a frame, a room, a plot, or a film. It is often sudden, unannounced, ex nihilo—like his entrance into Dorothy's apartment in *Blue Velvet*. It is matter of genre, but also something peculiar to Hopper in that he often plays characters without a past, without evident family ties—a kind of impossible monad wandering in the eternal present of the film's narrative. Most particularly, there is a magical, menacing, phantom-like quality (reminiscent of Joseph Cotten's part in Hitchcock's *Shadow of a Doubt*, 1943) to the way Hopper often just "appears" in scenes: most often (in *Red Rock West* and *Paris Trout*) he is found behind doors, his gun at the ready. His exits from a narrative (when they do not have the finality of death, which is often) can be just as sudden, ghostly, and mysterious as his initial entrances, especially in *The Blackout*, where Hopper is all at once an elusive "showbiz" Svengali, a symbol of conscience (prompting the hero to remember via his videotapes), and a sinister angel of death.

A similarly curious, and intensely figural, aspect of Hopper's screen presence is the astonishing extent to which it comes to us literally "mediated" within narratives. Hopper's image is insistently filtered via TV transmissions, home video cameras, surveillance screens, and the like in *The American Way, Reborn, Search and Destroy, Freddie the Fly*, and *The Blackout*. In *Speed*, most of the communication between Hopper and Keanu Reeves passes by audio-visual relays (phones, a video feed). Hopper, the eternally disconnected monad, exists (like Lang's Dr. Mabuse) solipsistically in techno-control rooms (*Speed*) or editing suites (*The Blackout*); he appears to have no private life beyond those moments when he is incarnated (like Cronenberg's Dr. O'Blivion) on a closed set (*Search and Destroy*) or a public stage (*Reborn*) for a TV camera, a "media guru" for a new age. (Another actor's less extensive screen career follows a similar pattern: Eric Bogosian in *Special Effects*, 1984; *Talk Radio*, 1988; and *Gossip*, 2000.) This ephemerality of existence spreads to the structure of entire narratives in which Hopper fleetingly, intermittently appears and re-appears: no exposition helps us understand how he pops up in a hotel room (with a long-missing Beatrice Dalle), on a beach (shooting a sex movie or a rock video?), or in his edit suite for the penultimate moment of truth in *The Blackout*.

Sometimes, in these films, it seems as if Hopper's fictional reality is on the verge of spluttering or flickering out altogether, that he has been reduced to the thinnest transparency of an image, jammed or imploded within the circuitry of a machine (an evocation most intense within the fractured, layered forms of *Reborn* and *The Blackout*). Hopper, avant-garde star? *Night Tide*, with its ghostly filterings of a former underground's mytho-poetic mode into a genre-based fairy tale, introduced this dream (the prospect of a remake, involving Hopper, was floated in the 1990s); and, unsurprisingly, Hopper asserted at the end of the 1980s that his own *The Last Movie* "has got to be seen, and reconsidered, particularly by the MTV generation who will understand its non-linear structure" (quoted in Bishop, p. 38).

I would like to add a final note on the transparent, mystic writing pad that is Hopper. Some reviews of the Patricia Highsmith adaptation, *The Talented Mr. Ripley* (1999), mentioned the fact that, long before Matt Damon, the title role had once been incarnated by Alain Delon (in *Purple Noon*, 1960). What almost no one mentioned was that, in 1977, guided by a celebrated and sympathetic director, Hopper also played Ripley. Wim Wenders's *The American Friend* presents Ripley as (in Thomas Elsaesser's description) an "ingenue cowboy" who behaves with "glad-handed joviality" (p. 249). Hopper is once more deployed as a grand emblem—of America itself, its attractions and repulsions, its pop culture and shady, capitalist adventuring.

As invariably happens in the screen versions of Highsmith stories, what begins as a clear-cut opposition between two very different men (Ripley and Jonathan/Bruno Ganz) turns into a reciprocal and rather phantasmatic swapping of traits, in which the loosely wound, wandering narrative engineers what Elsaesser calls a "crisscrossing": "paths converging and overlapping and separating again, without ever joining and merging" (p. 250). As always in Wenders, paranoia over losing one's ground, forgetting one's borders, and ceding one's territory—whether personal, cultural, or national—gives way to an experience of suspension and intermingling, not without its moments of dread and suspicion, but for the most part tender (and, as in all this director's films about male friendship, quietly homoerotic).

Ripley, as created by Highsmith, is bound to be a curious and compelling cinematic figure. He is always bleeding into and absorbing "others," like a Zelig. He mimics them through shame, through ambition, through a sense of personal incompleteness; invariably, his real-life homages also lead, Rupert Pupkin style, to the need and the drive to murder those he envies and emulates. Ripley is the ultimate replacement killer—transparent, chameleon-like, so unlike a fully formed self, and yet so charismatic, so physically present, so cunning and graceful in his fast moves. He is so empty, and yet so driven by feeling, by will, by razor-sharp instinct. As the 1980s approached, Dennis Hopper had already found his archetypal role as the misleading man.

NOTES

1. Respectively, Julie Harris in *Carried Away* (1996), and *Space Truckers* (1996).

2. The journal *Cinematheque* has also published an ongoing series of actor studies.

3. Recently, the best-read account of Hopper as Hollywood's "bad boy" of the 1960s and '70s is to be found in Biskind (1998).

4. Parts of this chapter thoroughly revise and update the analysis as first presented.

5. This is a sentiment almost identical to the actor's own: "There was a time in the 1960s when it was all working. Then organized crime took over and drugs started working against us. But by that time we had become addicted" (quoted in Bishop, 1989, p. 39).

6. It is possible that Hopper's own politics had changed by the end of the 1980s, if one can presume to judge from statements like this: "I don't think America has any major foreign policy problems at the moment. There aren't any Contras in Nicaragua any more. Have you considered that George Bush is okay? That maybe he's a good President? . . . Nor am I down on nuclear power—I still think it can be made safe" (quoted in Bishop, 1989, p. 39).

7. Keifer Sutherland said: "I have never worked with an actor as co-operative and as helpful as Dennis. For example, he's taught me how to act in mastershot, so that when it comes to the close-ups I don't have to work so hard to get the shots to match. You only learn that from someone with Dennis' experience" (quoted in Bishop, 1989, p. 40).

8. For examples of this kind of analysis, see Creed (1988, p. 108).

REFERENCES

Bishop, Rod. "Flashback" (interviews with Hopper and Kiefer Sutherland). *Cinema Papers* 76 (December 1989).

Biskind, Peter. *Easy Riders, Raging Bulls: How the Sex 'n' Drugs 'n' Rock 'n' Roll Generation Saved Hollywood*. London: Bloomsbury, 1998.

Brenez, Nicole. *De la figure en général at du corps in particulier*. Brussels: De Boeck, 1998.

Comolli, Jean-Louis. "Historical Fiction: A Body Too Much." *Screen* 19, no.2 (1978).

Creed, Barbara. "A Journey through *Blue Velvet*: Film, Fantasy and the Female Spectator." *New Formations* 6 (Winter 1988).

Dyer, Richard. *Stars*. London: British Film Institute, 1979.

———. *Heavenly Bodies: Film Stars and Society*. London: British Film Institute/Macmillan, 1986.

Elsaesser, Thomas. "Spectators of Life: Time, Place, and Self in the Films of Wim Wenders." In Cook, Roger F., and Gert Gemünden, eds., *The Cinema of Wim Wenders: Image, Narrative, and the Postmodern Condition*. Detroit: Wayne State University Press, 1997.

Flaus, John. "Thanks for Your Heart, Bart." *Continuum* 5, no.2 (1992).

Hopper, Dennis. "Personal Bio." Available at http://www.geocities.com/~thecinemaniac/denbio2.html.

Hopper, Dennis, and Quentin Tarantino. "Blood Lust Snicker in Wide Screen." *Grand Street* 49 (Summer 1994).

Lalanne, Jean-Marc. "Léaud the First." *Cahiers du Cinéma* 509 (January 1997).

Maltin, Leonard. *Movie & Video Guide*. New York: Signet, 1999.

Martin, Adrian. "Dennis Hopper: Out of the Blue and into the Black." *Cinema Papers* 64 (July 1987): 28–33.

Morin, Edgar. *The Stars*. New York: Grove Press, 1960.

Moullet, Luc. *La Politique des Acteurs*. Paris: Editions de l'etoile, 1993.

Naremore, James. *Acting in the Cinema*. Berkeley: University of California Press, 1988.

Pym, John, ed. *Time Out Film Guide*. London: Penguin, 1997.

Routt, William, and Diane Routt. "*Blue Velvet*." *Cinema Papers* 62 (March 1987).

Stern, Lesley, and George Kouvaros, eds. *Falling for You: Essays on Cinema and Performance*. Sydney: Power Publications, 1999.

Arnold Schwarzenegger in *Conan the Barbarian* (John Milius, 1982). © De Laurentiis (Kobal Collection).

———— Chapter 2 ————

The Replicator: Starring Arnold Schwarzenegger as the Great Meme-Machine

Louise Krasniewicz and Michael Blitz

INTRODUCTION

Who is the biggest star of all? The designation usually does not go to artistic achievement but instead is associated with movie box-office clout: who commands the highest fee, whose films bring in the greatest profits, who generates the greatest frenzy from fans. Several film industry organizations confer titles on stars that designate this honor: star of the decade, star of the century, star of the universe. These awards have gone to celebrities like Harrison Ford, Tom Cruise, and Arnold Schwarzenegger. For a while in the 1980s and 1990s, Schwarzenegger was often called the biggest star, commanding up to $25 million per film, starring in blockbusters that not only earned hundreds of millions of dollars but also achieved iconic status, especially the Conan and Terminator films. But with middle age, Arnold's box-office popularity in action films is waning and he is at the end of his days as the biggest of stars. Or is he?

We want to suggest that the biggest stars of all are the ones whose influence steps off the screen and beyond the box office to become pervasive in every nook and cranny of our lives. They become reference points for our actions, our decision making, our thoughts, and sometimes even our dreams. They generate prototypes for behavior that affect what people read, view, and buy, where they vacation, how they have sex, and how they deal with crises. Yet in many ways, paying undue attention to these celebrities can be seen as an enormous waste of time, energy, and money. How can we explain this discrepancy?

We are not identifying a new phenomenon here: movie and television stars have always been reference points for society, inciting fashion trends, inspiring speech patterns, and inflicting moral codes often at odds with those of the common folk. Even early on, Hollywood was aware of its influence. In the 1920s a Hollywood style of casual outdoor clothes spread to even the smallest American towns, in the process revolutionizing casual clothing (Eckert, p. 33). In her analysis of female film audiences, Stacey has shown that fans identify with stars in a variety of ways and imitate their on-screen hairdos, speech, singing, dancing, body language, attitudes, smoking habits, and so on in their "production of self" (pp. 154–57). In current Hollywood practices, the parallel marketing of music CDs, toys, clothing, food, and other merchandise related to a film unapologetically foregrounds the practice of using stars as vehicles for other agendas.

But what *is* new are the opportunities available to stars to extend their influence far beyond their status as cultural icons that function as desired objects or fashion models. Unlike most of the rest of us, stars have access to both public and private realms and media tools that can reach unprecedented numbers and types of people. How and why this happens is the subject of this chapter. We will explicate not just the particulars of a big star's success, but also will address the larger question of why we, as a culture, even have the category of stars in the first place.

THE END OF THE DAZE

There are a lot fewer of these movie idols than box-office receipts might suggest, and Arnold Schwarzenegger, we will argue, is one of the most significant ones. There have always been numerous angles to our research on Arnold Schwarzenegger, the cultural icon: Arnold as film superstar, political figure, generator of catch phrases ("I'll be back!" and "Hasta la vista, baby!"), purveyor of male reproduction, possible Nazi sympathizer, champion bodybuilder, famous in-law, fitness czar, commercial entrepreneur, and the embodiment of the American Dream. In order to bring these strands together, we have tried numerous approaches to studying Arnold, trying to understand how he came to be one of the scales against which we measured our highest values and principles, and why at the start of the twenty-first century we have created a culture that always seems to have a prominent place for him.

Arnold's ability to insinuate himself into any discourse or any metaphoric moment or any narrative thread is a remarkable feature of his stardom that we want to both observe and analyze. While we are certainly interested in how the particular person—the Arnold Schwarzenegger–immigrant–body builder– movie star—got transformed into a cultural icon, we are more concerned with the cultural process by which ideas about such an icon get circulated, recycled, reinterpreted, and incorporated into, for example, impossibly overbuilt and powerful bodies or shifted mindsets and attitudes.

We also want to bring studies of stars and celebrities back into the realm of ethnographic analysis, connecting notions about stars to social actions, showing, as anthropologist Clifford Geertz once said, "that cultural forms find articulation" (p. 17) in behavior. It is important to talk about stars not as an abstract category but as a real-world phenomenon that has consequences for everyday thoughts and decisions and actions. When we say that stars invade our dreams, we are talking literally as well as metaphorically. Because of this interest in developing a comprehensive, multidimensional study of celebrities, we want to propose a new approach to the study of stars that uses the emerging field of memetics to understand how and why stars come to be, and especially how some element of their stardom ends up invading multiple aspects of our lives.

Memetics, says Richard Brodie in *Virus of the Mind*, one of the first books to popularize the subject, is the "study of the working of memes: how they interact, replicate and evolve" (1996 p. 26). "Memes" is the term given by memetics to the basic units of culture that are transmitted by imitation and shared in the form of cultural knowledge. Memes are the plans or instructions or blueprints for creating, sharing, and dispersing what have been called the "memorable units" that human beings feel compelled to pass on to others (p. 30). We have thought of this form of transmission as "Lamarckian" (horizontal evolution by acquisition) but most scholars in memetics describe it as an exchange of instructions for carrying out cultural behavior (Blackmore, 1999, p. 62). The direction of transmission for memetics is claimed to be "predominantly horizontal" (Blackmore, p. 34), that is, it is not acquired by successive generations but is spread over large cultural entities at the same time, replacing or forcing out other cultural elements that may want to occupy the same cultural category or "space." But we believe that in an era of mass communication, transmission and reception are indistinguishable, spreading weblike up, down, and across generations and through the spaces they occupy. It is, Dennett says, "promiscuous," leaping from "vehicle to vehicle, and from medium to medium" (1995, p. 347).

Memetics is being called the interdisciplinary study of how "the mind works, the way people learn and grow, the way culture progresses" (Brodie, *Meme Central*, n.p.). It attempts to explain cultural changes over time in "evolutionary" terms (but not necessarily via biological evolution, as we shall see). Memetics tries to connect cognitive processes with social behavior as well as larger cultural developments; at various points in Brodie's book memetics is said to be the scientific theory unifying or even transcending such disciplines as biology, psychology, political science, anthropology, and the cognitive sciences.

Memetics is also called the "evolutionary model of information transmission" by the first academic journal of the field, *Journal of Memetics*.[1] Memetics deals with the spread of ideas via various vehicles, especially the human mind, but also various mechanical media, both old and new. For this reason the most popular version of memetics has used the concept of "viruses of the mind" to convey the notion that ideas and information are spread like a virus, often without our conscious effort or understanding—as is attested to by Richard Brodie's Web site and book that warn, "This book contains a live mind virus. Do not read further unless you are willing to be infected. The infection may affect the way you think in subtle and not-so-subtle ways—or even turn your current world view inside out" (*Meme Central* and *Virus of the Mind*).

Few academic disciplines besides anthropology and perhaps psychology have attempted such a comprehensive approach to explaining the whole range and evolution of human behaviors, especially those behaviors deemed nonproductive and inessential like celebrity worship. Anthropologists traditionally explained such nonproductive and nonreproductive behavior through the analysis of symbol systems, shared cognitive structures, cultural metaphors, ritual and myths, and all the other rich aspects of behavior that are peculiar to Homo sapiens. But when the field of academic anthropology essentially abandoned its comprehensive approach[2] to the study of human behavior, it paved the way for other researchers to take up the challenge of explaining why humans engage in behaviors that seem to have no practical purpose and do not contribute to their immediate welfare, advancement, wealth, reproductive success, or happiness.

When anthropology turned to models that claimed all human behavior conferred either an economic or biological advantage, it lost its ability to explain all the oddities of human behavior (including the worship of stars). As we shall see, there is no good economic or reproductive reason to worship a star, but there are plenty of good memetic reasons for it. In fact, the proof of the value of memetics, says Susan Blackmore, is what it can tell us about the subjects, like Arnold Schwarzenegger and celebrity culture, that we eventually define as trivial (1999, p. 184).[3] We are trying memetics instead of standard approaches like those in anthropology, film, or cultural studies because it promises something that the others do not: a way to explain the widespread and intensive penetration of some ideas, trends, and bits of action that do not seem to provide any benefit, advantage, or power to those who actually use and spread them (as opposed to those who, like agents, lawyers, and the stars themselves, might originate them).

While memetics is a form of evolutionary theory, its practitioners do not necessarily align themselves with biological, Darwinian evolution. Memetics is fond of pointing out that Darwinian evolution, based on natural selection and differential survival and reproduction of physical beings, is only one particular form of evolution and not the model for all forms of change over time. Natural selection relies on notions of a biological or reproductive advantage conferred on an entity because of some feature. Memetics is not about some biological advantage but rather the ability of a feature of culture to get itself replicated and spread well beyond its origins and practical purposes.

The process of replication in memetics is via imitation (Blackmore, p. 43). We pass on behaviors to others because they see, hear, or read about that behavior and for various reasons imitate and replicate it, sometimes faithfully, sometimes not. This is, of course, a classic idea of anthropology and memetics does, in fact, borrow more ideas from cultural evolutionary theories than it does from biological models.[4] This makes it a theory that is both retrograde and at the same time potentially revolutionary, for the return to cultural models, after years of the predominance of biological determinism in the social sciences (i.e., sociobiology and other models that say behavior is hardwired into either our brains or our genes) is a welcome change.

A sociobiological explanation of a phenomenon like Schwarzenegger might result in statements like, "We think that if we are like Arnold we will have a better chance of producing more offspring who will have a better chance of surviving and passing on our genes." Explaining it by cultural memetics would result in an understanding of why we use inordinate amounts of time and money perfecting an Austrian accent, pumping our muscles, going to violent and often bad movies, and reading magazine articles, tabloids, and newspaper accounts of our favorite, the Terminator. The purpose of all this, we will suggest, comes from the human need to connect, communicate, share narratives, and make meanings, not some animal drive to make little Terminators. It is the drama, as Donna Haraway has called it, of "touch across Difference," the desire to have contact with others in order to confirm our own humanity (1989, p. 149) combined with the fantasy of perfect communication and the "immediate sharing of meanings" (p. 135) that is always desired when humans come face to face.

While we do not subscribe to the entire range of memetic forms or theoretical directions, we do find it a useful approach for this subject. If memetics can help explain this phenomenon of star influence, it will be a valuable tool in the study of celebrity and culture. If the star culture can illuminate the sometimes murky field of memetics, all the better; it may provide a valuable tool for understanding such a pervasive and impressively influential cultural phenomenon.

MEMES

The unit of transmission for memetics is the "meme." The meme is "a contagious idea competing for a share of our minds," as Brodie describes it (*Meme Central*). Think of the meme as a catch phrase that automatically gets repeated ("I'll be back!"), or an accent that gets imitated (Ahnuld!), or a metaphor that gets incorporated into a discussion (He was as big/strong/powerful as Arnold Schwarzenegger). The meme is considered the smallest element of cultural activity that can replicate itself "with reliability and fecundity" (Dennett, p. 344). The meme passes on information or plans, the instructions for a particular trait, a trend or a potential, a set of actions, an interaction, and maybe even an attitude. According to Susan Blackmore, the meme is an instruction "for carrying out behavior, [that is] stored in brains (or other objects) and passed on by imitation" (p. 43). Memes are learned by copying something we have seen, heard, or read, something that sticks with us because it is pleasurable to repeat or share (an urban legend, a joke), because it is easy to remember (the jingle from a TV ad), because it reminds us of something else important, but not necessarily because it does us some good.

Arnold Schwarzenegger is the name we give to a collection of memes that has spread in our culture over the last 30 years. The meme complex called "Arnold Schwarzenegger" is not just referring to the actual person, but rather to the entire collection of ideas, images, actions, stories, metaphors, jokes, rumors, films, Web sites, fan activities, magazine covers, dreams, weight-training equipment, food supplements, T-shirts, interviews, photographs, memorabilia, film posters, newspaper articles, and so on that spread our perception of Arnold Schwarzenegger. Arnold's life, more than any example we can think of, represents the trajectory of a meme, an idea that spreads not because it is good or valuable or true, but because a place is available for it in the culture at a particular point in time and because it can find new niches and hiding places as it develops. How and why it does this reveal a tremendous amount about the culture that employs it. Like other forms of shared cultural activities—myths, rituals, symbols—memes that are this pervasive provide excellent entry points into the structure as well as the fluid features of a culture.

Our focus, as suggested by Derek Gatherer, will not be on proving that we have this Arnold meme in our brains; that is something that can never be proven nor is it likely that memes actually exist as a package that is measurable or quantifiable. Rather, we will show that memes can best be understood through "cultural events, behaviors or artifacts which may be transmitted or copied" (1998, no page). A meme does not exist in brains but is evident only through its manifestation in behavior, as the fallout from transmitted information and ideas. As Gatherer emphasizes, individuals do not *have* memes, they "build them, say them, do them, make them, assent to them, or deny them, but the memes are entirely outside the humans beings that generate them" (n.p.). In fact, says anthropologist Geertz, "Human thought is consummately social: social in its origins, social in its functions, social in its forms, social in its applications" (p. 360). Any human thought can only be seen in its actual manifestations: speech, visual representations, and behavior. For the meme, this manifestation is crucial because it is through imitation that memes get transmitted, and it is through "visible" evidence or fallout from behavior that we have an indication of the presence and success of a meme.

What we can show is not the meme itself (the complex informational schema that makes us think Arnoldian thoughts and act out Schwarzeneggerian actions) but only the behavioral manifestations of this phenomenon. We have no way of showing a transmission of beliefs (because, for example, not everyone must have the same feelings or attitudes toward Arnold to manifest his meme in their behavior), but can only retrospectively indicate the transmission of information that is part of the complex of memes called Arnold Schwarzenegger. What we will do by delineating this behavioral evidence and showing its cultural consequences is open up the field of memetics as well as the study of celebrity culture to a wider range of evidence than is usually admitted. In this indirect way, we think we can illuminate ideas about memes in general, and celebrities as a particularly clear meme form.

If memes are instructions for behavior, decisions and ideas that manage to get themselves replicated and spread, the most successful memes will be the ones that are memorable and flexible: they grab our attention for any number of reasons and then get "mentally rehearsed" and reused in variations that generate new and more extensive metaphors. "Effective memes," says Blackmore, are those that "cause high-fidelity, long-lasting memory" (p. 57). To formalize this, we would suggest that the most powerful memes do four things: they generate new metaphors; they readily invade numerous cultural arenas; they morph to adapt to different "environments"; and they eventually detach themselves from their origins. As one of the most powerful memes in the celebrity world, Arnold Schwarzenegger does all this, as we will show below, with ease.

MEMES AND METAPHORS

The ability to generate metaphors that get used by other members of a culture is a sign of great power and influence. Metaphors, in which we take one thing and make an often arbitrary association with something in a different arena, extend meanings, language, and categorization. The metaphor, explains Lakoff, is not just an element of poetic language. Instead, metaphor is the basis of our "ordinary conceptual system" (p. 3), affecting how we both think and act. To say, "The Dodge Viper is the Arnold Schwarzenegger of sports cars," as *Los Angeles Times Magazine* did in 1991, is to associate the car with great power, popularity, forceful direction, and overall importance. It is also to associate Schwarzenegger with more, better, and faster machines, increasing his appearance as a growing cyborgian entity and amplifying his star persona. It is a metaphor that extends the meaning of both entities. This further suggests that powerful memes are those that produce a kind of reciprocal metaphor. In the above example, neither "viper-ness" nor "Arnold-ness" are necessarily connected to vipers or to Schwarzenegger, but each quality, each metaphorically expressed trait, owes its force to this metaphoric oscillation triggered by the meme of Arnold's strength and ubiquity.

Metaphors create new categories of behavior, thought, and feelings, new connections that might not have been considered before. As George Lakoff has often pointed out in his years of work on metaphoric thought and language, making metaphors is a way to recategorize the world. We employ categorization when we reason, perform mundane or important actions, speak, listen, write, or do just about anything. Metaphors and categorizing are the basis of being a functioning human:

Without the ability to categorize, we could not function at all, either in the physical world or in our social and intellectual lives. An understanding of how we categorize is central to any understanding of how we think and how we function, and therefore central to an understanding of what makes us human. (Lakoff, 1987, p. 6)

Arnold Schwarzenegger, both the name and the meme, has been used as an adjective, a metaphor, an adverb, and a simile. He has contributed speech patterns and sayings to our everyday language, and has often dominated the speech of those trying to talk about things big, expensive, powerful, violent, tough, and successful. He is quite simply an easy-to-use reference point or perfect example, the prototype that is immediately understood and recognized. Prototypes, Lakoff explains, are powerful because they provide a standard against which other elements are measured (p. 446). Prototypes are the best example of elements that are in a category. Not everything in a category matches the prototype but rather they are compared to it and judged as being good or bad fits for the category. So, for example, the prototypical mother in contemporary American culture is the nonworking housewife who stays at home and is married to a man who financially supports her and her children. All other mothers are compared to her (even if she barely exists in reality) and are judged accordingly. Any meme that develops into such a prototype immediately extends its influence because it is used as a measure of right and wrong, good and bad, real and unreal, "real" and virtual, proper and improper, valuable and worthless. Everything in every category it can occupy uses it as a standard of measuring fit, value, design, direction, or sense. As such a prototype for a varied range of categories, Arnold Schwarzenegger is a very influential meme.

Schwarzenegger's prototypical meme is influential because of the importance of symbolic language in human life. Human beings are constructed and maintained through the narratives they develop, share, analyze, and contest. Our sense of belonging to a group as well as sense of being individual selves takes place through narratives. As Bruner (1984) expresses it, "Self and society are generated as they are expressed" (p. 10). The asking of, "Why are narratives so influential?" (p. 82), explicates for us the power of human exchanges through narratives:

Belonging is a primary human motivation: In order to belong, individuals adopt and use the narratives that surround them. Thus, the group's narratives organize the thoughts of its members, specifically the categories of their perceptions, especially perceptions regarding persons. (p. 82)

If language through narrative and metaphoric thought constructs our reality, then the place of Arnold Schwarzenegger in our language points to his significance as an influence on our cultural activities and actions. The meme Arnold Schwarzenegger has numerous metaphoric manifestations in everyday language. He appears as a reference point in an amazing array of fields, creating new ways to categorize experiences that, without the Arnold meme, might end up being associated with something entirely different: machines or natural disasters or Albert Einstein. Metaphors and analogies are most important because they show that the direction of thought has been modified to accommodate Arnold as a generator of best examples, as the prototype. These examples show the range and variety for this influence as well as the variation that takes place when a meme is employed so extensively.

As a measure of power:

- A radio announcer says of Russian leader Boris Yeltsin, "Y'know, he's not exactly the Arnold Schwarzenegger of world leaders."
- In a statement at a 1994 congressional hearing on medical fraud: "It's like sending Bambi out to meet the Terminator."
- From an article in a 1998 military newspaper: "The security forces here pack more firepower than Arnold Schwarzenegger in a Terminator movie."

As a reference for excellence:

- From a 1998 story on golf: "Imagine Arnold Schwarzenegger with a golf game."

As a purveyor of colloquial language that evokes violence:

- During the O. J. Simpson trial, the prosecutor notes that Nicole said to O. J. for the last time, "Hasta la vista!"

As a measure of individual persistence and determination:

- CNN announcer comments in a story on women leaving the military college, The Citadel: "Schwarzenegger could not have lasted longer."
- In a 1991 *Los Angeles Times* article on police chief Daryl Gates: "Even Arnold Schwarzenegger pales in comparison to Gates' cybernetic tenacity."
- At a talk in Los Angeles on computer file recovery: "It's like Arnold Schwarzenegger—it's destroyed, it won't be back."
- In a *Los Angeles Times* article on HIV research: "Every time the Arnold Schwarzeneggers of science have the virus in their sights for destruction . . ."
- On a 1995 episode of the *Today* show, the father of one of the hostages taken in Iraq comments that if he were Arnold Schwarzenegger, he would go in himself to rescue the hostage.

As a prime example of the immigrant experience:

- On NBC News, Los Angeles, 1992, in a story on the problems of Latinos having to change their names, Elizabeth Pena says, "They were able to memorize Arnold Schwarzenegger."

As a measure of physical strength and power:

- In a 1991 *Los Angeles Times* article on an Olympic weightlifting hopeful, the large man is said to "dwarf Schwarzenegger."
- In a 1991 episode of *Law and Order*, it was commented that you would have to be Arnold Schwarzenegger to pick up a big piece of equipment.
- In a 1992 *Los Angeles Times* article on the Lander's earthquake, one man's home is described as looking like "it had been trashed in a 'Terminator' movie."
- In two children's videos, one on construction equipment and one on trucks, powerful machines are given an Arnold Schwarzenegger accent.
- In an article on sea creatures: "An octopus in a lab can lift cinder blocks to get out of its tank," Forsythe said. "It's like having Arnold Schwarzenegger's biceps in your aquarium."

As an indicator of poor speech and acting styles:

- In a 1996 article on computerized speech: "So what if the computer-synthesized speech patterns include odd inflections? Arnold Schwarzenegger's fans never seemed to mind."
- In a 1998 review of the film *Firestorm:* "Long has the steroid-buffed look of an action hero. But his expressionless face and monotone delivery make even Arnold Schwarzenegger at his most robotic seem like a hypersensitive crybaby."
- In a review of a 1998 play: "The play might hold some interest as an acting-class assignment, but the Texas accents of the Willow Cabin cast are so forced and the staging is so stiff (Jed Sexton's Bus resembles Arnold Schwarzenegger's Terminator) that the exercise is almost an embarrassment."

As a sign of his own influence:

- In a 1990 *Newsweek* article on male pectoral implants: "maybe it's a sign of the Schwarzeneggerization of society."

Arnold Schwarzenegger is clearly a prototype for a number of concepts in our culture: fitness, power, strength, excellence, uniqueness, success, influence, positive action, violence and destruction, among others. On radio, in television, at congressional hearings, in magazines and newspapers, in children's videos and cartoons, in public lectures, and in courtrooms, he helps categorize and construct our perceptions. If the function of narratives is to "reveal and comment on the language of the social order" (Brothers, 1997, p. 80) then Schwarzenegger's widespread presence in our shared narratives means that we see the world, at least partially, through a lens constructed around his memes. He helps define what can count as experience, what can be seen as valuable, what can be allowed as truthful, and what can be acceptable as real.

It is hard to imagine other stars who could cover so much territory: Marilyn Monroe might suggest sexiness and vulnerability, foolishness and coyness, but not power, influence, and determination as well; and what, if anything, do "stars" like Brad Pitt or Julia Roberts, Sandra Bullock or Ben Affleck, evoke? Even enduring stars like Cary Grant (suave, debonair sophistication) or Bette Davis (bitchy woman, soulful eyes) had a limited metaphoric range and have not, over time, had that range extended.

MEMES AND DREAMS

A meme can be seen as particularly powerful if it extends its reaches outside its expected range and into unusual or unexpected spheres of influence. Schwarzenegger and his memes clearly have done this by moving beyond the obscure world of professional bodybuilding into Hollywood and politics and popular culture. In these arenas, we can make some conscious choices about whether to see a Schwarzenegger film, or repeat, "I'll be back," or read a magazine article. But when the Schwarzenegger meme reached into the world of dream narratives, we became acutely aware of what engaging a powerful meme means and how such memes really do move through all levels of cultural experience.

We were studying Schwarzenegger and his films in the early 1990s when we began having a series of vivid dreams about him and our research. Despite our awareness of Schwarzenegger's amazing reach into all aspects of the culture, we were nevertheless shocked when he began to appear in our dreams. For the next 10 years, we recorded over 150 dreams in which he was our adversary, lover, boss, friend, bowling partner, student, date, and the subject of our book. He was able to morph in our minds into all these different roles, placed in an equally varied set of scenarios.

On January 28, 1991, Michael Blitz had his first Arnold dream:

Arnold Schwarzenegger comes to my door and says, "I hear you are doing a book about me." He then tells me that Maria Shriver thought that she could find out about him by peeling away his layers like an onion. But he says that the only way anyone will find out about him is by breaking him into little pieces.

Taking Arnold's curious advice in this dream seriously, we did break him into little pieces and exposed ourselves to every form of Arnoldian culture. We watched his films, ate at his restaurant, read his books, perused the tabloids, collected "Arnold stories" from fans, photographed him, visited one of his film sets, attended his bodybuilding competition, and even tried bodybuilding ourselves. The meme Arnold Schwarzenegger, through the first instructions in this dream, seemed to set our fate.

We explored the little ways that he permeates social life—persistently, invisibly, quietly, insidiously. It is this amazing and often frightening reach into our actions, experiences, and thoughts that shows how an effective meme can extend its influence and its chance of spreading further. The dreams we had are the most obvious proof that this reach had made it all the way into even the seemingly most private aspects of our lives. But even these personal parts of our lives are used to create narratives that put the meme back into circulation. In the case of the Arnold meme, the dreams were a particularly effective medium because they have been reported by others in academic conferences, parties, books, essays, Websites, artworks, mealtime conversations, and e-mails. Like a good meme, they are memorable and pleasurable and these two features make a meme more likely to be spread.

Following are some of the over 150 Arnoldian dreams we have had in the past 10 years. They show the range and flexibility of the meme Arnold Schwarzenegger and demonstrate a remarkable combination, as do all dreams, of an internal logic with a wonderfully impossible set of juxtapositions and odd crossings. As Bert States (1997) points out, the "business" of the dream "is not to dream *about* something, even in a disguised form, but to make connections among memory networks" (p. 158). We look at these dreams, therefore, not for their meanings, but for what they say about the way Arnold Schwarzenegger, the meme, can cover a wide range of categories, make connections between categories, create new ones, and slay the significance of old ones. What the brain does in a dream, says States, is to move " 'mindlessly' from one image to another that is on some unfixable level related to it" (p. 157). This "mindless" movement, we think, is what memes are all about.

Louise's Dream (March 20, 1991)

For some reason Arnold Schwarzenegger is in my house. He is sitting at the kitchen table. We are talking about something. I say to him flirtatiously, "You know we are writing a book about you but we haven't been able to admit it face to face." I tell him I am interested in the President's Council on Physical Fitness. I show him something on a small piece of paper and he gets up from the table to look at it over my shoulder. I know he is looking down my cleavage and I am pleased.

Michael's Dream (March 8, 1991)

I am taking Arnold's photograph, using a wide-angle lens in order to somehow widen him. Arnold turns to a pal nearby and asks, "Why am I being photographed by such a ridiculous camera?" The friend comes over to confiscate my camera so I cut off his hand. For the rest of the dream I am running from Arnold's goons.

Michael's Dream (February 5, 1993)

Louise had found in a novelty shop a 78 rpm record of Arnold singing Elvis songs. One side was "Love Me Tender" and the other side was "Jailhouse Rock," which, she told me, when played backward, was also the "preamble" to *Mein Kampf.*

Michael's Dream (July 19, 1995)

Arnold and I are interviewing actors for recasting the *Bonanza* television show. Arnold is aloof, and after each interview mutters to me (about the actor), "Faggot!" He sits up suddenly when Bruce Lee comes in. Arnold says, "You're dead!" I am shocked. Lee cannot speak but does a flourish of karate moves, and Arnold stands up and shoots him. Lee is dead (again). Arnold says to me, "Fucking faggot!" and tosses his pistol onto Lee's corpse.

Louise's Dream (June 3, 1996)

I enter a talk show audience and hug a huge, blocky Lou Ferrigno, who looks like a refrigerator. Then Arnold arrives, also blocky. We are all younger. Arnold greets me like we know each other. Then we are backstage being interviewed by a sports reporter. She is a novice and nervous. She sucks a whole plastic bottle into her mouth. I make her pull it out. We go view a reenactment of a campus murder rampage. A man with a gun walks around and shoots people point blank. He goes up to one kid and shoots down his pants. The sports reporter asks us our theory about how this could happen. We say fear freezes people. Then the baby Arnold is holding has diarrhea and I change the diaper. Arnold is impressed.

Louise's Dream (November 5, 1998)

I am trying to get an interview with Arnold. I am outside his brownstone apartment. Maria comes rushing out, jumps into a big sports utility vehicle that has two steering wheels, and drives herself and the other surprised people inside away. Somehow I am then inside with Arnold. I just sit and he ignores me as I casually look at magazines and books that are about him. Then Maria sends up word that she will pick me up at four and gives back my bag, which I threw into the SUV. Arnold says forget it, he can get me back if I come to the airport field tonight at 3:20. He will give me a ride in his private jet. I show up there and as we all walk up to the jet there is a small group of fans ready. Then we have to march first in a funeral procession around the field. I have to carry a big American flag. It gets tangled in my feet but finally I carry it correctly. Then it is over and everyone rushes to put their flags down but I can't put an American flag on the ground.

Michael's Dream (December 7, 1999)

I was having a business dinner with Arnold and Patsy Kent. Patsy was an agent and was telling me that I should not have even been allowed to contact Arnold. I guessed that I tricked Arnold into attending this dinner, but I didn't remember how I did it. I tried to think of something that would make it seem worthwhile to him. I lied and I told him I'd seen his new movie, *End of Days*, and thought it was a real triumph. He snorted and said, "It's the saddest movie I evah made!" I was surprised by this moment of reflection on his part. Patsy looked disgusted with Arnold and slammed her silverware down. Some of my water spilled onto the table and I started to blot it up. Patsy said, "Now *that's* sad!" I hoped Arnold would not ask me about why I had done this. He was reading the label on his beer bottle and snapping his fingers as though to a song.

Dreams take our everyday thoughts and actions, our experiences and feelings, and try to categorize them in different ways, often creating the bizarre juxtapositions that we remember as dream narratives. The purpose of this is to bring our new experiences together with our old, creating new metaphors and reference points in the process, refining and reorganizing our categories. Bert States (1988) explains the process this way:

[F]ictions and dreams—remarkably similar in their content—are not simply ways these people amuse or instruct themselves; rather, they need fictions and dreams as complementary means by which they constantly monitor and index the diversity of their experiences. Through narrative they might, in a sense, remember experience—not in that trite way we say a novel is an accurate account of life in a certain historical period but, rather, the kind of remembering that has to be done over and over. If something is to be remembered at all, it must be remembered not as what happened but as what has happened again in a different way and will surely happen again in the future in still another way. And by this means, as Roger Shank suggests in his essay on memory models, a "commonality" can be built up among various versions of the same experience that might serve as the basis for forming a new knowledge structure or for modifying or confirming an old one. . . . So we keep writing the same old stories and having the same old dreams because we keep having the same old experience in different ways. (p. 119)

This suggests that dreams are an integral part of a meme's mechanism for spreading and surviving. The dreams are a remarkable example of what we mean by evolutionary mechanisms when we are in the cognitive realm. Ideas and concepts that are flexible, that can rapidly change to meet different circumstances and "environments," that can, essentially, morph like the T1000 in *Terminator 2* are those that will not become extinct. In our dreams (the entire collection is available on our Website, http://www.sscnet.ucla.edu/ioa/arnold.html) the Arnold meme appears as everything from a fireman to a voyeur and we give him/it every emotional reaction from fear to love to surprise to anger.

But Bert States prods us to remember that "if dreams were primarily instruments of communication, most dreams would be useless" (1988, p. 19). Because they are constructing new categories and metaphors, we cannot hope to "read" dreams like we can a poem or understand their point like we can with a joke. Dreams, when not remembered, are consolidating memes into the unconscious system we use to make meanings. When they are remembered, they are still doing this consolidation but are also giving the meme another vehicle, the dream account, for getting on with its work of spreading far and wide. Just as we are helpless in a dream to direct the progression of the meme's story (despite claims of "lucid dreaming"),[5] we are probably nearly as helpless when the meme in the dream wants to get expressed out loud. The compulsion of humans to share stories and create meanings is especially compelling with dreams that make no sense and need others to put them into a socially comprehensible context.

MEMES AND MORPHS

In addition to generating new metaphors and appearing in varied cultural arenas, powerful memes are also flexible enough to change seamlessly and invisibly to fit new needs and circumstances. Several of our dreams demonstrate this.

Louise's Dream (August 21, 1992)

Arnold and I get arrested by the Russians. We are taken to Russia and put into some kind of camp that has young people in it. They don't know that Arnold is there. We are waiting to be released and Arnold gets permission to have Maria come for a visit. Arnold takes Maria into the next room, which has a glass wall so that we can all watch. Arnold lies on his back on a Barcalounger and Maria sits on top of him. They kiss passionately but have all their clothes on. Meanwhile I am talking to all the young people as Arnold and Maria smooch in the background. They discover I have a Russian/Polish background when we dance, and they see I can do a mean polka. I say to them, "Do you know who that is in there?" One young woman says yes, but three others say no. Then Arnold suddenly comes out, takes me by the hand, and leads me off to another room. He sits down on a weightlifting bench and says to me, "Okay, what do I have to pay you to stop writing this book about my sex life?" I put out my hand and smile and say, "I am glad to finally meet you." He says, "We are not meeting. How much do you want?" We look at each other and start to kiss. He suddenly turns into someone else who looks like an old Tina Turner with small orange lips; maybe he is a drag queen. I think to myself that he is a bad kisser. I walk away and say, "I don't want to do this book anymore." Then I think about how much I could ask him for. I go back to the bench to kiss him again. His mouth is open and head tilted back and I look at a pool of accumulating saliva. I wished I hadn't kissed him and think about AIDS and all the lovers he has had. I decide not to kiss him again.

Michael's Dream (February 5, 1991)

Arnold was fighting Klan-types and had to dress as a firefighter with a long coat and hat, partly to hide his well-known balding head from several *Deliverance* types who were after him and me. At one point he becomes Gerard Depardieu, but he quickly corrected himself when I observed, "You look so much different in person than you do in my head." This prompted him to take off the firehat to prove that he still had a full head of hair and that my mental image of him was intact.

As our dreams demonstrate, a successful meme may become anything it needs to in order to spread. The dream is the perfect environment for a meme to both exert itself and to extend itself through new metaphors and new narrative forms. This is not symbolization, says States, but "primarily a mechanism of association, condensation and recall" in which things representative of something in a person's waking life are always "molested" and "contaminated" by their "similars" (1997, p. 157).

They can, in a sense, "morph" from one form to another. Morphing is a computer technology (with roots in mythologies of metamorphosis across cultures and time; see Krasniewicz, 2000) in which one entity transforms into another seamlessly, or two entities blend to form a third, entirely new entity. In either case, the morphing elements demonstrate a challenge to traditional categories and identities, as in the case of the Michael Jackson video (*Black and White*, 1991) in which people of many races change into one another. Morphing is so odd, in part, because it is a visible transformation rather than one hidden from our critical eyes. We are challenged by this process in which "an object seems to reshape and transform itself gradually into another object in full view of the audience, providing the same kind of pleasure one might find in a well-performed trick of stage magic" (Wolf, p. 83).

The process of morphing is best known from the Schwarzenegger blockbuster movie *Terminator 2* (1991) and from *The Abyss*, a 1989 film from *T2* director James Cameron. In the morphing that we see on the screen in *T2*, one terminator (not Schwarzenegger) seamlessly melts into others, constantly shape-shifting so that it is impossible to draw the boundaries between forms. In *The Abyss*, aliens take their form from water, moving effortlessly though spaces and with numerous faces. In *T2*, floors become men, arms become swords, cops become liquid blobs, and women find themselves duplicated as wounded twins.

Morphing is in a sense the behavioral (as well as visual) counterpart of the metaphor. Cultural morphing would thus mean taking disparate forms of behavior or the fallout of behaviors like artifacts or consumer goods, and blending them together to make an unheard of or a never before seen person or thing. In the case of his meme complex, "Arnold Schwarzenegger" is one big morphing machine, moving from inarticulate bodybuilder, to well-paid movie star, cultural icon, successful businessman, fitness czar, stern daddy, philanthropist for Jewish causes, and conservative statesman. While few people can articulate the precise history of Schwarzenegger actions, he has, become a prototype for many of these roles.

For example, during the elder George Bush presidency, Schwarzenegger was the chair of the President's Council on Physical Fitness and Sports. Despite years of reported steroid use and developing a bodybuilder's body that "represents" health and strength but in reality is neither, Schwarzenegger promoted childhood fitness, talking in the process to the governors of all 50 states about their fitness failures. At this same time, during the Gulf War, Schwarzenegger was mixed up with Norman Schwarzkopf, the commander-in-chief, Central Command (leader of U.S. forces and Western troops in the Gulf War from 1990 to 1991). While supervising exercises on the lawn of the White House for the annual Great American Workout, Schwarzenegger was interviewed by Willard Scott of the *Today Show*, the perfect foil of non-fitness. Scott asked Arnold, "This has been a big year for the Schwarzes. Are you two related?" Arnold replied, "No, but I am sure we have the same willpower." With that question, of course, they *were* related for Arnold had invisibly morphed into the military leader of the U.S. forces, a role reinforced by his appearance on a television special welcoming home and cele-brating the Gulf War troops. The two bigger-than-life men became not only each other but also symbols of a restored masculinity that encompasses mili-tary might and physical strength as well as caring about children, crying for women, and restoring order. As a student in one of Michael Blitz's classes asked at this time during a heated discussion, "We gotta get the Terminator in here to keep peace?"

Schwarzenegger has also moved across film genres, being the star of action films, comedies, disaster and horror flicks, and romances, sometimes within the same film. There is evidence of this morphing capability in many of his films, most explicitly in *Terminator 2* but also in *Twins, Predator, Kindergar-ten Cop, Total Recall,* and *True Lies.* Why do we call this morphing? Becausee, like the morph, it happens right in front of our eyes, we see the visible evidence of the change, and are fascinated by the impossible combinations put together. We see disconnected entities, twins who that look nothing alike, joined in some odd way to make perfect new components that we could not anticipate but who express the meme in totally acceptable ways. The morph, rather than the collage or the cyborg, is the vehicle of the meme because it eliminates the disconcerting evidence that comes from jumping types and categories.

THE DETACHED MEME

Although Arnold Schwarzenegger is associated with morphing, he is never, in fact, morphed in *T2*. Instead, his morphing spans two films (*The Termina-tor*, 1984, and *Terminator 2: Judgment Day*, 1991) separated by seven years of time, during which he changes from a killing machine to a caring machine. It can be argued that it is Linda Hamilton, as Sarah Connor, who takes on his old Terminator role. Schwarzenegger actually gets separated from the original Terminator meme; yet, every aspect of its significance, its power, its productiv-ity is still associated with Schwarzenegger. How can Arnold detach himself from, yet remain embedded in, this meme?

A meme that disconnects from its source but continues to evoke that source becomes, in effect, universally available for situations and expressions unen-cumbered by its original use but still spreading the meme of its origin. It is like looking for the origin of an urban myth (or an ancient one for that matter): it matters not whether there ever was a real precipitating event for a particular ur-ban legend. What matters is how they work, how they spread, how they change, and how they evolve into different, equally believable if bizarre leg-ends. "The defining qualities," says Brunvard, are not truth or fiction, but "oral repetition and variation," and any version of a story reinforces its basic message (1999, pp. 20–21).

Any version of Arnold Schwarzenegger, then, reinforces the meme Arnold Schwarzenegger. When someone says, "Hasta la vista, baby!" they do so with-out having to know specifically that this idiom, memeticized by

Schwarzenegger, is originally associated with a scene of brutal murder and, in later iterations, occasions of self-parody. In any case it evokes Schwarzenegger in many people, even in those who have never seen his films. As Arnold detaches himself from his familiar representations, it does not mean his meme is losing steam. Evidence of this can be seen in his continued ability to insinuate himself into new areas, morph into new entities, and generate new metaphors. His recent film, *End of Days* (1999), is a prime example. For the first time, Arnold presents himself in the context of a "religious memeplex," what Blackmore calls one of the most powerful and durable means by which people attempt to understand their world (p. 192).

In this end-of-the-millennium film, Arnold attempts this detachment by becoming the opposite of himself, turning as a result into Jesus Christ. First he is battling none other than the Devil himself, played by the appropriately named Gabriel Byrne. The Schwarzenegger in this film is amazingly weak: as the film opens he is about to commit suicide. Later he is beaten by an old lady as well as everyone else he encounters; he is guilty, uncertain, and finally has to pray to God to give him strength. The Devil, on the other hand, exhibits all the old Arnoldian characteristics: clever, witty, strong beyond belief, powerful, determined, and driven. He even states that "I don't do guilt," just as Arnold once said at a bodybuilding competition we attended. It is almost as if Arnold is actually battling himself on the screen, as if he were not just himself but is switching between several of the main characters. As the reincarnation of Jesus Christ (Schwarzenegger is quite literally crucified at one point), Arnold completes the millennial cycle, taking us back to the original battle between good and evil, Christ and the Devil in the desert (New York City). That original battle was one of wits and faith instead of brawn and bravery but the result is the same: nothing less than the redemption of humankind and the salvation of the human race.

We could also point to a scene in Schwarzenegger's film *Total Recall* as another critical moment in the displaced meme-life of Arnold. One of the protagonist's several personalities speaks from a computer screen to his alter ego (both played by Schwarzenegger): "You are not you! You're me!" Although it would be wild hyperbole to say that Arnold is attempting to implant the "total" meme by which the rest of us would recall ourselves to *be* him, it may be reasonable to argue that the constellation of events, cultural phenomena, images, recollections, dreams, consumer products, narrative references, and various manifestations of Schwarzenegger constitute such a meme's *potential* trajectory.

CONCLUSION

Arnold Schwarzenegger has always been off the evolutionary chart. He is bigger, more powerful, richer, more influential, and more pervasive than any normal human being. He is omnipresent (and has been for almost two decades) and insistent, remaking himself just when he seems to have disappeared. He has become, in a very short period of time, one of the major figures inhabiting both our private narratives (dreams, personal exchanges) and our public ones (films, politics, economics, cultural idioms).

In the 1998 Woody Allen movie titled *Celebrity*, one character states what has been the common wisdom on our interest in stars, both the famous and the notorious: our choice of celebrities "says something" about the society that picks them. But is there no more to celebrity than this, a simple reflective mirror held up to our desires, fears, and fascinations? We think that stars are the most vivid representations of some of our culture's most important memes. Because they are linked to traits we have come to value—power, fame, sexual desirability, money—stars are easier to swallow than other memes, but they are no different from the other meme complexes in a particular culture. They provide us with a way to make meaning, to interpret our own behavior and that of others, to place values on things and people, and to understand how the world works.

Some forms of memetics seem to suggest that the memes spread in association with stars are a classic form of thought contagion. We, instead, see the users of memes as more active than that, with memes as a tool in the hands and bodies of active participants in the creation of cultural interpretations. The memes associated with stars influence behavior, cause exchanges of power and wealth, affect concepts of self, and even infect our dreams. We have memes because humans are social creatures and memes are both the cause and the result of our need to test out, share, critique, and examine our ideas and behaviors in reference to those of others. Any meme complex that guides these meaning-making experiences, these interpretations of the world, is very powerful indeed and very likely to spread.

As a meme complex, Arnold Schwarzenegger has few rivals. Under the "new" evolutionary scheme presented by memetics, power, pleasure, money, influence, and admiration end up residing in those who can most effectively demonstrate their control of this second kind of evolution, the ability to spread memes, to get people to imitate and replicate a behavior or idea or action. Evolution is horizontal, spreading across people who exist in the same time and space (however virtual), rather than predominantly from parent to child (Blackmore, p. 34). Stars and other meme-machines, as parents already know, often seem to have more influence on meaning than they do.

Arnold Schwarzenegger is our model of this new evolutionary force, the one that favors the ability to spread viral thoughts, imitative speech, behavioral patterns, consumer behaviors, or dream content. What is the measure of this influence? It is becoming a reference point for important decisions and events of the culture, both on a personal level and in a more global communicative manner. Why do people go so much to Arnold Schwarzenegger movies? It is not just to see bodies blown up and bad guys defeated but to have more memes, to have an already desirable complex of feelings, ideas, and behavioral models expanded and confirmed. It is a cycle of reciprocity that continues until some other meme complex derails it.

If narratives, metaphors, and language are in constant motion in a culture, defining, refining, challenging, structuring, and deconstructing all at the same time our sense of who we are and how we make sense of the world, then the reference to a star in everyday language points to the significance of that entity in shaping our actions, decisions and focus. But not every celebrity is given the same accord, and certainly it is a small number who have penetrated the collective unconscious so deeply and thoroughly that they can be said to have truly turned the tide of a culture's inclinations and activities. Marilyn Monroe, Elvis, and John F. Kennedy come to mind as contemporary icons who serve as persistent reference points for our evaluations of love, hate, sex, power, death, and the other necessities of life. While it is impossible in most cases to trace a one-to-one cause-effect relationship between a celebrity and a cultural shift, it is possible, in the case of Arnold Schwarzenegger, to show both the breadth and depth of his penetration into the culture.

Many memeticists, especially Blackmore, talk about memes as if they have a life of their own, as if they can replicate, which they can (p. 7). Humans, for Blackmore, become merely vehicles or hosts for these virus-like memes. But in our desire to bring both memetics and the study of American popular culture back into the realm of social action and symbolic behavior, we cannot accept this idea. Memes, in their exchanges and replications and variation, actually serve humans in the most fundamental of ways. They reaffirm that we are human because the only way to substantiate our humanness is via exchanges with other humans: exchanges of thoughts, feelings, bodies, gifts, meanings. These "forms of social bonding," most explicitly seen in gifts but overtly present in every human act, are the foundation of the social fabric (Godbout). Verbal exchanges like those that carry and replicate memes are the most significant:

It is words first and foremost, sentences and arguments, that humans produce and exchange with others. Certainly, more and more, we speak only to pass on information or give orders. But before providing information or seeing that others conform to our wishes, we must first use words to establish a relationship. Through such shared exchanges humans avoid "social autism," or the kind of isolation that fails to confirm our definitions of self and society. (Godbout, p. 12)

Studying "trivial" meme complexes like stars, Susan Blackmore has shown, is important because these memes often "exert phenomenal power in modern society and are responsible for the movement of vast amounts of money. They shape the way we think about ourselves and, perhaps more importantly, they cause many people to believe things that are demonstrably false. Anything that can do all this deserves to be understood" (p. 184). But more significantly, they demonstrate a new view of evolutionary processes. Rather than seeing elements of a culture persist because they confer some reproductive advantage or survival value, memetic studies of celebrities support the notion that there are certain meme vehicles that are more efficient and effective because they are themselves good imitators, can tell or act in good stories worth passing on, or can get a podium from which to speak.

FUTURE THOUGHTS

It has occurred to us while writing this that there may not be an unlimited number of memes available to a culture. In fact, one way to define a culture is as a group of people who share a limited and particular set of memes. Our next goal is to delineate what the set of memes for our culture looks like and whether the Arnold Schwarzenegger meme complex is unique or simply just a vivid example of a larger cultural enterprise.

ACKNOWLEDGMENTS

Thanks to Bert States who made the connection about our dreams of Arnold Schwarzenegger and to Susan Blackmore for her take on memetics.

NOTES

1. Available at www.cpm.mmu.ac.uk/jom-emit. A bibliography of memetics was developed by Liane Gabora in 1997. It lists 190 of the major works in the field and can be found online at http://www.cpm.mmu.ac.uk/ jom-emit/biblio/.

2. Traditionally, anthropology in the United States along a four-field approach that combined cultural, biological, linguistic, and archaeological perspectives in the study of human cultures, and researchers were expected to be trained in all four fields even while specializing in just one. In the 1970s and 1980s, anthropology began to fall apart as a cohesive discipline, and today it consists of factionalized groups who have developed into specialists rather than generalists. These changes took place for many reasons but certainly the development of sociobiology was one key factor. Sociobiology attempts to put human behavior squarely in the biological rather than the cultural world, and human behavior is explained by comparing it to animal behavior, all of which is seen as maximizing reproductive strategies. Humans thus began to be compared to birds more than they were to each other, as had been the earlier cross-cultural tradition of the field.

3. For an anthropologist to be taken seriously, he or she has to conduct studies with two elements: it is done in a foreign culture and it covers "significant" subjects like economics, power, racial relations, and so forth. Despite its claim to be interested in all aspects of all cultures, anthropology generally still shuns American popular culture and media.

4. The culturally based memetics we want to employ developed, ironically, with a brief comment by one of the leading proponents of sociobiology. At the end of his 1976 book, *The Selfish Gene*, in which he promoted the idea that human behavior can be explained, like animal behavior, by the biological imperative to reproduce at all cost, Richard Dawkins briefly suggests that there might be a cultural equivalent to the gene that wants to get replicated; he called this cultural form the "meme." The

meme, he said, was the "new replicator" necessary to explain the additional complexity of humans. By the 1989 reissue of the book, Dawkins acknowledges that the meme was a "good meme" because the concept and term have now been so widely accepted (Dawkins, 1989, p. 322).

5. In lucid dreaming, the dreamer is supposedly able to direct the action in a dream. This is often promoted as a form of therapy. But it is questionable whether this is "dreaming" or another form of consciousness. See Flanagan, 2000, pp. 19, 126.

REFERENCES

Blackmore, Susan. *The Meme Machine*. Cambridge: Oxford University Press, 1999.
Brodie, Richard. *Virus of the Mind: The New Science of the Meme*. Seattle: Integral Press, 1996.
———. *Meme Central*. 1999. Available at www.brodietech.com/rbrodie/meme.htm.
Brothers, Leslie. *Friday's Footprint: How Society Shapes the Human Mind*. New York: Oxford University Press, 1997.
Bruner, Edward M. "Intoduction: The Opening Up of Anthropology." In Bruner, Edward M., ed., *Text, Play, and Story: The Construction and Reconstruction of Self and Society*. Washington, D.C.: The American Ethnological Society, 1984: 1–16.
Brunvald, Jan Harold. *Too Good to Be True: The Colossal Book of Urban Legends*. New York: W. W. Norton & Company, 1999.
Dawkins, Richard. *The Selfish Gene*. 2d ed. Cambridge: Oxford University Press, 1989.
Dennett, Daniel C. *Darwin's Dangerous Idea: Evolution and the Meanings of Life*. New York: Touchstone, 1995.
Eckert, Charles. "The Carole Lombard in Macy's Window." In Gledhill, Christine, ed., *Stardom: Industry of Desire*. London: Routledge, 1991: 30–39.
Flanagan, Owen. *Dreaming Souls: Sleep, Dreams, and the Evolution of the Conscious Mind*. Cambridge: Oxford University Press, 2000.
Gabora, Liane. *Bibliography of Memetics*. 1997. Available at http://www.cpm. mmu.ac.uk/jom-emit/biblio/.
Gatherer, Derek. *Why the "Thought Contagion" Metaphor Is Retarding the Progress of Memetics*. 1998. Online journal. 1999. Available at www.cpm.mmu. ac.uk/jomemit/1998/vol2/gatherer_d.html.
Geertz, Clifford. *The Interpretation of Cultures*. New York: Basic Books, 1973.
Godbout, Jacques T., with Alain Caillé. *The World of the Gift*. Translated by Donald Winkler. Montreal: McGill-Queen's University Press, 1998.
Haraway, Donna. *Primate Visions: Gender, Race, and Nature in the World of Modern Science*. London: Routledge, 1989.
Krasniewicz, Louise. "Magical Transformations and Metamorphosis in Two Cultures." In Sobchack, Vivian, ed., *MetaMorphing: Visual Transformation and the Culture of Quick-Change*. Minneapolis: University of Minnesota Press, 2000: 41–58.
Krasniewicz, Louise, and Michael Blitz. "Morphing Identities: Arnold Schwarzenegger—Write Us." In Smith, Sidonie, and Julia Watson, eds.,

Getting a Life: Everyday Uses of Autobiography. Minneapolis: University of Minnesota Press, 1996: 89–107.

Lakoff, George. *Women, Fire and Dangerous Things: What Categories Reveal about the Mind*. Chicago: University of Chicago Press, 1987.

Stacey, Jackie. "Feminine Fascinations: Forms of Identification in Star-Audience Relations." In Gledhill, Christine, ed., *Stardom: Industry of Desire*. London: Routledge, 1991: 141–63.

States, Bert O. *The Rhetoric of Dreams*. Ithaca: Cornell University Press, 1988.

———. *Seeing in the Dark: Reflections on Dreams and Dreaming*. New Haven: Yale University Press, 1997.

Wolf, Mark J.P. "A Brief History of Morphing." In Sobchack, Viviane ed., *MetaMorphing: Visual Transformation and the Culture of Quick-Change*. Minneapolis: University of Minnesota Press, 2000: 83–101.

Robert De Niro in *The King of Comedy* (Martin Scorsese, 1982). © 20th Century-Fox (Kobal Collection).

Chapter 3

Choosing Silence: Robert De Niro and the Celebrity Interview

Greg M. Smith

The celebrity interview seems to offer the fan fairly unproblematic access to the real person behind a film star's image. Yet when Robert De Niro refuses to answer questions or even to give interviews at all, the assumptions regarding access to the "real" De Niro are called into question. Who is Robert De Niro? Why is he so reticent about interviews? Is he merely shy, or is he trying to hide something? Or is it that there is nothing inside, that there is no Robert De Niro outside of his roles? The titles of articles in the popular press about De Niro often foreground the problem this star presents: " 'You Talkin to Me?' 'No!' " "Man of Few Words," "The Phantom of the Cinema," "The Return of the Silent Screen Star." It seems that the voice least heard from about De Niro is the actor's own voice. Robert De Niro becomes a structuring absence in the discourse about himself.

This chapter investigates the articles in the popular press that specifically feature Robert De Niro[1] and seeks to explain the significance of this silence. This breakdown in the interview process helps us to see some of the assumptions underlying the normally transparent workings of the system of film publicity. This silence has bearing on the nature of the film star, his or her status, and the literature concerning Western conceptions of the self.

Several important trends in celebrity publicity date back to the first constructions of film stars in the early 1910s. Richard de Cordova's (1985) work on the emergence of the star system reveals that players were first individuated as "picture personalities," coherent personae that could be read from actors' appearances across several films without reference to their off-screen life. When the player's existence outside the film was acknowledged, it was briefly depicted (according to de Cordova) as "merely an extension of an existence already laid out within films. The illusion that was operative was that the player's real personality (as presented in magazines) preceded and caused the representation of personality on the screen. . . . But actually the represented 'real' personalities were not primary; they were reduplications of a more basic representation of character within films" (p. 88). The filmic and extrafilmic texts maintained a careful redundancy.

Movie stars in the more modern sense began when the player's existence outside the film became the emphasis of the popular press. Fans began to gain access to information about the star's so-called private life, making explicit the distinction between the actors and the characters portrayed on screen. However, the two categories were still portrayed as being analogous, with no moral discrepancy between the professional and private selves.

Such portrayals of stars seem to be rooted in the prevailing understanding of the film medium's "realism." The mechanical nature of the film process is considered to decrease the effects of human intervention; therefore, film presents people "as they really are." The American film industry realized the necessity of maintaining continuity between the on-screen image and the "real" person depicted in magazines. To do otherwise would be to emphasize the apparatus's potential to lie.

But what about the actor, the professional liar? Not surprisingly, film realism has traditionally shown a preference toward what Barry King (1987) calls "personification" (limiting actors to parts consonant with their personalities and physical attributes) rather than "impersonation" (in which actors suppress the markers of their "real" personalities and take on the role's characteristics) (p. 130). King suggests that this tendency has an economic basis in the oversupply of actors available for Hollywood productions. The rational response to the actor oversupply (given naturalistic conventions) is "an emphasis on what is unique to the actor, displacing emphasis from what an actor can do *qua* actor onto what the actor *qua* person or biographical entity is" (p. 146).

A minimum level of acting ability is assumed to be present among Screen Actors Guild members; therefore, significant differentiation between members tends to be based on unique combinations of personal and physical traits. In King's terms, acting ability becomes a *continuous variable* (a criterion that is shared, however unevenly, by all members of a work force) and psychological/physical qualities are *discontinuous variables* (present in only some workers). The economics of oversupply favors choices based on discontinuous variables, which supports a preference toward personification. Because Hollywood is oversaturated with actors, casting directors can make choices based as much on physical characteristics, life histories, and personality traits as they do on acting ability.

Another widely held notion about acting emphasizes the opposite trend: impersonation, suggesting that only relatively unskilled actors have to be limited to playing parts similar to their own personalities. In this discourse film is generally considered to be less an actor's medium than theater. Film's editing capabilities can piece together a cohesive performance out of many different takes of a relatively unskilled actor. Editing can eliminate a performance entirely, leaving an actor's work on the cutting room floor. Control over the camera gives power over much of the signification of performance in the cinema, and this control is out of the actor's hands. In the theater the actor's control over pacing and so forth is perceived to be more direct and less mediated,[2] putting an emphasis on the actor's skills.

These notions concerning acting and film remained fairly stable until the revolutionary arrival of Method acting[3] on the screen, most importantly in Elia Kazan's and Marlon Brando's works. When American practitioners adapted Constantin Stanislavski's Method, they emphasized how actors should call on their life histories to provide source material to use in creating characters. This technique grounds the acting in a real-world base, purportedly giving the actor's performance a new realism and emotional truth. At first glance it would seem that the Method as it appeared in film emphasized personification over impersonation. Lee Strasberg, the primary popularizer of the Method in America, describes Kazan's strategy in selecting his actors: "He casts people who he thinks have a certain something deep inside them—which if it could come out would be essential to the role. To succeed, then, he would have to find some way of bringing this something to the surface" (Cole and Chinoy, 1970, p. 623).

The Method emphasized the unique set of experiences that each actor as an artist could draw upon as affective memories. Awareness of these memories gave the artist access to the materials of his or her trade. Stella Adler, De Niro's primary teacher, says: "The first idea [at the Group Theatre] asked the actor to become aware of himself. Did he have any problems? Did he understand them in relation to his whole life? To society? Did he have a point of view in relation to these questions?" (Cole and Chinoy, p. 602). The Method could be seen as an economic strategy to emphasize the qualities that make personifying actors unique. If an actor has a "certain something" inside, he or she can market his or her unique appeal.

But the Method is not simply a reassertion of personification. Stanislavski's Method is a complex combination of the physical and the psychological, with the intent of bringing these factors under the actor's conscious control. Actors develop physical and psychological discipline so that they can use the raw material of their experiences to create a variety of characters. "Craftsmanship," the artistic ability to forge characters consciously using one's memories instead of merely duplicating those memories, is the other central idea of the Group Theatre's American Method (in addition to the artist's individual self-awareness mentioned above), according to Adler. The Method's emphasis on an actor's memories is not intended to limit the actor to a simple reenactment of personality but is meant to give the actor a means of consciously reworking his or her affective memories into different characters.

Though discussions of the American Method have perhaps shown somewhat of a personifying emphasis (after all, Adler says that the actor's self-knowledge is the *first* step in the Method), the Method contains a counterbalancing influence foregrounding impersonation. Strasberg admits that the American Method has been construed as overly psychoanalytic when he says: "The emotional thing is not Freud, as people commonly think. Theoretically and actually, it is Pavlov" (quoted in Roach, p. 216). But this quote also points out a significant oversight in the American version of Stanislavski's Method. Partly because of the English publication history of Stanislavski's works, the American Method focuses more on earlier Stanislavski ideas and shares his early emphasis on psychological work rather than his later stress on physical work. This causes the misconception that the Method is rooted in a psychology of the mind (like Freud's) rather than a mind/body theory (like Pavlov's). As Joseph Roach notes, "[It] has been assumed that the process begins with work on the *psychical* aspect of the instrument, then emphasizes the preparation of its *physical* aspect, and finally brings both together in the creation of a role" (p. 205, emphasis added). The version of the Method discussed in pop culture publications generally shares this relative emphasis on the psychological, rarely getting to the second step of the actor's preparation (the physical).

Barry King cites De Niro as "an interesting case in this regard, since he appears, paradoxically, to combine to a stunning level of virtuosity the capacity for impersonation with a drive, role by role, to transform himself physically into the substance of the signified, e.g., Jake LaMotta in *Raging Bull*" (1987, p. 144). De Niro has come to represent an extreme of both impersonation (foregrounding his versatility) and personification (foregrounding his body). Though the writings on later Method film actors (like Dustin Hoffman, Robert Duvall, and De Niro) have emphasized the virtuosity of their impersonations, "the self-referentially of Method acting—the so-called personal expressive realism of Brando, for example—rather than representing the triumph of the actor as impersonator can be seen as a successful adaptation of impersonation to the pressures of personification, deploying impersonation to refer back to the person of the actor, the consistent entity underlying each of his or her roles" (King, p. 147). Thus the focus of acting that foregrounds impersonation points us back to the "real" personality of the actor just as surely as personification does. The question of the "real" personality of a virtuosic actor like De Niro becomes even more fascinating because it contains the variety of characters he depicts. This is the promise proffered by De Niro interviews in the popular press: that we can get to know a personality rich and varied enough to produce such a wide range of characters.

The central difficulty with getting to know this "real" personality through the print medium, however, seems to be De Niro's reluctance to be interviewed unless "pressured" (always by unnamed forces) to do so. When he does submit to an interview, his reticence to disclose private information and his discomfort with the entire interview process silences the expression of his "true" voice. It is this silence that is foregrounded in the press.

When reporters do manage to pin him down for an interview, he appears uncomfortable, as if "each question tossed at him were some sharp-edged object and he's unable to duck" (Fine). His answers are partial at best, as Bruce Kirkland notes: "Robert De Niro never completes a sentence but he rarely starts one, so you hardly notice" (p. 81). The reporter is often left with little to give an account of except for a string of unreadable gestures ("He starts to say something, hunches forward, taps the table, sighs, rubs his chin." [Terenzi]) or inarticulate mumblings (when asked by the *Toronto Sun* what was left for him to accomplish, De Niro reportedly said, "I, uh, can't, ah, umm. . . . Well, let's, ah, see, uh, I, uh." [Thompson]). The resulting articles pay as much attention to the frustrating, intimidating task of the interviewer as they do to the subject himself.

The primary explanation offered concerning De Niro's desire for privacy is to allow him to create a tabula rasa onto which he can project his different impersonations. In *Video Review*, he is quoted as saying: "I just don't care to be known as a celebrity. I think the more people know about you personally the more they see into your performance, and that often distracts from the performance" (p. 50). Larry Terenzi puts it this way: "His magic is sparked internally, and, like any magician, he'd like to keep its secret from being revealed." De Niro's silence becomes a kind of sleight of hand in which we are asked not to pay attention to the man behind the curtain so that our illusions about the characters may be maintained. De Niro's rejection of the interview process can be read as an attempt to promote impersonation over simple personification. He suggests that knowledge about the actor encourages an audience toward personification-reading strategies, and impersonation is easier if the audience does not know the "real" person. I want to concentrate on a less-commented-on feature of these interviews: those subjects that De Niro *will* talk about without reticence. In all the hullabaloo about what De Niro is "hiding" from the press, one tends to overlook what is freely communicated to the interviewers.

The articles on De Niro feature anecdotes about his "obsession" with preparing for a role. He gained weight for both *Raging Bull* and *The Untouchables*; he drove a taxi for *Taxi Driver*; he went to Sicily to learn Italian in the proper dialect for *Godfather 2*, and he also went to Brando's dentist to get a mouthpiece made for the part of Vito Corleone (played by Brando in the original *Godfather*); he trained as a boxer for a year (and became good enough to be a ranking middleweight, according to LaMotta) for *Raging Bull*; he learned to play the saxophone proficiently for *New York, New York*. Over and over these stories appear in the articles, full of details about the lengths De Niro will go to prepare for a part.

These anecdotes function to promote the "realness" of De Niro's acting. Because these stories are in popular circulation, they strategically help De Niro establish the verisimilitude of his performance. A member of the audience who knows about De Niro's extensive preparation for a role is predisposed to evaluate his performance as being really "real." Whether De Niro's research methods actually affect his on-screen performance is open to question, but the importance of this information about De Niro rooting his acting in real life can strongly affect viewer impressions. Note that the preparation that De Niro emphasizes is not psychological preparation but physical preparation, exemplified by the boxing training and weight gain for *Raging Bull*. To say that De Niro is silent in the discourse about his own stardom is to overlook the fact that De Niro offers his body fairly freely into the discourse.

De Niro is not portrayed as being notably camera shy to reporters, though there is a tradition of actors who dislike being photographed in situations beyond their control (from Katharine Hepburn, Greta Garbo, and Marlene Dietrich to Sean Penn).[4] Instead, De Niro is shown as being blatantly tape recorder shy, as being reluctant to have his *voice* captured.[5] Celebrity interviewers are accustomed to actors expressing themselves vocally, not bodily. Some respond to De Niro's vocal silence by offering a fairly detailed transcription of De Niro's body language, further asserting that De Niro's participation in the discourse is done bodily, not vocally.

However, having access to an actor's body is assumed to be a given by the dominant conception of the celebrity interview, and it is not enough. After all, we have access to images of the actor's body in the films themselves. The fan requires the celebrity body to speak, to reveal the inner truths it contains. Obviously the celebrity interview operates as part of the modern Western pursuit of the secret truths held by the body, as described by Michel Foucault. The desire for scientific knowledge of sex is the desire to make the body speak, to elicit its confessions.[6] De Niro's body clearly is communicating both in films and in interviews, but it does not give the satisfying answers we seek because it does not provide us with interior access.

The relatively free access we are given to De Niro's physical preparations is emphasized when compared to the little information we glean about psychological preparation. We are told that he prepares for a part by asking real people incessant questions, but we never learn what kinds of questions he asks. Jake LaMotta says that De Niro learned so much about his inner psychology that he told him things he never knew about himself, but he never revealed what those things are (Kroll, p. 86). De Niro's silence extends not only to private information about his personal life but also to the psychological methods of preparation. By telling us that he talked to real people but giving us no more information, De Niro further imbues his acting with "realness" while simultaneously mystifying the process.

The discussion on De Niro, therefore, may be seen as an attempt to reassert the importance of the actor's *physical* preparation to the American Method. Actor Chazz Palminteri says, "Marlon Brando changed acting when he walked across the stage in *A Streetcar Named Desire*. De Niro changed it with *Raging*

Bull. At that time, no actors transformed themselves the way he did. They do it now. But they do it because of him" (Cortina, p. 85). De Niro's assertion of his body, but not his psychology, into the discussion is at odds with the psychological orientation of pop culture's version of the Method. De Niro's refusal to give us psychological insight may be seen as an attempt to reclaim the body of the actor as the basis for impersonation, not mere personification. His silence regarding psychological preparation forces us to renegotiate the dominant conception of an actor's tools.

This silence extends even to the psychological processes of characters. De Niro talks about the process of developing the characterizations for *Raging Bull* with Martin Scorsese: "We did not feel a need for the old cliched psychological structure. He hated his brother so therefore he did . . . that sort of thing. Why should anybody say anything came from anywhere? Reasons? We never discussed reasons" (Ferretti, p. 28). According to Hal Hinson, "De Niro is the least psychological of Method actors. He doesn't appear to be as interested in puzzling out a character's inner life as he is concerned with expressing the mystery of personality. In *Raging Bull*, De Niro tells us that a man like Jake LaMotta is impossible to know, and that we are wrong to expect to understand a character's drives and motives" (p. 203).

When asked at a seminar for filmmakers what he was thinking at a pensive acting moment in *New York, New York*, De Niro replied: "I hate to disappoint you—I don't know. You probably thought I was really working. That's what I mean: It's very simple. . . . The audience knows how you feel. The less that you show the better" (quoted in "Dialogue," p. 43). De Niro's advice to actors tends to emphasize simplicity. While this may seem to be an attempt to make Method acting less intimidating and less mystical, the vague advice to "simplify" is more mystifying than it is instructive, particularly when balanced against a sizable publicity about De Niro's very complex preparations. Such mystification gives power to those who already have achieved "simplicity." Even De Niro's advice may be construed as giving more power to his own imposing stature.

De Niro passes along only one piece of advice from either of his well-known acting teachers, Stella Adler and Lee Strasberg. Several times he quotes Adler as saying, "Your talent lies in your choice" (quoted in "Dialogue," p. 40; Grobel, p. 85). This quote has a very specific meaning in acting contexts, but De Niro also seems to be using it in a larger sense, positing an ego that makes life choices. De Niro portrays himself as making choices as to who has access to what kinds of information. Reporters and fans can have access to data about his body, but he denies access to information about his private life, his psychological preparation, and his characters.

His extraordinary physical preparation becomes a discontinuous variable that distinguishes him from other actors, giving him what Robert Brady calls a "personal monopoly" (p. 129) with the accompanying economic power. Articles consistently emphasize his hard work, and this entitles him to a kind of status traditionally denied to film stars in a capitalist country founded on the Protestant work ethic. Film acting is not considered to be "real work" because of the tendency toward personification acknowledged in the pop song: But De Niro sweating and punching is a man obviously at work.

These attributes work in conjunction with the silent psychological discourse to make De Niro a more valuable commodity, one that allows him to exert a kind of control rarely extended to film actors. His hard work differentiates him from other actors, while his silence creates a mystery that this entire discourse wishes to solve. Normally film stars have to trade privacy for control. Stars like Clint Eastwood become producers of their own images, but they must follow the traditional rules of star publicity to do so. De Niro's choices have given him a collaborator's status with Martin Scorsese and more recently as head of an ambitious Lower Manhattan film collaborative. Elizabeth Kaye situates De Niro's recent interest in directing and producing as "an extension of the interests and skills that preoccupied him from the start, when he sat through long production meetings, paying rapt attention to discussions on where to store the costumes, where the trucks should be parked" (p. 45). Stars usually have to trade increased public visibility for the power of directing, but De Niro has used his silent acting mystique to gain status as a director (A Bronx Tale).

His strategy has given him power over things that are outside the normal film actor's control, but it also seems to imbue De Niro with discursive power over portions of the self that are traditionally considered very difficult to change. His refusal to discuss his past in detail allows us to assume one that seems to fit his persona. He is often believed to have grown up in a lower-class New York environment, but actually his father was a fairly successful modern artist (Dickey, p. 70). An emphasis in the popular press on the cultural capital of his upbringing might make playing Johnny Boy in Mean Streets difficult, but his silence frees him discursively from the class constraints of his past. Usually the actor's body is thought to provide the actor's basic "look," a given that can only be recast slightly through cosmetics. However, De Niro demonstrates an ability to break free of the traditional restraints of the body, reshaping it for different roles.

De Niro's ability to change the unchangeable (his past, his body) functions as part of a larger set of present-day discourses on altering one's own past (recasting it through psychotherapy) and one's body (through exercise and dieting regimens). These discourses acknowledge that society makes judgments based on the same assumption underlying personification in actors: that there is a unity between the body/personality and the social identity/role. People judge you when they see your body or when they detect traces of your past in your personality. Modern society posits that we, like De Niro, can change our pasts and our bodies, and therefore we can choose a different social identity: "In America it is almost as if, democratically, any actor can play any role naturally, just as any citizen can aspire to be President" (Le Fanu, p. 49).

The positing of some entity who is following Stella Adler's advice, choosing to speak or to be silent, choosing discursively a past or a body, still leaves the principal celebrity interview question open: Who is the "real" Robert De Niro? Who is doing the choosing? One common answer is disturbing for reigning Western conceptions of the self, even ones that acknowledge the possibility of reshaping a modern social identity. The explicit answer provided by some interviewers is that there is no "real" Robert De Niro, that there is no one at the wheel choosing life directions. An old girlfriend suggests: "The thing is, once you penetrate all the paranoia and secrecy that Bobby surrounds himself with, you'll find out that at the bottom of Bobby is really . . . nothing" (Brenner, p. 118). This De Niro is perhaps nothing but the roles he portrays. Shelley Winters says, "In between pictures, Bobby doesn't exist. I don't know where the human being is" (Brenner, p. 121). Michael Moriarty, who worked with De Niro on *Bang the Drum Slowly*, passed up an opportunity to speak to De Niro on the *Taxi Driver* set: "I don't know that guy at all. I knew Bruce Pearson [De Niro's *Bang the Drum Slowly* role]. I don't know Travis Bickle or Bob De Niro." Elizabeth Kaye suggests, "No one, perhaps, is better suited to being an actor and less suited to being a personality" (p. 45). Interviewer Paul Gardner muses: "The Method school uses acting for self-knowledge. De Niro's acting runs closer to self-escape" (p. 34).

This silence poses a threat for one of the founding Western beliefs: the utilitarian egoism of the individual. According to the philosophical tradition of Hume and Hobbes, a person's identity can be determined without reference to roles and social positionings, and this person can be trusted to act to promote his or her own best interests. The possibility that De Niro is nothing but his roles, that there is no central agent making decisions based on his own self-interest, is a very modern phenomenon. Clearly this is where De Niro's celebrity differs from that of other reclusive film stars to whom he is sometimes compared (Garbo, Brando). In the publicity about these stars, the existence of a "real" though elusive personality is never brought into question. With De Niro the silence is portrayed as a lack of an ego at the center of the individual.

On a somewhat less earth-shaking scale, the silence also calls into question the normally invisible workings of the Hollywood film industry publicity apparatus. When denied access to De Niro himself, the reporter often has to put secondary communications at the center of the piece. Several articles have more quotes by other people about De Niro than they have quotes by De Niro. When De Niro refused to talk to *Vanity Fair*, the interviewer (Bosworth) pieced together a portrait, "The Shadow King," from interviews with 50 of De Niro's associates and friends. For an *Esquire* article, Mike Sager prowled the Tribeca area, asking residents about their famous neighbor, some of whom were about as forthcoming as De Niro himself (" 'Whaddya, stalkin' him? . . . Why don't you fucks just leave him alone? Everybody knows: Bobby

De Niro don't do interviews."). This strategy further emphasizes the absence of the star's voice as it tries to fill that absence with other voices.

Another strategy is to focus on the difficulty of the De Niro interview process. One article in *Gentlemen's Quarterly* (Richman) consists of a long discussion of the reporter's trepidation at the task of interviewing such an elusive figure, followed by a brief chat with De Niro in which the star auditions the interviewer and turns him down. In his *Playboy* (Grobel) interview, De Niro turns off the tape recorder 11 times, looks at his watch seven times, and indicates he wants to leave five times. Here the awkwardness spotlights the assumptions we carry concerning the celebrity interview. The reporter does not have to justify his or her right to ask questions, but De Niro must justify his right to refuse them.

A related strategy (briefly noted earlier) is to emphasize De Niro's inarticulateness by delivering a fairly literal transcription of his words: "Yeah, well . . . I think that . . . umm . . . you know . . . uh-hah" (Schickel, p. 68). Usually a reply in such halting "naturalistic" speech would be cleaned up, and awkward false starts would be edited out. The inclusion of such markers of distinct speech patterns transforms the interview subject into an Other (for instance, when someone provides a phonetic transcription of Southern accents or African American speech patterns). Thus the considerably-less-than-smooth interactions between star and interviewer emphasize the constructed nature of the seemingly seamless interview usually proffered by the film publicity apparatus. Even though De Niro's silence problematizes both the film celebrity interview and Western conceptions of a unified utilitarian ego, these ideas still exert their power. It is possible to recoup much of the popular discourse on De Niro into a unified concept of self. In spite of the emphasis on De Niro's versatility of impersonation, one can reincorporate his work as personification.

The prototypical De Niro role is an angry, violent, obsessive, urban, alienated, lower-class, repressed loner, epitomized by *Taxi Driver*'s Travis Bickle and *Raging Bull*'s Jake LaMotta. De Niro comments in some interviews on characters that he would not play, particularly historical figures (he turned down the part of Jesus in *The Last Temptation of Christ*). This acknowledges that, despite the discourse on versatility, there is a recognizable core to the De Niro persona. This on-screen persona bears great resemblance to the De Niro depicted in the interviews: a silent, brooding, obsessive loner.[7] Paradoxically, De Niro's off-screen silence, which supposedly allows him the freedom to remake himself into many different on-screen characters, also ties him to those characters in a rather straightforward personifying manner.

The on-screen and off-screen De Niros differ from each other in a key way. In an off-screen situation, De Niro's silence is read as nonsignifying, as a refusal to communicate. However, when De Niro is silent on screen, his silence speaks. The magnified scrutiny of close-ups allows a film actor to signify without words, with very subtle movements. "If De Niro's silences tend to be a little awkward at parties, they explode on the screen. . . . In his silences, I see storm clouds on the horizon" (Braudy, p. 13). Barry Paris notes:

Robert De Niro's sentences—his *thoughts*—are like his acting. Grammar, syntax, and vocabulary are all there, but not always in words. . . . It's ironic that the very thing that draws people to De Niro on the screen—this powerful, largely nonverbal projection of character, emotion, and meaning—is what baffles and annoys some people about him offscreen, particularly the scribes who create his "image." (pp. 30, 33)

De Niro, the man who will go to extraordinary lengths to make his character fit the dramatic situation, refuses to change in acknowledgment of the difference between the interview situation and the dramatic situation. The more cooperative interview subject helps the celebrity publicity apparatus maintain the fiction that the two situations are not that different. We are promised access into the actor's psychology through interviews, and we seemingly get into the character's psyche through close-ups. But the discourse hides the fact that the interview and dramatic situations call for very different forms of communication. De Niro maintains a quiet reserve in both situations, perversely refusing to impersonate a celebrity interview subject, and, by doing so, he spotlights the invisible expectation that an actor will transform into a unified speaking subject during an interview.[8]

Here is where the signifier "De Niro" takes on one of its most radical critiques of modern society. The silent De Niro, not a utilitarian agent yet not purely reducible to situational roles, acknowledges the omnipresence of impersonation in our society. In order to survive, one must be able to adapt oneself to an increasingly varied set of situations. In such a society, older conceptions of self-interested agency may get lost in the chaos. De Niro, by carving out a structuring absence in his own discourse, is "released, at last, from producing an identity card in an absurd world where, he knows, most lives are fraudulent anyway" (Gardner, p. 33).

NOTES

1. This chapter will only deal with De Niro's interviews and celebrity profiles in print. Interviews in other media (which are quite rare) and reviews of his films would provide interesting insights into the phenomenon of De Niro's stardom, and certainly they interact with the print discourses dealt with in this chapter, but they lie outside this chapter's focus.

2. I do not wish to make the romanticized case that theater actors actually do have more control over their work than do film actors. To call theater an actor's medium is to ignore the power of the director, who can occupy a dictatorial space in the theater just as he or she can in filmmaking. Obviously a range of ideologically and interpersonal power issues are at play in any theater or film process, and these factors can vary widely. I only wish to acknowledge the presence of a thread of discourse that romantically (though not always accurately) locates more control in the theater actor than the film actor.

3. Important texts concerning Method acting include Stanislavski (1989a, 1989b, 1989c); Chekov (1985); Hagen (1991); Strasberg (1987); and Adler (1988).

4. There is some evidence about De Niro's anger toward unauthorized photographs. In 1995 he was charged with assaulting a cameraman outside a Manhattan bar. However, the tables turned when the photographer allegedly said he would drop the charges in exchange for money, and De Niro helped police set up a sting to trap the extortioner (Wulf, p. 102). There is no indication that De Niro is reticent to have his picture taken by reporters in interview situations. In fact, he has posed for several magazine covers, most notably dressing up as George Washington for the December 1995/January 1996 cover of *George*.

5. Notably, Julia Kristeva (1980) considers the voice to provide access to interior states.

6. According to Foucault (1985), Western societies seek to penetrate the external restrictions of the body, not only to gain sexual pleasures but also to gain the pleasure of knowing that body. Western cultures seek to know the truth about the body, and that knowledge then gives the feeling of power and control over what would otherwise be unruly. He calls this desire to know *scientia sexualis*, allying this desire with the pursuit of scientific knowledge, and he locates this impulse in a range of discourses, including pornography, law, medicine, and psychiatry. The impulse to know the truth about De Niro, a truth that his body stubbornly withholds from us, is rooted in this broader context (pp. 51–73).

7. In a humorous sidebar in *Entertainment Weekly*, Jake Tapper (1997) presented a Robert De Niro quiz that asked readers to match De Niro's films with a brief description of his role. The joke is that they all sound the same ("Cutesy gangster, Satanic psycho gangster, Repentant gangster cop, Psycho messenger, Psycho boxer, Patchwork psycho") (p. 66).

8. De Niro's refusal to employ different strategies when situations change flies in the face of Erving Goffman's (1959) theories of agency, where a social actor changes his or her role to fit a change in situation. The social actor tries to maintain what Goffman calls "synechdochic responsibility" (p. 51), which is both a consistency of manner and a fit between setting, costume, and behavior. By maintaining his core silence despite a change from dramatic to interview situation, De Niro refuses to play-act according to Goffman's (and society's) rules.

REFERENCES

Adler, Stella. *The Technique of Acting.* New York: Bantam, 1988.

Agan, Patrick. *Robert De Niro: The Man, the Myth, and the Movies.* London: Robert Hale, 1989.

Bosworth, Patricia. "The Shadow King." *Vanity Fair.* October (1987): 100–107+.

Brady, Robert. "The Problem of Monopoly." In Watkins, Gordon, ed., *The Motion Picture Industry.* Annals of the American Academy of Political and Social Science. Vol. 254 (November 1947): 125–36.

Braudy, Susan. "Robert De Niro—The Return of the Silent Screen Star." *New York Times.* March 6 (1977): sect. 2, pp. 13+.

Brenner, Marie. "What's Robert De Niro Hiding?" *Redbook.* May (1977): 116–21.

Butler, Jeremy G., ed. *Star Texts: Image and Performance in Film and Television.* Detroit: Wayne State University Press, 1991.

Canby, Vincent. "In Films, Acting Is Behavior." *New York Times*. December 12 (1976): sect. 2, pp. 1+.

Carrithers, Michael, Steven Collins, and Steven Lukes. *The Category of the Person: Anthropology, Philosophy, and History*. Cambridge: Cambridge Univeristy Press, 1985.

Chekov, Michael. *To the Actor*. New York: Barnes-Harper, 1985.

Cole, Toby, and Helen Krich Chinoy, eds. *Actors on Acting: The Theories, Techniques, and Practices of the World's Greatest Actors, Told in Their Own Words*. New York: Crown, 1970.

Cortina, Betty. "Robert De Niro." *Entertainment Weekly* 510 (Winter 1999): 85.

de Cordova, Richard. "The Emergence of the Star System in America." *Wide Angle* 6, no. 4 (1985): 4–13.

"De Niro Is Shy, but His Art Is Probing a Role's Psyche." *People*. April 2 (1979): 15.

"Dialogue on Film: Robert De Niro." *American Film*. March (1981): 39–48.

Dickey, Christopher. "The Second Time Around." *Newsweek*. May 31 (1999): 70.

Dyer, Richard. *Stars*. London: British Film Institute, 1979.

Fehren, Henry. "Real Make-believe Belief." *U.S. Catholic*. September (1981): 41–43.

Ferretti, Fred. "The Delicate Art of Creating a Brutal Film Hero." *New York Times*. November 3 (1980): sect. 2, pp. 1+.

Fine, Marshall. "De Niro May Be Good—but He's No Pacino." *Detroit News*. December 15 (1995).

Fiske, John. *Television Culture*. London: Methuen, 1987.

Flatley, Guy. "Look—Bobby's Slipping into Brando's Shoes." *New York Times*. November 4 (1973): sect. 2, pp. 13+.

Foucault, Michel. *The Uses of Pleasure*. Vol. 2 of *The History of Sexuality*. Translated by Robert Hurley. New York: Pantheon, 1985.

Gardner, Paul. "It's Dilemma, It's Delimit, It's De Niro." *New York*. May 16 (1977): 33–37.

Goffman, Erving. *The Presentation of Self in Everyday Life*. New York: Anchor, 1959.

Gordon, Meryl. "Grill Power: Robert De Niro Builds His Dream Restaurant." *New York*. April 9 (1990): 76–83.

Grobel, Lawrence. "*Playboy* Interview: Robert De Niro." *Playboy*. January (1989): 69–90+.

Hadenfield, Chris. "New York, New York: In Which Robert De Niro Trades His .44 for a New Axe." *Rolling Stone*. June 16 (1977): 36–44.

Hagen, Uta. *A Challenge for the Actor*. New York: Scribners, 1991.

Haskell, Molly. "People Are Talking about Robert De Niro." *Vogue*. May (1981): 282+.

Hibbin, Sally. "Star Profile: Robert De Niro." *Films and Filming*. May (1984): 6–7.

Hinson, Hal. "Some Notes on Method Actors." *Sight and Sound* (Summer 1984): 200–205.

Hutchinson, Curtis. "Newsreel Special: Robert De Niro at the NFT." *Films and Filming*. April (1985): 3.

Kaye, Elizabeth. "Robert De Niro." *New York Times Magazine*. November 14 (1993): 44+.

Kehr, David. "A Star Is Made." *Film Comment*. January–February (1979): 8–9.

King, Barry. "The Star and the Commodity: Notes towards a Performance Theory of Stardom." *Cultural Studies*. May (1987): 145–61.

Kirkland, Bruce. "The Good, the Bad, and the Brilliant." *Toronto Sun*. December 3 (1995): 81.

Kondo, Dorinne K. *Crafting Selves: Power, Gender, and Discourse in a Japanese Workplace*. Chicago: University of Chicago Press, 1990.

Kortarba, Joseph A., and Andrea Fontana, eds. *The Existential Self in Society*. Chicago: University of Chicago Press, 1990.

Kristeva, Julia. *Desire in Language: A Semiotic Approach to Literature and Art*. Translated by Thomas Gora, Alice Jardine, and Leon S. Roudiez. New York: Columbia University Press, 1980.

Kroll, Jack. "De Niro: A Star for the '70's." *Newsweek* May 16 (1977): 80–86.

———. "De Niro as Capone: The Magnificent Obsessive." *Newsweek*. June 22 (1987): 64–65.

Le Fanu, Mark. "Looking for Mr. De Niro." *Sight and Sound* (Winter 1985–86): 46–49.

McKay, Keith. *Robert De Niro: The Hero behind the Masks*. New York: St. Martin's, 1986.

Meyrowitz, Joshua. *No Sense of Place: The Impact of Electronic Media on Social Behavior*. Oxford: Oxford University Press, 1985.

Modderno, Craig. "De Niro: Man of Few Words." *Video Review*. March (1989): 50.

Paris, Barry. "Maximum Expression." *American Film*. October (1989): 30–39+.

Pfuetze, Paul. *Self, Society, Existence: Human Nature and Dialogue in the Thought of George Herbert Mead and Martin Buber*. New York: Harper, 1961.

Richman, Alan. " 'You Talkin to Me?' 'No!' " *Gentlemen's Quarterly*. January (1991): 92–97.

Roach, Joseph R. *The Player's Passion: Studies in the Science of Acting*. Newark: University of Delaware Press, 1985.

Sager, Mike. "The Man Who Acts like God." *Esquire*. December (1997): 74–80.

Schickel, Richard. "The Quiet Chameleon." *Time*. January 27 (1972).

Schruers, Fred. "*De Niro*." *Rolling Stone*. August 25 (1988): 43+.

Silverman, Kaja. *The Acoustic Mirror: The Female Voice in Psychoanalysis and Cinema*. Bloomington: Indiana University Press, 1988.

Stanislavski, Constantin. *An Actor Prepares*. New York: Routledge, 1989a.

———. *Building a Character*. New York: Routledge, 1989b.

———. *Creating a Role*. New York: Routledge, 1989c.

Strasberg, Lee. *A Dream of Passion: The Development of the Method*. Boston: Little, Brown, 1987.

Tapper, Jake. "You Talkin' to Him?" *Entertainment Weekly*. January 31 (1997): 66.

Terenzi, Larry. *Once upon a Time in Tribeca*. Available at http://homearts.com/depts/pl/movie/18deniro.htm.

Thompson, Bob. "The De Niro That Wags the Dog." *Toronto Sun*. January 6 (1998): 26.

Watters, Jim. "Raging De Niro: A Fighting Actor Tackles a Tough Role." *Life*. November (1980): 89–94.

Wolcott, James. "Loose Cannons." *Vanity Fair*. April (1990): 54+.

Wulf, Steve. "Lights, Camera, Reaction." *Time*. November 13 (1995): 102.

Part II

The Cultural Impact of Star Images

Keanu Reeves in *Speed* (Jan De Bont, 1994). © 20th Century-Fox (Kobal Collection)/Richard Foreman.

Chapter 4

The Keanu Effect—Stardom and the Landscape of the Acting Body: Los Angeles/Hollywood as Sight/Site

Carmel Giarratana

Hollywood is indeed the city of the marvelous, in which the heroic ideal of life is real and real life mythic. Here are the Elysian fields: a legendary city, but also a city living its legend. A ship of dreams anchored in real/reel life. A Californian Shangri-La from which flows the elixer of immortality.
—Edgar Morin

A movie star is mythic—like no-one you've ever seen in your daily life.
—John Waters

THE LANDSCAPE THAT IS KEANU AND THE SPACES THAT ARE *SPEED*

Keanu Reeves's films are almost always about locating spectacle and display: of his actual body, of the acting body, of the body of the star. We cannot, however, begin to comprehend the phenomenon of Keanu Reeves's stardom without understanding the ways in which, upon the body of the star—and this star in particular—reside several discourses about site and sight, about notions of landscape and spectacle. Because both the Hollywood landscape and the body of the actor are discursive spaces that act out notions of utopian and dystopian space, the actor's body as readable landscape is therefore a metaphor entirely appropriate to the discussion of Hollywood and its stars. This chapter will explore some of the landscape dimensions associated with the body of Keanu Reeves.

Cinema, from its inception, has been a rich source of spectacle and of the representation of actual and mythic landscapes. And Hollywood, with "more stars than there are in heaven" has always been its premier site.[1] From the be-

ginning, it has been a place for "stars" and for filmmaking and that has continued to be its raison d'être. As a site, "Hollywood exists . . . as a state of mind,
not [just] as a geographical entity" (Carey quoted in Davis, 1999, p. 392). Indeed, for writers in cultural geography, the term "landscape" means more than
just an actual site or a pleasing view of scenery. Landscape is about the interaction of people and places. It speaks about a social group and its spaces, particularly the spaces to which the group belongs, and from which its members
derive some part of their shared identity and meaning (Groth, 1997, p. 1).

According to cultural geographer Denis Cosgrove (1991), "landscapes are
cultural images, whether we are speaking of actual topography or of its representation in words, pictures or even music [and film], moreover, the representation of landscape can help share feelings, ideas and values, most particularly
those which refer to the relation between land and life" (p. 8). The actual and
mythical place that we understand as "Hollywood" functions exactly as this
sort of multilayered landscape, so much so that, as Mike Davis has noted, the
concept of Hollywood as a place is "difficult . . . to come to grips with, [it is]
elusive and elastic at the same time" (1992, p. 394).[2]

In the Western world we do not just inhabit or see landscapes, we "per-
ceive" them. We are the point from which the "seeing" occurs. The Western
landscape is therefore an ego-centered landscape, a perspectival landscape, a
landscape of views and vistas. In cinema, the depicted figures/characters act as
mediators between the viewer and the events portrayed. Like other visual artists, filmmakers (i.e., screenwriters, directors, actors, cinematographers, and
production designers) create ego-centered landscapes through their manipulation of time and space. Sometimes these created spaces are mimetic representations of real spaces endlessly rearranged or re-envisaged, and other
times they are "new virtual worlds" designed to (re)present or (re)place reality. As both a producer of culture and a cultural production, cinema is one of
the preeminent manipulators of subjectivity, of vision and visuality, and of
time and space, and therefore, it partakes in both the politics of vision and of
dispossession.

Cinema creates and offers up both utopian and dystopian landscapes. In the
essay "Of Other Spaces," Michel Foucault outlines the distinction between
utopian, heterotopian, and dystopian spaces to show how particular types of
space enact social and power relations. In this essay, Foucault names "utopias"
as sites with no *real* place. They are theatrical sites that have a general relation
of direct or inverted analogy with the real space of society. They present society
itself in a perfected form, or society turned upside down; but in any case, these
utopias are fundamentally unreal spaces (Foucault, p. 24).

Individual films are capable of presenting us narratively and visually with
many such utopias and their opposite—dystopias. Heterotopias, on the other
hand, according to Foucault, are the siting of the partial, the contingent, the
specific, and the peculiar. They are capable of juxtaposing in a single real place
several spaces, several sites that are in themselves incompatible. In effect, they

disallow a utopian claim to universality and completion. And though it is often utopian in a narrative sense, cinema (i.e., the operation of cinema as an activity) is a heterotopian space par excellence. In other words, it is a contradictory site that brings together a whole series of places that are foreign to one another. It is a three-dimensional space in which one sees projected on a two-dimensional space, three-dimensional images. Filmed landscapes, and the characters who inhabit them, are always at the same time utopias (since utopias are sites with no real place) and heterotopias (which are simultaneously mythic and real).

The geography of the cinematic landscape is, therefore, imbued with the spatial and the spectacular and not just the psychic.[3] In this way one can talk about the body of the star as being tied up with materiality, with spectacle, and with the geography of the "surface" and not necessarily, or exclusively, with the psychic identification that is the basis of much psychoanalytic film theory. Being open to multiple readings and desires, Keanu's body, for example, is both a utopian and a dystopian landscape. He can be seen/perceived in a variety of ways depending on one's point of view. A visit to some of the Web sites devoted to him reveals that he has been heroized by Asians, Anglo Saxons, and African Americans alike, and his sexuality and/or sexual appeal is variously interpreted as being gay, bisexual, or heterosexual.[4] Likewise, as a box-office drawing card, he can be both mainstream and marginal.

It is in its representation of utopian, heterotopian, and dystopian spaces that cinema is able to present both the hegemonic and the oppositional. Such simultaneity may be found, for example, in the film *Speed* (1994) in which, to use Michel de Certeau's rather evocative phrasing, "Every story is a travel story—a spatial practice" (p. 115). What is most striking about the film is the way it moves the body of its star, Keanu Reeves, through its spaces and the kinds of political messages that this might consciously and unconsciously suggest. For example, *Speed* is about the laterality of Los Angeles. It could only have been filmed in L.A. with its extensive freeways and its ineffective public transportation system, which, in the film, becomes a metaphor for poverty. The film presents us with a cartography of the often intangible social relations that are acted out in its spaces. It is like an atlas that reveals some of the invisible spaces that are not locatable on official maps.[5]

In *Narration in the Fiction Film* (1985), David Bordwell begins his chapter, "Narration and Space," by outlining the various approaches taken in film theory to account for the effects of filmic space on the viewer, and also for the formal, spatial manipulations and operations that are intrinsic to it as a medium. He argues that "each adjustment of distance and perspective in cinema is invested with exquisite sensibility" (p. 99). *Speed*, like many other popular fictions, chooses the spaces of the city, in this case Los Angeles, as its narrative and actual site. This film shows transgressions of the boundaries of city spaces as well as those of genre. It is part detective film, part melodrama, and part action film. But primarily, this film is an exploration of the landscape of Los Angeles and of the body of its star, Keanu Reeves. The screen's exploration of his body and its operation in the landscape is a narrative that spills out above and beyond the "action" of the story. And while the city itself is one of the major "characters" in *Speed*, it is Keanu's movement through the city that is of most interest.

While landscape and cityscape shots construct a narrative space in which the characters in a film can perform the various actions of the plot, these location shots, which are more than just neutral spaces, often demand to be read as real historical places (Higson, p. 3). At the same time, as Andrew Higson argues, the narrative compulsion in films works continually to transform specific *place* once more into abstract *space*. In the case of *Speed* this means that over and above the narrative, the visuals, including our vision of the actor/star body, are often the film's real stars. This tension is "transcended by the incorporation of landscape shots into, and as, the movement of the narration itself: place becomes a signifier of character, a metaphor of the state of mind of the protagonist" (p. 3).[6] Via the body of Reeves's character, Jack Travern, Los Angeles, through its transportation systems, becomes not a utopian vista but a dystopian place to be investigated, intersected, interrogated, surveyed, and policed, a space that is full of social and criminal dangers.

Bordwell and Thompson have argued that

in the classical paradigm, the system for constructing space (that is, the continuity style) has as its aim the subordination of spatial (and temporal) structures to the logic of the narrative, especially to the cause/effect chain. Negatively, the space is presented so as not to distract attention from the dominant actions; positively, the space is "used" up by the presentation of narratively important settings, character traits ("psychology") or other causal agents. Space as space is rendered subordinate to space as a site for action. (quoted in Higson, p. 8)

It may also be argued, however, as Higson does, "that the narrative system of a film is never as simple as Bordwell and Thompson's formalism would allow. There is [as both Stephen Heath and Steve Neale also suggest], always an undertow of meanings pulling against the flow of the narrative, always more than the narrative can use, whether it is in the form of the spectacular, or in the form of descriptively authentic detail" (p. 8). In other words, because there is a surplus of "realistic detail" in the film's narrative, we tend to read the narrative space of the film as a real historical space, even though, as Higson suggests, much of that detail is actually structurally redundant to the narrative. This immediately raises the problem of the relationship between character and environment, between the protagonists of the fiction and the spectacle of the real historical conditions of the place that they inhabit (p. 8).

Speed is very much a film about the fragmentary spaces through which characters interact (usually in a transgressive way), with environments both visibly represented and unrepresented. David Bass has suggested that "a movie has neither presumptions nor obligations to encyclopedic completeness, and so its choices of fragments and their mode of assembly is relatively free. What is selected for inclusion is often less revealing than what is excluded—lost, as it were, in the interstices between chosen fragments" (no page). Where we *are not* taken in *Speed* is just as interesting as where we *are* taken. We are not driven through Bel Air or Beverly Hills, for example, because the public transportation system has no social, cultural, or political place in these neighborhoods.

According to Diane Ghirado, professor of architecture at U.C.L.A., the city bus system is used mainly by the Hispanic population. It is significant, therefore, that the white, obviously middle-class, Annie (Sandra Bullock) is only riding the bus because she has lost her driver's license—for speeding! *Speed* becomes about the spectacle that *is* Los Angeles; and that spectacle, I would argue, is finally caught up in a vision that traverses/constructs not only the narrative spaces of the film, but also situates and conflates our vision with that of the narrative protagonists. This view forces us to investigate the space of their actions, to interrogate the kinds of political messages and anxieties that are implied in the film's use of space, because, ultimately, the "identity" of Los Angeles has often rested on its being a space that is continually contested and recontested.

That Los Angeles has an enormous social and material complexity makes the number of possible literary, historical, and cinematic takes on the city limitless, and its history as a cultural palimpsest has been well documented by various writers, including Mike Davis and Merry Ovnick. But it was Reyner Banham who prophetically claimed that Los Angeles' polymorphous landscapes and architectures were given a "comprehensible unity" by the freeway grid in a metropolis that "spoke the language of movement not monument" (quoted in Davis, 1992, p. 73). As a film *about* Los Angeles, *Speed* maps a baroquely layered and multidimensional reality in which the city and its star, Keanu Reeves, are both liminal and endless texts—always promising meaning, but ultimately only offering hints and signs of a possible and final reality. It is like an unfinished freeway—one of the most common actual sights in Los Angeles, and one of the most potent metaphorical sites in the film. As Richard Dyer writes in a review of the film, "this is the movie *as* roller-coaster: all action and next to no plot" (p. 8). But, rather than seeing *Speed* as mindless entertainment, Dyer argues that what is just as important as narrative is its function as spectacle. For Dyer,

the cinema has always had the potential to be like this. Whether or not it is true that the first audiences for the Lumiere Brothers' film of a train entering a station ducked in terror as it advanced towards them, the idea that they did has often seemed emblematic of what film is about. The Lumieres ushered in a new technology, that has become ever more elaborate, reveling in both showing and creating the sensation of movement. *Train Arriving at a Station* and *Speed* belong to a distinguished lineage. . . . The celebration of sensational movement, that we respond to in some still unclear sense "as if real," for many people *is* the movies. (p. 7)

As Dyer notes, the price is not just in people but elsewhere in things and places. In *Speed* it is the transportation system itself that is smashed about: cars, trucks, freeway barriers, planes, and even the roadway in a final eruption of a subway train from below the city. This spectacle of destruction makes visible one of the great frustrations of modern urban living—moving through space and time (Dyer, p. 8). However, through the body of its star, Keanu Reeves, we are guided triumphantly through the dystopian spaces of Los Angeles, which, as Matt Wray has noted, construct public space as a restrictive and dystopian zone of conflict (p. 2). It is no wonder that we relish the way *Speed* takes us through public spaces that still bear the traces of "openness" and "danger," and that the film seems so much like a wild theme-park ride, complete with a fantasy ending on Hollywood Boulevard.

The ironic, self-reflexive ending where Reeves and Bullock end up beneath a movie marquee and a Hollywood "Tours of the Stars' Homes" bus, doubly conflates star/landscape and site/sight. It thereby undercuts the political and social dilemmas of the film, and presents Hollywood cinema and the star body as appropriate utopian solutions to deal with the dystopia that is the real Los Angeles/Hollywood. In other words, the "not real" heterotopia of filmic space undercuts the politics of real place, suggesting utopian fantasy as a solution to real social problems. As the film-producer character played by Steve Martin says in Lawrence Kasdan's *Grand Canyon* (1992), "All of life's riddles are answered in the movies." In that film, the proliferating symptoms of social collapse can only be counteracted by small acts of individual well-meaning, while in *Speed*, the "buffed and beautiful" action hero Travern/Reeves saves not only the people on the bus (including co-star Sandra Bullock) but also prevents the imminent destruction of Hollywood (symbolized here by its namesake, Hollywood Boulevard) as a site/sight.

Through its astounding success *Speed* made Keanu a legitimate star; it reinvented the "action hero," and it revitalized Hollywood cinema through its massive box-office takings. It shows its viewers (particularly the residents of Los Angeles) that the only safe space is cinematic space. As Matt Wray notes,

The ideology of the film shows itself in how it constructs and resolves conflicts in public space. The narrative first works to create a moral panic and paranoia about violence in the public realm, conjuring up fantastic dangers and frenzies of violence, in large part caused by and visited upon both the underclass and working-class psychopaths. (p. 3)

Wray suggests that for the spectator the meaning of this film is clear: no one, including the middle class, is safe in Los Angeles. The solutions offered by the film include increased surveillance of the public realm along with more police "force," masked as rugged individualism in the figure of Reeves's Jack Travern (Wray, p. 3). Ultimately, despite the entertainment appeal of its spectacle, and the utopian cinematic fantasies it offers about the resolution of social conflict, *Speed* also draws our attention to the role of space in defining and maintaining divisions and hierarchies of power, and is thereby a part of the culture and politics of space.

Along with the political aspects of cinematic space, another advantage to thinking spatially about film is that our physical environment matters so much because it shapes both our material and our psychic lives. Siegfried Kracauer has convincingly argued that "spatial images are the dreams of society. Wherever the hieroglyphics of any spatial image are deciphered, there the basis of social reality presents itself" (p. xv). Thus, the real and imagined spaces we define in man-made landscapes, in architecture, in literature, or in films *produce* us at least as much as we produce them. Politics and social relations do not merely use the organization of space to their own ends; politics *is* the organization of spatial relationships.

This is particularly so in Los Angeles/Hollywood where the identity of "place" both actual and narrative, is so much tied to the economics of the film/entertainment industry.[7] There is an implicit politics of identity in the way that all cinema, but particularly Hollywood cinema, represents certain spaces and landscapes. Los Angeles/Hollywood is a literal "mediascape" in which the politics of identity and space are played out. As Giuliana Bruno (1993) has noted in relation to the Neapolitan city films of Elvira Notari, there is a strong comparison to be made between our aesthetic experience of the cinema and our subjective experience of the city (pp. 35–38).

THE SITE AND SIGHT OF BEAUTY

As a Hollywood star, Keanu Reeves's star/acting body functions, in Richard Maltby's (1995) terms, as a dialectic of cinema's warfare between personality and mechanism (p. 237).[8] His body is both a literal (real/reel) and a metaphorical (not real) landscape on which is inscribed the politics of place, the aesthetics of beauty, and the act of performance. Underpinning each of these is the economic imperative of "stardom" as a function of the Hollywood film industry and its global networks. His "star" body, like the literal and metaphoric landscape of Hollywood, is both a utopian and a dystopian place, while remaining at the same time, like the screen upon which it appears, a heterotopia, a nowhere land. Keanu's body, because of its actual and potential beauty, is utopian, like the Los Angeles/Hollywood sites it occupies, but also dystopian in its potential for violence and acts of transgression, and finally, heterotopian in its literal nonreality.

Keanu's bodily presence on the screen is an important feature of his function as "star." Most critics and many viewers tend to agree that he has no real acting range.[9] His performances are notable for their poor critical reviews. However, despite his reputation for "poor acting," it appears talent has little to do with his being cast in a role. Although he has been a convincing clown in *Bill and Ted's Excellent Adventure* (1989), an angst-ridden teenager in *River's Edge* (1987) and *My Own Private Idaho* (1991), and a cartoon-like action/sci-fi hero in *Point Break*, *Speed*, and *The Matrix* (1999), in actuality, his body acts as a liminal space that can cross genres and defies critical reception. The question needs to be asked: Why do we continue to want to *see* Keanu on the screen despite his notorious "lack of acting talent?" The answer lies not in the act of performance, but in his performance of beauty. It is his appearance that seems most attractive to both the lesser- and well-known directors he has worked with. For these directors Keanu Reeves is more than just an actor—he is a star![10]

The myth of stardom was created by Hollywood from the beginning, and it continues to be supported by Hollywood's restructured studio system. Stars guarantee financial success and, as was noted in *Premiere* magazine, "In Hollywood today, a star's endorsement is often the only real fairy dust that can make a project spring to life" (Horne and Spines, p. 62). In an age where film budgets have skyrocketed, the studios have come to rely more heavily on the pre-sold popularity of stars in an attempt to make their corporate strategies as risk free as possible, and this has led ultimately to a complete realignment of Hollywood power structures (Horne and Spines, p. 59). As Richard Dyer notes, "Hollywood wants the sure thing—the genre, the star—but people don't want exactly the same thing; they want the same only different." As a star, this is what Keanu Reeves does best. He is literally a body of variable expectations, and his body functions as a textual, narrative (cinematic), and economic (box-office) device.[11]

The star/acting body is also constructed for maximum economic return so that "artistic performance" is not the only, or even a necessary, precondition or measure of a star. In Keanu Reeves's case, like many stars before him, including the legendary Greta Garbo, beauty, in fact, works against any objective evaluation of performance. As a star, Reeves often appears merely to be *present* on the screen. His *acting* ability does not seem to be paramount, even though from time to time a director like Kathryn Bigelow in *Point Break* manages, some would argue, to wring out of him a genuine "performance" rather than just a "presence." The aesthetics of beauty of the star/acting body, like the beauty of the filmed landscape, are the fodder of narrative cinema, and Keanu Reeves's beauty/face/body have been utlized for maximum narrative potential in films like *Point Break*, *Speed*, and *The Matrix*.

Speed, in particular, appears to conflate the acting body of Keanu Reeves with the narrative and actual landscape of Los Angeles/Hollywood. It is a film about the disjunction between utopian and dystopian spaces, where the freeway and other transport systems act as heterotopias—no man's lands—spaces existing between the violent dystopia of the city and the apparently safe utopia of the suburbs.[12] In the same way that this film charts the differing cultural and political aspects of Los Angeles, Keanu's body is a map on which are written the differing desires or needs of the audience. His body "acts" as a safe place on which can be written many different discourses—gender, sexuality, fandom, economics, aesthetics, and politics.

Perhaps part of the intense interest in him lies in his "mysterious" racial appearance—part Asian and part European—which gives him the malleable features out of which several directors have seen fit to construct a persona. Or perhaps his universal appeal lies in the way his face is changeable in the same way that a landscape is changeable and open to interpretation. As his co-star in *Speed*, Sandra Bullock noted, "Everything about him is laced with mystery—that's his charm" (quoted in Bassom, p. 74).

Unlike Tom Cruise whose acting persona always seems to be a fixed social, cultural, political sign (Cruise excels at portraying variations of white, middle- and upper-class manhood), Keanu's performances have been shaped and framed in various ways to express a variety of social, cultural, and political roles (gay, straight, ethnic, working class, and middle class). He is, in effect, a variable landscape that directors like Bertolucci, Bigelow, Coppola, Branagh, and others have seen fit to place within a frame. Indeed, in the majority of Keanu Reeves's films the most successful performances by him are those where he is allowed to "be beautiful" rather than to "act."

If, then, presence rather than performance is one of the conditions of stardom, then so is the beauty of the star. In *The Most Beautiful Woman on the Screen—the Fabrication of the Star Greta Garbo*, Michaela Krützen establishes a close connection between human beauty and the specifics of the film medium. "Film shapes the production of the star through the characteristics inherent in the medium; its affinity for the surface, the possibility of close-ups or the filmic interpretation of a role" (p. 4). Like Siegfried Kracauer, she believes that film defines itself as an art form more suited than any other to the visual representation of physical reality. As such, film is "*the* representative form for Beauty" (Krützen, p. v). Krützen argues that in addition to its capacity for showing reality in great detail, film, in contrast to theater, can incorporate the close-up, a device by which the human face can be reproduced in previously unknown perfection. Therefore it is no accident that the myth of Greta Garbo is most concretely expressed in the evocation of her face (Krützen, p. v). "By means of the close-up," Krützen writes, "the human face aquires new and special meaning. Actors know this and they energetically insist upon the greatest number of close-ups before signing a contract" (p. v).[13]

The affinity of film for showing the superficiality of things, whether a landscape or a face, is a feature of cinematography that cannot be matched by any other medium, including still photography. It acts as an exemplar for the filmic representation of beauty, because the beauty of the star is almost always external, despite its occasional presentation in fan magazines as "inner quality." Beauty is, in Krützen's terms, "an element of the surface splendour of the star" (p. 15). The technical possibilities of film for producing beauty are its affinity for the surface, and the possibility of the close-up—two features that have been used to good effect by those directors who have worked with Keanu Reeves. Although lingering close-ups of Keanu's face are consistent features of most of his films, *Speed*'s love affair with Keanu's face prompted one critic to note:

Keanu Reeves' Travern lacks not merely a tragic dimension or even an ironic one, but any dimension at all; experience has left no imprint on his beautiful features. . . . Dennis Hopper is almost more than the movie can survive. . . . It is extremely difficult to connect this pudgy, vacant-eyed ranter with the sophisticated devices that the movie is all about. (Berardinelli, n.p.)

Likewise, in *Point Break* Kathryn Bigelow consistently makes Keanu's face and body the constant object of the camera's movement. In this film when he is pursuing or being pursued through the landscape, it is he who is of prime visual interest. He seems to transgress the borders of the frame—because when he is not in the frame we momentarily lose interest, and so we are forced to search him out. His body, therefore, is not only of prime visual interest, it also moves the narrative forward—it literally constructs the landscape of the film. When his body is threatened with violence and breach, as in the stakeout scene where Utah is thrown to the ground and nearly meets his end pinned underneath a slicing lawn mower, the crisis for the viewer seems to be, "Oh no, what will happen to Keanu's beautiful face?" In scene after scene in *Point Break*, Keanu's co-stars, Patrick Swayze, Gary Busey, and the female lead Lori Petty, act as mere mirrors reflecting the power of his "star" presence. This is the essence of the "Keanu Effect"—his is the power of the surface, where the display of physical beauty achieves the level of a dramatic act.[14]

To say that someone is superficial almost always means to devalue him or her—it suggests a lack of depth, of subtlety, or meaningful content. Many critics have made it clear that this is true of Keanu's ability, or lack of ability, as an actor, whether on screen or on stage.[15] However, in Krützen's terms, "The surface is always only a totality of edge points, the shell of a core which is understood as essential . . . philosophical reflection then means penetrating and going beyond the surface" (p. 285). Siegfried Kracauer also assesses the surface as the place that exhibits the fewest solidifications. He assumes films mirror society and therefore "film finds medial fulfilment in the depiction of the external—the cinema seems to come into its own when it clings to the surface of things" (quoted in Krützen p. 285). Though arriving at their conclusions from different angles, both Kracauer and Krützen believe (and it seems, so do most of Keanu's critics) that "the basis of the work of a film perfomer is appearance [rather than performance]" (Krützen, p. 94).

Australian cinematographer Ellery Ryan (1999) notes, for example, the difference between the impression a cameraman may get of an actor whose performance seems lackluster or even ordinary on the set, and the filmed dailies of that performance, which often reveal a perfection or radiance not obvious in real life. According to Ryan, sometimes the "beauty" of the most beautiful of "real" faces (especially some television or soap stars) does not necessarily translate to the big screen, while on the other hand, someone who appears "ordinary" in front of the camera actually suprises, and shines, on the screen. Mystically he or she appears to become a star.

Mysticism is a trait that has often been associated with the star. Hollywood invented the star, and while the supremacy of Hollywood's celebrities in cinema worldwide is a testament to the marketing skills of the industry, there needs be a more coherent explanation of what makes a star, to explain why particular actors are stars and others are not. It cannot simply be marketing, or inherent beauty, or sex appeal that creates stars—there must also be other forces at work.[16] If acting ability is not a condition of stardom then what is it that makes Keanu Reeves a star? What is the essence of the Keanu Effect? I would argue that apart from beauty, "largeness" is the key. The largeness of the cinema screen, as opposed to the smallness of the television screen or the photograph, changes the dramatic weight of everything.

In his discussion of what makes a film star, Ellery Ryan suggests that cinema works with the dimensions of faces and bodies in a way that no other medium, including large-scale painting and billboards, can. This "mythical and technical largeness" has significant repercussions for the representation of cultural and political spaces not only within the imaginary or narrative space of cinematic representations, but also for the way in which we identify with actors/characters, and the spaces—both metaphoric and literal—that they inhabit. Ryan suggests that what is larger than life on the movie screen becomes smaller than life on television.

Leaving aside considerations of story situation and setting, which in practice are also considerably diminished, the size of the screen also limits the visual style of the medium.[17] The long shot and the extreme close-up are rarely used in television production. There is an over-reliance on the two shot, the head shot, and the zoom. The aim is most often to present an "easy" image, one that the eye can easily accommodate without disorienting the viewer. There is always an emphasis on a smooth continuity of images with few surprises and no real difficulties (Ryan).

"Largeness" appears to affect which people are considered cinematic stars and why. Writer Bruce Cook notes, "In the movies everybody is bigger than life . . . one is either a movie star or a television star—never both" (p. 58). Although one might question this dictum in light of the successful transition recently of some television stars like George Clooney and the cast of the U.S. sitcom *Friends* to the big screen, Cook's anecdote about the actor Richard Dreyfuss is still a rather telling one in this respect. He notes that "when *Jaws* was being shot on Martha's Vineyard, [Steven] Spielberg was said to have become miffed that Dreyfuss was so much more successful than he was in getting dates with girls on the island. Dreyfuss, who had already been seen in *American Grafitti*, consoled Spielberg: 'Look at it this way, Steve. I've got a face that's forty feet high. You haven't' " (quoted in Cook, p. 58). Like Ryan, Cook also suggests that "largeness" has done much to dictate the technique of the film actor who must become a reductionist, and who has to discipline himself or herself to hold his or her histrionic effects down to an absolute minimum (p. 58).

In the same vein, most writers on stardom, including Edgar Morin and Richard Dyer, also argue that the movie star is one who "behaves" rather than "acts." Cook suggests that

it is his [*sic*] vocation, his function, to serve as a vessel for the fantasies of the audience. The more he can contain, the greater star he will be. There is almost necessarily an element of the mythic in every movie star . . . like all mythic heroes, his character must remain somewhat generalized and undefined, even perhaps (in an odd way) sexually neuter. (p. 59)

As a condition of stardom, Keanu Reeves has definitely been characterized in this way. Rumors and anecdotes about his sexuality abound, and continue to be the core of most stories written about him. Keanu appears to be living proof of Cook's belief that a star chooses a role to fit the persona he or she has created (p. 69). This may certainly have been the case in his choice of roles with a "gay" subtext like *My Own Private Idaho* (1991), or grunge roles in *Feeling Minnesota* (1996) and *The Last Time I Committed Suicide* (1997).

According to Morin, "The star is more than an actor incarnating characters, he incarnates himself in them, and they become incarnate in him" (p. 44). Because of his choice of roles, Keanu has consistently been constructed as aloof and unintelligent or misunderstood. So effective was Keanu's incarnation as Ted in *Bill and Ted's Excellent Adventure* that the persona of the "himbo" has dogged him ever since and has become a stereotype that he is not able to shake off—in the eyes of most critics at least.

However, following the enormous worldwide box-office success of *Speed*, which prior to its popular discovery by fans was known derisively in industry circles as "that bus movie,"[18] both the quantity and quality of writing about its undoubted "star," Keanu Reeves, has reached hagiographic proportions. Even film critics and cultural theorists whose aim it often is to analyze and deconstruct such phenomena appear to have bought into the Keanu Effect. Many respected critics and film theorists seem mystified and yet still caught up in the mystery that is Keanu's stardom. Almost all appear to be seduced by the beauty of his face.

Even more interesting is the hagiographic turn taken by many writers and critics on Keanu. His fan worship has reached cult status and, befitting such a status, his life (or "vita") has been constructed (part truth and part myth) and embellished by his followers who view him as having on saintly virtues. In the same way that the Renaissance art historian Giorgio Vasari traced and elevated to heroic stature the lives of the great artists Michelangelo, Raphael, and others in his *Lives of the Artists*, Keanu's life has been charted and described like that of a great painter or sculptor. This is a mode of talking and writing about stars that has persisted throughout the history of Hollywood cinema. As Edgar Morin noted,

The star is profoundly good, and this cinematic goodness must be expressed in her private life as well. . . . The idealization of the star implies, of course, a corresponding
spiritualization . . . the mythology of the romantic stars associates moral beauty with
physical beauty. The star's ideal body reveals an ideal soul. (pp. 47–48)

Keanu's "goodness" and "moral beauty" are depicted in writings on
Keanu, like the unauthorized biographies by Sheila Johnston and David
Bassom, which follow the traditional "rise and fall" cycle attributed to performers—usually artists and saints—but now more commonly celebrities and
cult figures like Mother Theresa, Princess Diana, or Kurt Cobain. In this manner of writing everything associated with the star, whether quirky or mundane,
takes on significant meaning. Hence, Keanu's unusual name has been consistently examined for its mystical meaning.[19] His rise to success, fame, and worship as star is meticulously charted and sprinkled liberally with quotes from his
"followers" and true believers. For example, Johnston quotes John Macken-
zie, who directed Keanu in the television movie *Act of Vengeance* (1986), as
having said, "I bet that guy's a star in five years. I cast him as soon as I saw him.
The instant you put him on film, he burns up the celluloid. He's not consistent; I don't think he's a very good actor. But when he hits the moment, he's
just got a God-given thing" (p. 44).

Keanu's path to fame follows the traditional trajectory outlined in such art-
ist/star biographies. First, glimpses of raw talent in the untutored youth are
spotted early by the cognoscente; and it merely remains to be discovered by
some master or great director (and he has worked with several). An apprenticeship for the novice "star" follows, which includes several flawed but significant
works, such as *River's Edge* (1987), *My Own Private Idaho* (1991), *The Prince
of Pennsylvania* (1988), and *Point Break*. This apprenticeship is then followed
by a breakthrough performance (*Speed*), which cements his reputation and/or
star status and brings his asking price (commensurate with his newly emerging
box-office appeal) up to $7 million per picture.

Like many stars and artists, much of what is written about Keanu is apocry-
phal and intended to show his "specialness," his ability to rise above the rest.[20]
What are consistently noted and lauded are his beauty, his modesty, his unful-
filled talent, his patronage by noted directors, and, of course, the inevitable fall
from grace. This "fall" comes about because Keanu fails to live up to his star
status (refusing to do *Speed II*) and bastardizing his talent by making less than
spectacular—or "quirky" and "personal"—films like *Feeling Minnesota*
(1996), *The Last Time I Committed Suicide* (1997), *Chain Reaction* (1996),
and *Johnny Mnemonic* (1995).[21]

The decline and fall of the star presages a triumphant return in the tradition of
all Hollywood legends. As Jeannie Basinger notes, "enduring stars keep re-mak-
ing themselves" (quoted in New York Center for Visual History, "The Star"). In
the words of Dyer, "Star images themselves have a history. The successful star career endures by finding new inflexions—by doing something that is basically the
same but different enough to be interesting" (quoted in New York Center for

Visual History, "The Star"). Accordingly Keanu's star rises following the reprise of his "action hero" role in the huge critical and box-office success of *The Matrix*. As a result, Keanu makes it to number 78 in *Premiere* magazine's "The Power List—The 100 Most Powerful People in Hollywood" in the June 1999 issue, behind Sandra Bullock, his co-star in *Speed*, at number 76 but *ahead* of Hollywood "legend" Robert De Niro at number 79.[22]

Despite his rise in the star firmament, Keanu refuses to play by stardom's rules, which, according to Morin,

in the dialectice of actor and role, the star contributes her own beauty to the heroine of the film form [from] whom she borrows imaginary moral virtues. Beauty and spirituality combine to form the mythic. This super personality must unceasingly prove it[self] by appearances, elegance, clothes, possessions, pets, travel, caprices, sublime loves, luxury, wealth, grandeur, refinement—and seasoned to taste with exquisite simplicity and extravagence. (p. 48)

So while Keanu is noted for his collection of classic Norton motorbikes and his love of vintage French Bordeaux, he refuses to conform to star "elegance" and deliberately eschews it, cultivating instead an anti-glamour. He dresses badly, has no permanent address, and lives in the seedy and "fashionably" unfashionable Chateau Marmont, home of the notoriously "dark side" of Hollywood. As James Kaplan notes in *Premiere*,

[In real life] for a movie star, Reeves has a surprisingly neutral presence. He doesn't suck the air out of a room; he hangs back and ponders the options. In his scuffed hiking boots, wrinkled black jeans, black V-neck sweater, and dark grey T-shirt, he might be your brother, home from college for the weekend, or the painter from down the hall, over for a friendly game. (p. 68)

Ironically, it is Keanu's stardom that allows him to refuse to buy into the "public needs to know all about my private life" game, and he makes himself deliberately inaccessible in that sense, so much so that it has led to consistent speculation about his sexuality.[23] For the star, unapproachability is an important quality and is maintained through the attributions of loneliness, mysteriousness, and melancholy (Morin, p. 48). Keanu is known to be obsessively reclusive—to say little about himself; therefore, in the manner of all saints, artists, and cult heroes, his "true" self has to be "divined," sought out by journalists and fans.

However, the truth is rarely ever apparent and what emerges in published articles and Internet sites is most often a version of Keanu that is most desirable or applicable to a particular individual or group. The strength of his appeal as a star lies in this malleability. As Kaplan notes,

More than most of us, Keanu Reeves is a mass of ambiguities: He's masculine and feminine; decisive and waffling; focused and goofy; crisp and turgid. Some men become movie stars by dint of their looks, a scrap of talent, and sheer, dogged persistence. But every once in a while, a star comes along—a Montgomery Clift, a James Dean—who has such an elusive, help me quality that audiences are drawn into the vortex of an enigmatic soul. Keanu Reeves has all this, but what he has in addition, as the world first discovered in *Point Break* in 1991, is the ability to play action heroes, men of little hesitation, anti-Hamlets. His easy physicality is a side of him that—in an age of action pictures, and layered over the subtext of his sensitivity and good looks—is pure gold. It's an ability Reeves confirmed three years later with *Speed*. (p. 69)

But while the film medium guarantees a distance between the Hollywood star and the audience, stars nevertheless can have no secrets. Film magazines, popular culture magazines like *Vanity Fair*, *The Face*, *Details*, infotainment programs like *Entertainment Tonight* and *E!*, and fan sites on the World Wide Web transform film viewers into voyeurs who behave as if they are continuously present in a virtual landscape/movie of the star's private and professional life. The reader/voyeur is able to persecute the star in every sense of the term, because there is no hiding place for the star.[24] Keanu is a captive of his fame because, as in the early days of the film industry, the Hollywood studio/star system demands the systematic organization of the private-public life of the stars.[25] In a 1995 edition of the "hot" celebrity magazine *Vanity Fair*, a reporter asked Keanu how he coped with the constant attention of fans and the media. Keanu allegedly shrugged and said, "I'm Mickey [Mouse]. They don't know who's inside the suit." Kamen replied, "But you're a movie star." Keanu laughed, "So's Mickey" (quoted in Shnayerson, p. 112).

Despite Keanu's protests to the contrary, however, as an actor he can never entirely immerse himself in a role because the viewer's prolific knowledge about him unconsciously influences his performance on the screen. Director Gus Van Sant is said to have cast River Phoenix and Keanu Reeves in *My Own Private Idaho* (1991) not just because of their beauty, but because he believed the audience would be captivated by an intensity that came from their past lives (Kaplan, p. 66). In fact, Keanu's public "largeness" is inescapable, and in Bruce Cook's terms, "it is his vocation, his function, to serve as a vessel for the fantasies of the audience" (p. 59). Several writers have argued that like some of the legendary stars of the past—Humphrey Bogart, Henry Fonda, and John Wayne—Keanu has an open stony-faced quality that asks, indeed demands, of the moviegoer that he or she fill in the details. In the legendary stars this was thought of as a quality of mystery or of innocence; in Keanu it is variously seen as an absence of qualities or a lack of talent.

A supposed lack of talent notwithstanding, Keanu Reeves continues to legitimate his stardom by what is considered to be in today's terms the only true marker of stardom—success at the box office. In Keanu's case, his unusual beauty compensates for what is understood to be an imperfect acting technique. What is of interest to us on the screen is the geography of his face—a face that appears to conform to a canon of beauty that can be Hellenic or Oriental, exotic or ordinary. His very blankness allows directors, cinematographers, and viewers to construct upon his "star" features the richest human geographies.

According to film historian Joseph Boggs,

The grammar and vocabulary of body language include a vast array of non-verbal communication techniques, but the motion picture is perhaps unique in its emphasis on the eloquence of the human face. Although the face and facial expressions play a part in other storytelling media, such as novels and plays, in film the face becomes a medium of communication in its own right. Magnified on the screen, the human face with its infinite variety of expressions can convey depth and subtlety of emotion that cannot be approached through purely rational or verbal means. (p. 263)

Given the largeness of the cinema screen, the art of film acting (particularly for the star) is in *reacting* rather than acting. It is in this sense that Keanu's "acting" is a spectacular form of non-acting and, consequently, in the reception of his "performances" there are almost unlimited possibilities for scenic interpretation.[26] His face is the same but somehow always different. This sameness/difference is what audiences look for in stars. As Rick Nicita, head of CAA (Creative Artists Agency) says, "In this business, stars are human nature exponentially magnified."[27]

KEANU AS STAR AND HOLLYWOOD AS SITE

I return to the connection between Keanu, the body of the star, and the landscape of Los Angeles/Hollywood via Louis Marin, who argues that a particular site is the result of a product, of a construction that is at once real, imaginary, and symbolic (p. 164).[28] Marin's argument, that "body" and "site" are conflated, is entirely applicable to Hollywood as a site, and Keanu's presence there as "body/star" (p. 168). Marin asks the question, "What is a place and how is a place different from space?" (p. 169). He notes the extreme polysemy of the notion of place in the seventeenth century where "place is a primary and immobile surface of a body which surrounds another or, more clearly, the space in which a body is placed. A spot intended for setting something either by nature, or by art" (p. 169). Los Angeles and Hollywood, as sites of stardom, are polysemic in just this sense.[29]

The key to any city is literally and metaphorically linked to an architectural notion of place—to the sociocultural understanding of the term—and therefore a place is distinguished by the privileges attributed to the various uses it is intended for (Marin, p. 170). Like Marin's example of Versailles, and its situating of the body of the prince, Los Angeles/ Hollywood, too, is a place for situating stars and for filmmaking. It is a place that, in Michel de Certeau's terms, "obeys the law of the proper and of property" (quoted in Marin, p. 170). Thus, there is present there, as Marin argues, "a classicism of [the] place" (p. 170). In just this sense, Los Angeles/Hollywood appears to be the only legitimate site for stars. It is a place determined by its industry and its subjects—that is, the stars and the narratives of the films it produces, and of the industry it supports—whether as a site of industry with its studios and production facili-

ties and narrative locations; or as a tourist location that feeds off the former in
the form of commercial theme parks/locations like Disneyland, the Universal
Studios Theme Park with its utopian quasi-urban Universal City Walk, tours of
the stars' homes, or the re-development of specific sites/sights like Hollywood
Boulevard, the Beverly Hills shopping precinct, and Santa Monica's Third
Street Promenade.

As Marin suggests, the act of "representation is thus essentially an organization of movements in space, movements whose effects are spaces" (p. 171). In
other words, in the case of Hollywood and its stars the acting body of the
"star" would appear to designate Hollywood space in every sense of the term.
The star's body points to the strategic site it occupies by becoming one of Hollywood's sights/sites. It is not surprising, therefore, to find an overt
self-reflexivity in the final sequence of *Speed*, making reference to Hollywood
Boulevard as both a utopian and dystopian street of dreams. As Marin suggests, place, space, event, and the dialectic at play between these three notions
are what constitute any idea of place (p. 171).

Los Angeles, for example, constructs itself literally in *Speed* as a dialectic between a real place as Hollywood narrative space and as Keanu's body as specta-
cle/event. As star, he too is doubly of the landscape—as actual actor, star,
beautiful face, and fictional character. *Speed*'s narrative and ending on Hollywood Boulevard right outside a movie marquee and a studio tour bus, also
doubly conflate the site and sight of both Los Angeles/Hollywood and of
Keanu as its narrative protagonist and actual Hollywood star. Utopia and
dystopian spaces meet in this filmic finale in the heterotopia (not real) of the
cinema screen.

Through its narrative representations Hollywood cinema literally and metaphorically constructs Los Angeles as theatrical sight/site, which, because of
its global exposure, literally subjugates the eye of the beholder—whether that
beholder sits in a theater miles or even continents away from Los Angeles, or is
actually present on site. According to Marin, "representation develops a visual
theatricality which strikes the eye and subjugates the gaze" (p. 173). So, for
Marin, "to represent means also to show, to intensify, to redouble a presence"
(p. 174). This is the same for cinema. It is the legitimating force or paradigm in
which stars (both living and dead) can operate. For example, both Marilyn
Monroe and Humphrey Bogart continue to signify "Hollywood" many years
after their deaths.

It is the site of Los Angeles/Hollywood as home of cinema that legitimates
the activity and the function of stardom—it is the physical and metaphorical
site that gives the "sight" of the star its power. "Through 'place' space is
transubstantiated into a body" (Marin, p. 178) and the star's body, and thus
the functioning of the apparatus of cinema as industry is located and revealed.
The layout of Los Angeles/Hollywood as playground to the stars presents the
geographic space of Los Angeles/Hollywood as a matrix, or as a universal metaphorical cinematic space that can be transported outside Los Angeles and

Hollywood through film and its byproducts, and still retain its meaning and power.

> Through topographic representation, the architecturally visible is totally legible and the descriptively legible is visible; image and symbol are founded and merge in a same *reality* of discourses and places, that of a perfect simulacrum which manifests an identical prosopography, the portrait of the [star] Sun-King. (Marin, p. 181)

The star carries the site/sight of Los Angeles/Hollywood with him or her wherever he or she goes. So, one might legitimately ask, what did Keanu's visit to Australia for major location shooting of *The Matrix* in 1999 mean for the law of place that signifies "Los Angeles/Hollywood star"? Did it simply mean the transportation of Hollywood to Australia in the very literal sense of industry and physical star body? Ian Sands, the managing director of its distributor, Roadshow Film Distributors, gave the power of Keanu Reeves's presence in Australia as one of the key reasons for that film's huge box-office success there. "We hope people will want to see *Mission Impossible 2* for the same reason" (quoted in Bodey, p. 6). Meanwhile, United International Pictures' marketing manager, Sam Hamilton, noted, "the result also shows what a year of pre-publicity can do. That reason being that Keanu was in Australia and his location and whereabouts were under constant scrutiny" (quoted in Bodey, p. 6).

Reeves's and his co-stars' presence became, in fact, the preoccupation and fodder of the entire spectrum of Australian publishing and broadcasting—from women's magazines to infotainment programs, including the national nightly news. Even stories of Keanu's ill health (presumably as a result of his enforced "relocation" from "home") made tabloid headlines, suggesting perhaps that, although you can try to take the star out of Hollywood, you can't take Hollywood out of the star without affecting his or her bodily and symbolic "presence."

Foucault notes, "the spaces in which we live, which draw us out of ourselves, in which the erosion of our lives, our times and our history occurs, the space that claws and gnaws at us, is also, in itself, a heterogeneous space. . . . [W]e live inside a set of relations that delineates sites" (p. 26). Foucault's notions of "sites," whether literal or metaphorical representations, may help us to understand landscape as organizing metaphorical representations, as an organizing principle in culture, and in film, where space and bodily action are integrated with the question of identity and spectatorship. In this sense, Los Angeles/Hollywood, and the bodily presence and mobility of its stars, like Keanu Reeves, provide us with a richly symbolic experience of landscapes that are ambiguously utopian and dystopian, one fully orchestrated in relation to the surrounding environments and their rich history as sites that manufacture spectacle and attractions.

ACKNOWLEDGMENTS

The theme and general argument of this chapter are indebted to Michel Foucault's (1984) essay, "Of Other Spaces," and to Louis Marin's "Versailles and the Architecture of the Prince" (1991). Both these authors argue strongly for the body "in situ" as signifier of meaning. They suggest that we can neither understand nor see the body as *not* being implicated politically and, aesthetically in the spaces in which it resides, moves and acts.

NOTES

1. This has long been the motto of MGM, a studio once synonymous with Hollywood stars. Its logo continues to identify the studio along with its trademark lion across all of the studio's inter- and intra-corporate structures, including the MGM Hollywood Grand hotel/casino complex in Las Vegas.

2. In the chapter, "Beyond Blade Runner," Davis (1992) argues that today Los Angeles/Hollywood, or rather its idealization, has become the subject of simulation and caricature. Mega-corporations like MCA and Disney have turned both the actual sites and sights of Los Angeles and Hollywood into theme parks. In this sense, there are multiple hyper-realities known as "Hollywood": (1) "Hollywood" as social reality (slum); (2) Hollywood as movie-made spectacle; (3a) Hollywood as Disney-MGM (Florida); (3b) Hollywood as Universal (Florida); (4) Hollywood as City Walk (Los Angeles); and (5) Hollywood as redevelopment project (pp. 393–94).

3. Henri Lefebvre uses the term "spatio-analyse" for its echoing on an alternative to "psychoanalyze" or psychoanalysis (pp. 1–2).

4. There are hundreds of sites devoted to Keanu, including these very specific sites from certain interest groups: The Asian American Celebweb at http://geocities.comTokyo?temple/1500/reeves.html; Keanu Reeves' Italian Fans at http://www.keanu.simplenet.com/menu.html; and the Keanu Reeves Island Surfing School at http://geocities.com/SoHo/square/7335/surfing.html.

5. For an interesting discussion of the "intangible cartography" of cities, see Doug Henwood (1994). This is an acute analysis of how atlases although they present the official and statistical often fail to represent the political hierarchy of spaces.

6. Higson (1984) makes this point in relation to the British "kitchen sink film."

7. Foucault (1984) makes this point about space in general, but I think that it applies as much to the categories of space making that I am suggesting.

8. Maltby (1995) refers here to Frank McConnell's paradox of film presence, "the presence of absence, a 'reality' which is not there" (p. 174).

9. Typical of these kinds of reviews is this one for *Johnny Mnemonic*. "Just in case you hadn't realized, Keanu Reeves is in imminent danger of brain collapse. It's the twenty-first century, the planet Earth is in lousy shape and not only does everyone want to chop off Keanu's head and freeze it, but if he doesn't get rid of what's stored inside it on micro-chip, then basically, he'll blow up. Or melt down. Or possibly both. Reeves is Johnny, a jet setting courier of top-secret material, which he loads into his re-modeled brain through a little hole drilled in his head. In order to perform this unpleasant but well-paid task, J. J. has jettisoned his childhood memories and therefore has no real personality—a made-in-heaven role for Reeves, who attacks it with gormless voracity" (Paviour p. 56).

10. Typical of the response to Keanu's performance in *Speed* is the following from a review by Scott Renshaw. "Since the dawn of time, three Great Questions have defied the greatest minds: Is there a God? Is there existence after death? And how does Keanu Reeves continue to get work as an actor? All right, that might be a slight exaggeration; I have some ideas about that life after death thing. Reeves remains a mystery, a physically striking but mush-mouthed thespian who has been cast by Coppola, Bertolucci and Branagh. A post *Bill and Ted* star-making vehicle has eluded him, however—until now. Arriving with more buzz than a swarm of killer bees is *Speed*, and you can believe the hype. Thrilling and relentless to a fault, *Speed* seems destined to score big box office and make Reeves a very hot property." Later on in the review, he notes, "Jack Travern is the perfect role for Reeves. He is asked to do little more than set his jaw and look good in a tight T-shirt, and he's good at both."

11. Richard Maltby (1995) has noted that "a movie performance is also constructed out of the performance of the camera, the editing, the mise-en-scene. . . . A movie is a performance and not a text. If movies were texts, we could write about them with much more critical confidence than we do. But all attempts to reduce movies to texts, whether through analogies between film language, shots and words, or through formal analysis, ultimately fail to resolve the interpretive complexities of performance signs and thus to resolve the dialectic of cinema's warfare between personality and mechanism" (p. 237).

12. In "Of Other Spaces" (1984) he outlines the distinction between utopian, heterotopian, and dystopian spaces to show how particular types of space enact social and power relations. Foucault's essay, along with the works of de Certeau, Bachelard, Focillon, and Lefebvre, and the writings of phenomenologists have each in some way tried to deal with the changing conceptualization of space in cultural life and/or art.

13. It is also worth noting that in a recent interview series for the Australian Cinematographers' Society, award-winning cinematographer John Seale spoke about the increasing control being taken by actors of their screen images, especially of close-ups. "You have to look after your leading ladies. That's the little edict of the studio system and producers are very adamant about that—that's the money up there and they want to see it. Meg Ryan demanded that a tight close-up of her from *City of Angels* be pulled unless it was digitally enhanced, because she believed it showed her in an unflattering light—with pores and creases." He is speaking specifically of women but the same trend can be seen in the control of image by male actors. For developments of this trend, see Horne and Spines (1999).

14. Krützen (1992) makes the same point about Greta Garbo's "non-acting" style (p. 27).

15. See review of *Johnny Mnemonic* in Paviour (1995). But almost any review of a Reeves's film will be sure to mention either the wooden quality of his acting or the fact that his acting is not acting at all.

16. For a discussion of the economic imperatives of "stardom," see Sherwin Rosen. Rosen notes: "The phenomenon of Superstars, wherein relatively small numbers of people earn enormous amounts of money and dominate the activities in which they engage, seems to be increasingly important in the modern world. . . . The elusive quality off 'box-office appeal,' the ability to attract an audience and generate a large volume of transactions, is the issue that must be confronted" (pp. 845–46). However, Rosen also notes the limits of his economic model and warns that "prospective impresarios will receive no guidance here on what makes for box-office appeal, sometimes

said to involve a combination of talent and charisma in uncertain proportions" (p. 846). For an interesting legal and cultural approach to celebrity and stardom, see Rosemary J. Coombe.

17. One could argue that some mini-series, which often present us with sweeping historical sagas, are an exception to the rule.

18. Sandra Bullock, in an interview with David Letterman, *The David Letterman Show*, ABC Television, United States, 1994.

19. Almost all writers on Keanu make mention of his unusual name, which is meant to translate from Hawaiian as "cool breeze over the mountains," a claim that is under some dispute, but that nevertheless gives rise to much talk about his mystical "specialness."

20. There is even a college course on Keanu Reeves. In the unauthorized biography, Sheila Johnston (1996) notes, "In 1994, the artist-lecturer Stephen Prina launched a course on 'The Films of Keanu Reeves' at the Art Center College of Design in Pasadena, California, a few kilometers down the road from San Dimas, Ted's stamping ground. . . . In a similar spirit, in the spring of 1995, London's Institute of Contemporary Arts asked its members to name any one person they would like to hear lecture. Keanu topped the poll by a comfortable margin; the runner-up was Slavoj Zizek, a Lacanian philosopher and Intellectual arch-guru based in Ljubiljana" (pp. 4–5).

21. See especially, the review of *Johnny Mnemonic* in note 9.

22. Reeves's entry reads as follows: "Title: Dude Awakening. Status Report: Carried kickass *Matrix*, his first studio movie in two years, to huge business. Fee will soar to $12 million for next project, the football comedy *The Replacements*. Yes It's True: Gave up $1 million of his *Devil's Advocate* salary to help pay for Al Pacino's" ("The Power List," p. 95).

23. The most famous and most prolific of these rumors concerned an alleged secret "gay marriage" between Keanu and producer David Geffen. Asked about the rumor, Geffen replied: "It's just an ugly, mean-spirited rumor meant to hurt him because he's a movie star" (quoted in Shnayerson, p. 112).

24. One need only look at some of the innumerable Keanu sites on the Web to note the range of responses to his stardom from adulation to total vitriol. Some of the sites post "hate" messages of such vehemence that they need to be seen to be believed. One such site is *The Keanu Report*, which argues that Keanu Reeves is the manifestation of evil on earth, the anti-Christ. See http://www.geocities.com/Hollywood/6608/keanu.html.

25. The precursor to many of the "star at home or on the town" genre of articles that we see today in magazines such as *Instyle* was the annual "Hollywood" issue of *Architectural Digest* (the special issue continues to this day), which featured stars in their homes—where both star and home became synonymous fixtures of the Los Angeles/Hollywood landscape, in much the same way that stars are now associated with specific fashion designers, hairdressers, and makeup artists who are themselves celebrities, testifying to the longevity of the notion of Hollywood as premier site of stardom/celebrity.

26. Krützen (1992) notes that this is exactly the case for Greta Garbo (p. iv).

27. Rick Nicita, head of Creative Artists Agency, is quoted in *The Stars* (television series).

28. It is real, in that the palace (place) exists: one can still visit it today. It is imaginary, in that it reveals "baroque" desire, the fantastic, the phantasmic desire to show (oneself) as absolute power. It is symbolic—since in some manner it is the sovereign norm, the "classic" law of universal subjection to signs, which constitute a transcendent cultural and political universe devoid of civil and natural exteriority.

29. A potent example of the "laws and powers of place" was the 1999 strike in Hollywood by technicians protesting the increasing move of film production away from Los Angeles to locations like Canada and Australia. The newsworthiness (both in Australia and in the United States) of this highly visible and emotionally charged protest is testament to the uneasiness that is seen to be brought about by the possible relocation of "Hollywood" to "other" places/spaces including what in some circles is being called "Aussiewood." The technicians' protest seemed to suggest that "Hollywood" cinema cannot be made anywhere else except the actual physical site that is Hollywood, that is, that the Hollywood film industry is seen (in Marin's terms) as a condition of place.

REFERENCES

Bass, David. "Insiders and Outsiders: Latent Urban Thinking in Movies of Modern Rome." *BFI—Cinema & Architecture* (forthcoming).

Bassom, David. *Keanu Reeves—An Illustrated Story.* London: Hamlyn, 1996.

Berardinelli, James. "*Speed.*" (Review.) Available at http://www.cybernex. net/~berardin listed in http://www.imdb.com.

Bodey, Michael. *The Sunday Age.* July 18 (1999): 6.

Boggs, Joseph M. *The Art of Watching Films.* Mayfield, CA: Mayfield Publishing, 1991.

Bordwell, David. *Narration in the Fiction Film.* Madison: University of Wisconsin Press, 1985.

Bordwell, David, and Kristin Thompson. "Space and Narration in the Films of Ozu." *Screen* 17, no. 2 (summer 1976).

Bruno, Giuliana. *Streetwalking on a Ruined Map: Cultural Theory and the City Films of Elvira Notari.* Princeton, NJ: Princeton University Press, 1993.

Cook, Bruce. "Why TV Stars Don't Become Movie Stars." *American Film* 1, no. 8 (June 1976).

Coomby, Rosemary J. "The Celebrity Image and Cultural Identity: Publicity Rights and the Subaltern Politics of Gender." *Discourse* 14, no. 3 (Summer 1993): 59–87.

Cosgrove, Denis. *The Palladian Landscape—Geographical Change & Its Cultural Representation in Sixteenth Century Italy.* Philadelphia: Pennsylvania State University Press, 1991.

Davis, Mike. *City of Quartz—Excavating the Future of Los Angeles.* New York: Vintage Books, 1992.

———. *The Ecology of Fear—Los Angeles and the Imagination of Disaster.* New York: Vintage Books, 1999.

de Certeau, Michel. *The Practice of Everyday Life.* Berkeley: University of California Press, 1984.

Dyer, Richard. "*Speed.*" (Review.) *Sight & Sound* 4, no. 10 (October 1994).

Farber, Stephen. "Writing in Action." *Movieline.* August (1998).

Foucault, Michel. "Of Other Spaces." *Diacritics* 16 (spring 1984).

Ghirado, Diane. "Identity and Place in Los Angeles." Lecture, School of Architecture and Planning, University of Melbourne, August 1998.

Groth, Paul, and Todd W. Bressi, eds. *Understanding Ordinary Landscapes*. New Haven: Yale University Press, 1997.

Henwood, Doug. "Making a Social Atlas." *Bad Subjects* 17 (November 1994).

Higson, Andrew. "Space, Place and Spectacle." *Screen* 25, nos. 4 & 5 (July–October 1984).

Horne, John, and Christine Spines. "Actors Rule." *Premiere*. August (1999): 58–67.

Hunter, Stephen. "Reeves Hot and Cold, Hopper Overblown, but *Speed* Is a Wild Ride." *Sun Times*. October (1994). Available at http://www.cinemedia.com/Speed/html.

"John Seale ACS, ASC, Discusses *The English Patient, City of Angels* and the DOP & CGI." The Australian Cinematographer's Society Video Series, ASC, 1999.

Johnston, Sheila. *Keanu*. London: Sidgwick & Jackson, 1996.

Kaplan, James. "Why Keanu Won't Sell His Soul." *Premiere*. September (1997).

Kracauer, Siegfried. *Theory of Film—the Redemption of Physical Reality*. New York: Oxford University Press, 1966.

Krützen, Michaela. *The Most Beautiful Woman on the Screen—the Fabrication of the Star Greta Garbo*. Berlin: Frankfurt and Main, 1992.

Lefebvre, Henri. *The Production of Space*. Cammbridge, MA: Blackwell, 1991.

Maltby, Richard. *Hollywood Cinema*. Oxford: Blackwell Publishers, 1995.

Marin, Louis. "Versailles and the Architecture of the Prince." In Hampton, Timothy, ed., *Baroque Topographies*. *Yale French Studies* 80 (1991).

McConnell, Frank. *The Spoken Seen: Film and the Romantic Imagination*. Baltimore: Johns Hopkins University Press, 1975.

McDonald, James. "The City, the Cinema: Modern Spaces." In Jencks, Charles, ed., *Visual Culture*. London: Routledge, 1995.

Morin, Edgar. *The Stars*. Translated by Richard Howard. New York: Grove Press, 1960.

Neale, Steve. "Triumph of the Will—Notes on Documentary and Spectacle." *Screen* 20: 1 (spring 1979).

The New York Center for Visual History. "The Star." *American Cinema* (series), Fox Video, 1995.

Ovnick, Merry. *Los Angeles: The End of the Rainbow*. Los Angeles: Balcony Press, 1994.

Paviour, Andiee. "*Johnny Mnemonic*." (Review.) *Who Weekly*. July (1995).

"The Power List—The 100 Most Powerful People in Hollywood." *Premiere* (June 1999).

Renshaw, Scott. "*Speed*." (Review.) Available at http://www.rec.arts.movies.reviews.

Rosen, Sherwin. "The Economics of Superstars." *American Economic Review* 17, no.5 (1981): 845–58.

Ryan, Ellery. Personal interview with author, June 26, 1999.

Shnayerson, Michael. "The Wild One." *Vanity Fair*. August (1995).

Soja, Edward W. *Thirdspace—Journeys to Los Angeles Other and Real and Imagined Places*. Cambridge, MA and Oxford: Blackwell, 1995.

Wray, Matt. "Speed and Politics." *Bad Subjects*. April 20 (1995).

Princess Diana. © AP/AAP.

———— Chapter 5 ————

More Sign Than Star: Diana, Death, and the Internet

Michael Punt

Diana, Princess of Wales, was undoubtedly a star who was created by the media into a magnificently popular figure. Nonetheless many were surprised by the way vast numbers of people used the occasion of her death to express deeply felt grief. This chapter will highlight how ordinary people also used the funeral for other, tangentially related purposes. It is particularly concerned with the way that some of these uses meshed with a number of other recent trends that are evident in the popular success of the *X-Files*, conspiracy theory bulletin boards, and so-called slash fan fiction (Internet facilitated revisions of narratives in the public domain). Diana's own cosmetic independence and the renunciation of her own historical destiny as Queen revisited a populist existentialism, which, by coincidence, was the thematic of the summer blockbuster *Men in Black*. Understanding the extraordinary intersection of determinants of the public grieving may, paradoxically, lie with a perceived loss of intellectual and psychological control that, it is argued, is induced by the centralization of power and the efficiency of the media in gathering news.

WHAT HAPPENED?

On August 31, 1997, the news that Diana, Princess of Wales, had been killed in a car crash was unavoidably thrust upon the majority of people in the United Kingdom. Every public service broadcast station canceled its programs and devoted the day's output to the Princess and the accident. Very little other news was covered and the impulse to explain the random fate and absurd accidents that affect an individual life was focused on Diana and produced hours of biography and speculation about the causes of such an event. The excesses of the media—especially the BBC—were later explained to some extent by an extraordinary twist of fate. John Morrison, editor of BBC TV news programs, claimed:

Our business is to satisfy the hunger for information, working to a strict protocol laid down in a BBC manual. We rehearse rolling news stories and we had worked to a fictional scenario involving the death of a leading royal in a car crash in a foreign country recently. It proved amazingly prescient. At times it seemed like I was dreaming.[1]

This did not quite explain the full bandwidth of coverage and rumor at the time (contingency plans for the death of the Queen Mother, who was then in her ninetieth year, were simply brought into play for this unexpected bereavement—something that John Morrison may have found difficult to admit to in public).

The Queen Mother, who has lived through a century thought to have encompassed the most dramatic period of change in history, would no doubt have provided editorial copy to fill twenty-four hours. Diana was different; she had led a relatively ordinary life for the late twentieth century—early marriage, children, affairs, divorce, a series of lovers, and so forth. There had been nothing to match the wars of her great-grandmother-in-law, except perhaps the human tragedy of AIDS, which was not quite a topic to unpack in a panegyric directed at the more conservative sections of British society. But perhaps more restricting for journalists having to fill the hours was the immediate implication of the paparazzi in the accident, which constrained the press from filling columns with the adventures of a personality whose chief claim to public attention was its apparently voracious appetite for the intimacies of her private life. In one of the more myopic examples of the coverage that was symptomatic of the dilemma her death posed for reporters was a BBC commentator complaining in a voice-over about the presence of the press and cameras in live news footage of the scene outside the Hôspital de la Pitié-Salpétrière.

In the circumstances overstatement was inevitable, and her identification with the underdog led to copy that was nothing short of hagiography. Diana, of course, had been the wronged woman of the House of Windsor for many years. She had aligned herself with various intractable causes, which were self-evidently worthy and carried a certain cache of radical chic. Her humanitarian reputation and the copy it produced ensured that in five days the Princess of Wales Memorial Fund exceeded £100 million (about the same that Oxfam and the Red Cross combined could expect in a year). This visible identification with the underdog guaranteed that, from the very first announcement, the causes of the accident and third-party involvement became a dominant topic for reporters. Because of the delicacy of the relationship between British broadcasters and the state (and no doubt Al Fayed's high profile as a litigant), this speculation was for the most part highly coded and oblique. The Internet, however, was less guarded and in the following days when the immediate known circumstances of the crash were temporarily exhausted, thicker histories of the Princess—her loves and life—were welded together in a congested amalgam of fact and speculation about various high-level conspiracies. By the time she was buried five days later, the "Death of Diana" had become a popular political cause as the media hagiography seemed to be confirmed by what the press never appeared to become embarrassed at calling "the public outpouring of grief."

Explanations for this extreme manifestation of popular affection encouraged commentators to assume that Diana occupied a place in people's hearts and had "star" appeal like Rudolph Valentino or Marilyn Monroe. Indeed there was some relief (possibly surprise) that nobody took his or her own life in a pathetic gesture of solidarity. As it was, the funeral passed without further tragedy, although two people were killed in a coach accident on their way to London. Two million people turned out on the streets to watch the cortege, and the event was witnessed on television by 59 percent of the population in Britain (31.5 million), which was nearly 20 percent more than watched the Euro 96 semifinal between England and Germany. This was regarded as exceptional although some commentators attributed this to the fact that many women do not watch football and, by that reckoning, the audience was possibly less than expected. Not withstanding this, the event was covered with such intensity that for some who did not tune in and took a late summer stroll there was a rather strange "Stepford" creepiness to the streets for several hours.

The press, along with book publishers, assumed that here was a copy "gravy train" good for a decade. Ambitious schemes were proposed to name airports, hospitals, and bridges after her. In the atmosphere of a national consensus overburdened with media hyperbole, hesitancy about these ideas was often confused with criticism of the Princess, and wary commentators and cautious government spokespersons who were sceptical of the public affection were vilified as unfeeling and unpatriotic. They were somewhat vindicated when only one year later, however, the planned five-day media bonanza to mark the first anniversary of her death collapsed on the first day through obvious public apathy, and broadcasting schedules had to be quickly changed. In the week before the burial it was common to read that millions of bouquets of flowers were left (an exaggeration to be sure); two years later flowers were left at the gates of Kensington Palace to mark the second anniversary but this time they could be counted in the hundreds rather than the thousands and covered less than 50 meters of the fence.

For all the quasi-academic cultural analysis that has been devoted to her popular apotheosis, little has been written about her descent. Diana's fall from public attention may be less newsworthy than the spectacular scenes as she was lying in state but it is no less important to understand. This chapter is intended to open that question and, using evidence from the national coverage of the death of Diana and from local sources in the United Kingdom, I argue (as I did in a magazine article published just after her death and reprinted below [see appendix] in translation) that the stars of the "Princess Diana Show," in the

movie sense, were the individual mourners who were invested by the media
with a unity of purpose but seemed to use the opportunity that her death offered for their own diverse ends. In this economy Diana was more Zodiac constellation than the Hollywood tragic movie star that some thought.[2]

The focus of this chapter is almost exclusively on the United Kingdom,
where I happened to be at the time. The underlying claim is that the event,
which was often described as common experience, was for most people essentially subjective, and as a consequence the voice of what follows is willfully
unacademic. Although I speak mainly of the United Kingdom and use the first
person, the conclusion, I believe, has a more widespread significance in identifying a category of star that emerges from the power relationships of contemporary culture, serviced as it is by a complex international network of data
distribution systems in which there is currently an imbalance between the delivery capacity and the available content.

WHERE WERE YOU?

In November 1963 I was standing on a railway station in London, returning home after some heavy adolescent drinking, when I heard that John F.
Kennedy had been shot. I bought a newspaper, which I think I left on the train.
Later, when I was grown up, I played the Abe Zapruder footage of the shooting over and over again, tormenting my students with questions about media
specificity. I was always unable to reconcile my experience with what I saw on
the screen. The horror of Jackie Kennedy crawling across the trunk of the car
away from the blood had no bearing on my personal memory of the event.

Early one morning 30 or so years later, I was standing barefoot on quarry
tiles in the kitchen, waiting for the kettle to boil when I sensed that something
was wrong. Instead of the usual baiting of politicians and the carping criticisms
of the European Union, the radio was telling me about the royal family, Princess Diana, and Dodi Fayed. Then "for those of you who have just tuned in" (a
phrase to be repeated at 10 minute intervals), the slim facts of the news of the
crash in the Pont d'Alma tunnel were reiterated, followed by more family detail. In the intervening years the world had become electronic, and instead of
buying a paper I switched on all my radios and televisions just to hear it all over
again simultaneously. Perhaps because the crash was in a tunnel and hence out
of sight, and certainly because all stations were using a single news source, the
broadcast media suddenly seemed inadequate: somewhere above it all in a ker-
nel of ethereal technology that fused image, sound, and text—one message
beamed up from central Paris. There was no opinion, no post-modern collapse
of history; the one story had to be reread like a love letter or legal summons as
though a concealed truth was embedded in the punctuation.

I was indeed back on the railway station, a slightly fuzzy, reluctantly passive
consumer of the news making up my own story. None of this reaction was especially unique to me nor evidently were my subsequent responses of (1) find-

ing someone to tell who did not know, (2) telephoning someone else to see if they knew, and (3) logging onto the Internet to check Reuters and CNN, in order to see what I was not being told and regain some control of my own opinion. These news agencies, of course, were calling the shots and it was quickly clear that a Web search was called for to see if there was any inside story that the lawyers had repressed. The first 50 hits for "Diana, Princess of Wales" that the search brought up were "fan" sites sprinkled with obscene and erotic content—this was shocking to me although, as a Web journalist, perhaps it should not have been, but it simply had not occurred to me that anyone would be interested in her in that way. Within hours, however, these sites quietly dropped off the search engines and new sites opened in which people expressed condolences, shock, and sadness. Later new pages began to appear that contained conspiracy theories ranging from the simple to the elaborate and the plausible to the apparently outlandish (e.g., establishment coverup of Diana's abduction by aliens). It appeared that the more unrestrained reactions to violent death and all the more dramatic ideas that the broadcast media were constrained by law and convention to leave unspoken found expression in the less regulated public space of the Internet.

WHAT DID YOU DO?

As the week progressed more extraordinary things happened, most of which were so well represented in the press that they do not require extensive exposition here. Suffice to say that huge crowds gathered outside Kensington Palace, and many new arrivals brought a gift of flowers with a message or personal mementoes—soft toys, religious images, candles and so forth—to leave at the gates. Visitors tied cards and favorite photographs to the railings, lined up to sign the official book of condolence, and whiled the day away distracting themselves reading the personal thoughts of others posted in a moment of apparently private reaction to the sudden news. The Palace opened an Internet Web site and was obliged to break further with tradition by lowering the flag on Buckingham Palace in what was interpreted as a response to people power.[3] Initially the crowd was comprised of mainly a socially defined group of middle-brow Royalists, working-class citizens embedded with the idea of national identity, and lonely people at home with the myths constructed by the Princess's public relations office. Republicans, intellectuals, the "chattering classes," and the more restrained sectors of British society stayed away. But gradually those who in the normal course of events saw the "Diana cult" and her subsequent media hagiography as yet another expression of manipulative bourgeois ideology were drawn to the fascination of the crowd and began to subscribe to the myth. Take, for example, the British writer Alan Bennett. The extracts from his diaries published in the *London Review of Books* (Jan. 1, 1998) show the gradual slide from distant sardonic cynicism and witty observation to a personal emotional involvement:

2 September. Hysteria over the death of the Princess continues, people "from all walks of life" queuing down the Mall, not merely to sign the book but to sit there and write for up to 15 minutes at a time. Others presumably just write "Why?," which suggests a certain cosmic awareness while at least having the merit of brevity.

3 September. The order of service is published for the funeral, the music to be played, Albinoni, Pachelbel and Elgar's "Nimrod." It's the apotheosis of Classic FM. The Dean: "And now from Elgar's *Enigma Variations,* 'Nimrod,' which is on page two of your Order of Service and No 17 in this week's Classic Countdown." The poor Queen is to be forced to go mournabout. I suppose it is a revolution but with Rosa Luxemburg played by Sharon and Tracey.

The following day, however, not even Bennett could resist the draw of the scene, and, although he keeps his usual ironic distance, something of his tone lacks the Republican confidence of the previous days. On September 5, after expressing some more sympathy for the Queen for having to perform for the crowd, he writes,

After supper we go down to look at the scene in the Mall, which is full of people not particularly silent, no mood at all, really, just walking up and down as if coming away from an event, though it's also like a huge passeggiata. . . .
The evening redeemed by an extraordinary sight. Despite the hundreds and hundreds of people trooping past, there, on the grass by the corner of Stable House Street, is a fox. It's just out of the light, slinking by with its head turned towards the parade of people passing none of whom notice it. It's quite small, as much fawn as red, and is, I imagine, a vixen. It lopes unhurriedly along the verge diving under the hedge into St James's Palace grounds. Besides us only one woman notices it, but that's probably just as well: such is the hysteria and general silliness it might be hailed as the reincarnation of Princess Diana, another beautiful vixen, with whom lots of parallels suggest themselves.

Bennett's diary is worth quoting at such length because it is typical of nearly every account of the week before the funeral that has been told to me by people who do not include themselves as part of the "mass" (i.e., everyone). Many went to the Palace not to remember Diana but to "see the crowds" as an unusual, if not unique, social phenomenon; many also used the experience in personal ways and were slightly changed.

The first reaction was often that, given that the event was a massive public mourning, it was extraordinary how happy people appeared to be. The second was often to personalize the experience as unique. Like Bennett, they found the media mawkishness redeemed in an image or a special personal moment. The simplest, and by no means uncommon, reaction perhaps came from a woman who had lived in London all her life and went every evening (during this time of mourning) to the Palace because she had never before been able to walk in the parks after dark for fear of violence. The crowd, the likes of which we usually see at football matches and political demonstrations, was uncharacteristically sober and considerate, which meant that for a week women could (and did) stroll in the early hours, seeing London as never before. Street vendors stayed away (there is, in any case, a law against trading in royal parks) and Harrods' vans distributed free cups of tea. Others said that the smell of flowers and wax in the evening air was an unforgettable experience, and yet others remarked on the heat from the candles (a comment one often hears about the Catholic masses from atheist onlookers).

Most people spent their time reading the messages on the railings, which had the same enigmatic fascination as inscriptions in a derelict graveyard: messages to whom? from whom? for what? For a week the park was like a massive open-air Baroque cathedral, an overwhelming entertainment for the senses that encouraged many to rather casually slip into the journalistic jargon of the moment and describe Diana—who, as stars go, was an unexceptional-looking woman with an eye for fashion—as beautiful, just as Alan Bennett did in his diary. The quasi-religious adoration persisted after the burial, and on the day following the interment at Althorp House, three million people—a third more than actually attended the funeral—walked the route, chatting in some unique social festival. Most returned to normal life the following Monday although some stayed on, only to be finally discouraged by park attendants anxious to avoid the health and fire risk of tons of rotting flowers and cellophane.

For those unable or unwilling to travel to London, there were opportunities to share in the mood of the moment. Throughout the British Isles floral tributes were placed in piles at suitable sites. Often war memorials were thought to be the most appropriate places: an odd choice since they are generally dedicated to those who fell in action, and driving at breakneck speed from the Ritz to your pad for a nightcap with your best boy hardly seemed to fit into this category. Cynics had it that the local florists were the first to make a show there in order to stimulate sales (the more determinist conspiracy theorists attributed the whole disaster to Interflora). Whatever the origins, a national convention developed and soft toys, photographs, and flowers appeared among last year's poppy wreaths, as if by magic.

Most of all there were texts—poems, letters, and obituaries—but violent accusations against the British establishment were also common. In view of Diana's media presence and her relationship with the Palace these responses were to be expected, but more difficult to account for were messages that simply included the sender's name. One of many that I read was typical, in ballpoint pen was written, "from Arnold and Winifred." Apart from the handwriting there was no clue to the sender's identity, no sense of who was the intended reader and, except for the location, no clear idea of why it was written. Similar lines, personal but anonymous, appeared on Internet message boards. The most that can be inferred from such slender texts was that something quite personal and heartfelt was made manifest in a way that was beyond the rationality of everyday life. Such enigmatic expressions were reductively dismissed as a sentimental unity with the moment or, less charitably, as mass hysteria.

WHAT DID YOU THINK?

The crowds and the floral tributes appeared to me to be a confluence of confused and even contradictory messages that were ultimately inscrutable. They were inevitably quite locally specific (as Bennett predicted somewhat ironically), and I began to think that perhaps the Internet, as an expression of a collective unconsciousness, might yield a broader body of evidence to be examined. Of course, as I expected, it provided a rather skewed image of the world since in 1997 the World Wide Web was still essentially an enthusiast's environment. Originally a defense strategy with a subculture of academics and artists, the U.S. National Science Foundation, which had been subsidizing the expanding network, began to withdraw its funding in 1990 in exchange for commercialization. Over the two year period of this transformation, the Internet became public, and a community of some 20,000 grew to around 30 million by 1997. The constituency expanded exponentially and figures of 200 million were spoken of in the following two years. If things have changed since 1990, it is not so much the commercialization and larger constituency that is important but the profile of the users.[4]

Whereas the network was initially used by academics, who could call on technical support from computer enthusiasts, in 1992 it was sufficient to be enthusiastic about anything to get (and stay) online provided that you did not mind text-only data. Search engines—Mosaic and Netscape (1994)—changed the mode and appearance of Internet data. By 1997 although the pioneers were becoming the invisible strata of an undertaking about to be made profitable, the Net still had the whiff of the intellectual avant-gardism and street-wise anarchy that began colonizing it in the 1960s. Consequently, although I was dismayed to find invitations to view erotic pictures of Diana, I was not the least bit surprised that the first hit in a search for "Princess + Diana" was

1. HOROSCOOP VAN DIANA, PRINCESS OF WALES! Jaargang 2 editie 8 September 1996. De Horoscoop van Diana, Princes van Wales. Op basis van de basisgegevens uit de geboortehoroscoop van de Princes van . . . [http://aaa-mainstreet.nl/journal/2/8/diana.html—size 6K—14–Sep-96 - Dutch].

The third was what I was looking for,

3. Diana Princess of Whales [*sic*] died car crash Paris. Diana Princess of Whales has died in a car crash in Paris [http://www.bestware.net/vink/public/dianacarcrash.html—size 33K—31–Aug-97].

And others followed,

4. Condolences on the Death of Diana, Princess of Wales. To Prince William, Prince Harry and the British Royal Family, My condolences to you and your family. The world

will mourn in the departure of this . . . [http://webstars.net/diana.htm—size 1K—31–Aug-97—English].

5. Diana, Princess of Wales—Condolences. Condolences from Jens du Plessis, Terry du Plessis, Lindsay du Plessis and Jason du Plessis [http://www.safari-iafrica.com/diana.htm—size 2K—31–Aug-97—English].

10. Lady Diana Princess Diana pictures nude . . .

Following this brief link to nude images of Diana, I returned to pages of condolences,

12. Diana Princess of Wales. Leave your messages of support and condolences for the family and friends of Diana Princess of Wales diana princess of wales di diana dies died Died Dies [http://members.aol.com/miamiint/diana.htm—size 1K—31–Aug-97—English].

By the following day salacious pictures of her had disappeared and in their place, albeit from different sources, well-established conspiracy theory sites began to come up in the searches. Typically these blamed the British secret service, accused the French government of coercion, and speculated about a Muslim connection.

These conjectures were fueled, no doubt, by the summer blockbuster just hitting the screen, starring Mel Gibson and Julia Roberts, called *Conspiracy Theory*. It was a taut and telling movie of sex and violence (what else), which chimed in well with the earlier box-office hit *Men in Black* in which alien busting is not so much a covert operation but a major international industry concealed from the public for their own good and with their tacit consent.

Other sites condemning tabloid journalism also grew and when it became apparent that there were indeed photographs of the crash, a militant campaign began to boycott newspapers, in particular the German publication *Bild*, which supposedly had bought them. As people were doing "whatever" in the royal park—taking the night air, watching foxes, experiencing a moment of transcendental union, remembering a fellow human being—a tumultuous melange of news, cultural paranoia sentiment, sex, and the occult was also churning away in the worldwide consciousness of the "next big thing" to hit capitalism—the Internet.

TRYING TO MAKE SENSE OF IT

In terms of public reaction, Princess Diana's death was a startling and perplexing mixture of sentiment, irrationality, and contradiction. Although the scale of the public expression was unusual, perhaps even unique, some of its features were not unfamiliar. The least welcome resonance of such collective behavior could be seen in recent political history. The hysterical glorification of a Wagnerian hero/savior figure used to rally the crowd inevitably raised questions about how different Diana's following was from other "charismatic leaders" in recent history. She was politicized from the start as the modern face of the royal family, and after her divorce she had been used by various factions as a rallying point for a new republican movement—particularly in Australia.

For some sections of the press intent on republican reform she was the perfect vehicle to drive the cause. She was the wronged woman badly treated by the most privileged class. She would never be able to replace the monarchy (which, contradictorily, the press argued she was trying to dislodge) because the public staging of her amorous affairs eliminated her from the possibility of ever becoming Queen—at least as we currently know the function. Her romances had involved some rather sordid telephone stalking of married men; her lovers had included stereotypes of bounders guaranteed to raise the public hackles: her bodyguard (Barry Mannakee—a mere sergeant), a gormless cad of an army captain, an English rugby player who was handsome but dumb (allegedly), and to cap it all for racist Britain a Muslim.

Diana, the deposer, could be discredited at any moment that was convenient to those manipulating her image as a loose woman with a penchant for rough trade. It was this double bind that gave a woman who had political influence and considerably more, emotionally and materially, than any individual might expect out of life the air of being a victim. On top of this, something about "the big lie" and the massive following by people who were apparently oblivious to the manipulations was vaguely sinister for Europeans with an eye on recent history. In her life she was a vulnerable and dangerous victim with a massive material advantage.

The uncomfortable parallel between the crowds in a public park mourning a powerful person claiming to be a victim and other totalitarian cult hero worship of the past did not pass without comment. The anxieties were dispelled, however, by the theatrical excess of the sentiment over a person who was clearly subject to widespread and variable interpretation and lacked gravitas. What was for some people a glamorous heterosexual woman's role model was for others a gay icon of self-definition; for still others she was intelligent and cultured but also someone who liked pop music and was at home with the stars from *Hello* magazine. Yet others saw her as a caring human being only with thoughts for others despite her evident self-obsession as she succumbed to eating disorders, worked out in Chelsea, and subjected herself to all kinds of quack treatments.

From the popular newspaper archives alone as much evidence could be staked against any of these claims ("real" photographs, fashion victim, a selfish shopper, health freak, etc.) as could be marshalled to support them. She was too fragmented to be a new Rienzie but such inconsistencies and contradictions did not lead to incoherence; the very gaps in the Diana story, it seems, gave rise to a following devoted to weaving narratives around personal detail, however irrelevant or prurient. She was both fashion plate and pinup—an image waiting for a text—a star shaped by individuals and the press, less for her own qualities than the needs of those who modeled her. This kind of interest precipitated the sort of fan fiction usually reserved for soap operas, which interprets and reinterprets every shred of evidence to produce a coherent whole that is quite independent from the original (indeed, some of slash fan fiction willfully distorts the original material by insisting on cross-dressing the characters). In her death the contradictions that constituted the public Diana (actually no more than a consequence of the way data about her was organized) became the perfect topic for conspiracy theorists.[5]

As the more prurient Internet sites dropped out of sight, they were replaced by conspiracy bulletin boards, which had a number of declared functions. The first was to collect any and all data on Diana, Dodi, bodyguard Trevor Rees-Jones, and Henri Paul (the driver). The second was to weave this information into a narrative that appeared to explain those elements of the story that were (1) unknown, or (2) thought to be concealed by some agency of the British government. On some sites the more creative explanations supported other stories posted there about UFOs and contaminated breakfast cereals. The list below is typical of what was available. Here are the Network News Top Ten Theories concerning Diana's death:

(1) The deaths were orchestrated by the royal family, outraged by the likelihood that she would (1) leave the country and set up in the States (2) marry a Muslim (3) prevent Charles becoming king/marrying Camilla (4) become a feminist icon; or (5) Dodi had cheated the Queen in a cocaine deal; or (6) all of the above.

(2) Landmine manufacturers did it.

(3) Diana was hounded to death by greedy paparazzi in the pay of media moguls. Just because they were 200 metres behind the car when it crashed doesn't mean they weren't hounding her.

(4) Diana did it herself—she faked the crash so that she and Dodi could live in private. The Mercedes brake system does not leave skid marks and yet there were skid marks: why? Or did she do it for real because she was mad? Or did her implant make her do it? Or the passengers and driver of the Mercedes were all off their heads on booze and drugs and their youthful exuberance got the better of them.

(5) It was the Bank of England, in league with Ghostly Shock Troops of the Situationist International. Paris is the traditional Masonic home of regicide, and this also explains why early reports said the bodyguard's tongue had been severed in the crash.

(6) It was a psychic attack from Chumbawamba; [and] that's why Elton John recorded "Candle in the Wind" to push them out of the charts.

(7) The deaths were a spiritual retribution for the theft of the head of Yagan, nineteenth-century Aboriginal warrior.

(8) The satellite navigation system on the Mercedes was interfered with by (1) computer hackers or (2) the crew of the space station Mir.

(9) Agents from Interflora tampered with the brakes when the car was stolen earlier in the summer.

(10) It was all a dream.

Many were simply absurdist irrelevancies, some were tasteless black jokes, but most contained an undisguised criticism of the power that Western cultural and economic imperialism is thought to wield.

Assistance with these narratives was at hand, not only from Mel Gibson, Julia Roberts, and others, but also in the popularity of television conspiracy shows that had a cult following in the United Kingdom. Where the post-modernist *Twin Peaks* flirted with the union of the state and the supernatural in studied post-modern unclosure, the *X-Files* returned to the modernist idea of truth and made the abuse of power a fact that was "out there" waiting to be exposed. By 1996 the last of the series was screened in America, and after 76 episodes the cult status, merchandising, and Internet traffic connected with the program was fading, but the appetites that it had developed were cultist obsessions with conspiracy theories that involved extraterrestrials and state coverup. According to Lavery, Hague, and Cartwright, however, the attractions of stories like these are more than escapist fantasy. They claim it represents a cultural moment and cite John Mack's 1992 article on the connection between UFOs, alien abduction, and New Age spiritual and ecological awareness:

For Mack, the essence of the abduction experience is nothing less than an epistemological crisis in which abductees experience ontological shock and require another ontological paradigm after realising the limitations of a chronological, physically based interpretation of reality. . . . According to Mack, the UFO abduction experience radically undermines the assumptions of a culture that seeks to place human beings at the centre of the universe, able to control and predict all events: "to a large degree, the scientific government elite and the selected media that it controls . . . determine what we are to believe is real, for these monoliths are the principle beneficiaries of the dominant ideology." (1996, p. 11)

Mack's provocation may seem too speculative, but it suggests that we should not overlook the evidence from within and without the Court, where Diana's life was deeply implicated in a discourse of power—not just the petty squabbles of a divided House of Windsor, but a larger cultural conflict in which the ownership of one's destiny was at stake. Her apparent willingness to be photographed while at the same time taking court action against photographers testifies not only to what some critics referred to as the confused ambivalence of a star-struck exhibitionist, but also more generally to the complex personal struggle necessary to control one's own image. It is a power struggle that, since the invention of the photo album, is one that every child has had to win in order to claim adulthood. Through the filter of the personal struggle for power versus subjugation, the apparent irrationality of the public mourning in all its various manifestations, both tasteful and distasteful, sentimental and genuine, can be seen as a moment when the higher authority of the state and court, despite their best efforts to destroy someone (in fact or fiction), are made to appear puny. Whether she was a privileged princess who died in the kind of daft accident that affects us all, or she was assassinated by the monarch who was then made to lower her own flag, Diana's death became a moment of mass triumph.

A SIGN MORE THAN A STAR

Perhaps the most striking correspondence Diana's death had with other cultural phenomena was in the first hit that the search engine came up with—the horoscope. Theodore Adorno's famous study of the horoscope in the *Los Angeles Times*, published in 1974, is ostensibly an investigation of astrology to show its cultural subterfuge. Its subtext, however, never far from the surface, is the relationship between organized irrationality and paranoia. The type of people who accept astrology take it for granted: "much like psychiatry, symphony concerts or political parties; they accept it because it exists without much reflection provided only that their own psychological demands somehow correspond to the offer" (Crook, 1994, p. 36). Adorno finds most troubling the incompatibility between progress in the natural sciences and a belief in astrology, and he argues that the reconciliation is only achieved because some strong instinctual demand cancels the rationality of our own experience. Consistent with his regard for Freudian explanations, he also suggests that

indulgence in astrology may provide those who fall for it with a substitute for sexual pleasure of a passive nature. It means primarily submission to the unbridled strength of absolute power. However, this strength and power ultimately derived from the father image [have] become completely depersonalised in astrology. Communion with the stars is an almost unrecognisable and therefore tolerable substitute for forbidden relation with an omnipotent father figure. People are allowed communion with absolute strength in as much as it is considered no longer human. (Quoted in Crook, p. 36)

There is perhaps enough critical work on Adorno's contemporary relevance and questionable methods to side-step it here. The contradiction that needs to be reconciled, however, is that the majority of casual horoscope readers engage with this notion of higher forces in newspapers that apparently shape our interpretation of events. For Adorno there is evidence that they are written in ways that valorize the very ideological assumptions of the news media that carries them. However, there is also sufficient work to suggest that audiences use cultural productions in much more personal and subversive ways. But Adorno's insight that the relationship with the horoscope is one of unequal power in which forces greater even than humankind shape the minutia of daily life is still valuable. Carol Clover and Linda Williams, for example, have used an anthropologist's approach to question ideological readings of slasher movies and stag films respectively, preferring instead to show how each is used in a process of reconciling the powerlessness of an individual in the face of relentless power. Jane Juffer more recently has asked what (outside the rhetoric of well-rehearsed positions) pornography means. She chooses to regard it as reconciliation between the erotic and the everyday by carefully placing it between the mundane and the profane. According to Laura Kipnis in this precise positioning,

[p]ornography provides a realm of transgression that is, in effect, a counter-aesthetic to dominant norms for bodies, sexualities, and desire itself. . . . What shapes these genres [of pornography]—their content, their raw material—are precisely the items black-balled from the rest of culture. This watchful dialectical relation pornography maintains to the mainstream of culture makes it nothing less than a form of cultural critique. It refuses to let us so easily off the hook for our hypocrisies. Or our unconsciousness. (Quoted in Juffer, p. 17)

What these theorists share is the premise that audiences are not quite the passive receptors that some cultural theorists have assumed. Their approach suggests that to understand the compulsion of horoscopes we should consider that for most people they *fail* to predict the future as much if not more than they actually hit the mark. Princess Diana's own astrologer, for example, predicted that Prince Charles would die in a road accident (was it this, one wonders, that motivated John Morrison's contingency plan for the BBC?). By dint of their very failure, horoscopes—even the one chosen by the "princess of chic"—may be in Kipnis's terms as much a cultural critique as pornography.

CONCLUSION

The apparent continuity between horoscopes and conspiracy theories in subscribing to an intelligence that is not humanly centered needs to be reconciled with the apparent necessity for the transparent absurdities that are characteristic of both. Whether an Internet account of the crash in the tunnel, or Mulder and Scully's skirmishes as they uncover U.S. involvement in a conspiracy with former Nazi and Japanese scientists to assist alien beings in performing experiments—including hybridization—on American citizens (to quote the blurb), an essential factor for success, it seems, is the precise distance between the erotic and the everyday.

Diana's stardom in her lifetime was a horoscope fantasy and/or a strap line for an *X-Files* episode. The narratives that informed us about her were written in the same terms as both: a larger power was always at force shaping her destiny. This ranged from the irrational forces of her love for dreary old duffers like the Prince of Wales (a weakness that appeared to stay with her even when she should have known better), to the machinations of the Royal Court, the gladiatorial struggles between press agents, and the power of the tabloid press to find her wherever she was in the world.

When she died the narratives that had made her were reversed: the fantastic and elaborate stories of her life (usually developed from a paparazzi snap) that made claims to super powers, beauty, grace, humanity, and even intelligence became exaggerated even more as stories showed her as both powerful and powerless. The public mourning may have been as much a confirmation of the fickleness of power as an "outpouring of grief"—it may have been a callous celebration of the ultimate unity between star and worshiper. In an erotic exchange, the horoscope narratives—ambiguous one liners—through which she was made known, became necessarily definitive. She had died. As much as anything this strange reversal might go some way in explaining the irrationality of a large number of people in response to her death. It was a confirmation that even the omnipotent are finally without power.

Diana was never beautiful, never witty, not especially intelligent, nor particularly human-spirited. She was a transparently ordinary person invested with a star quality that was a self-evident simulation. With an eye on *Hello* and Hollywood she looked the part that both she and the press willingly played for the power and influence it gave them. Her real cultural significance, however, is as a sign—a star sign. She was, and possibly still is, a figure caught in the conflict between the rational and irrational in a power struggle in which neither side is especially worthy. Not surprisingly then her moment came and went with her interment in September 1997. There was little popular interest in the first anniversary of her death and less at the second. Althorp is a place for enthusiasts and fortunately very little was named after her to embarrass us (and her memory).

Perhaps the most intriguing aspect of the five days between the announcement of her death and her funeral was the displacement of erotic pictures of Diana on the Internet by conspiracy theory bulletin boards. I wrote about this briefly at the time and since then the puzzle has continued to intrigue me. The explanation of public decorum did not immediately seem to be consistent with the evident paranoia that replaced it, and as the Diana story has unwound over the past several years the question of the reconciliation forms the central question of this chapter. The conclusions are inevitably speculative but, since writing a caution in 1997, two years after Diana's death, it appears that in the current power/information equation when we have more bandwidth than data we might need to rethink the idea of a popular "star" and at least differentiate between the stellar and the Zodical.

POSTSCRIPT

On the occasion of the second anniversary of Diana's death, I went to Kensington Palace. In the sparse crowd a pretty woman I did not know approached me with a smile and began talking—I thought it was my own moment of celebrity—as she walked past me toward the video news camera saying something about the atmosphere that would be forgotten before the next item in the program. Elsewhere a few people, mostly couples, read the notes tied to the railings, pointing out interesting phrases to one another. I had only one Polaroid film left in my camera to take a picture—an unprofessional oversight that I rationalized might force me to sum up what was going on in a single image. The gods smiled down: there foursquare in front of the flowers tied to the gates a couple met. They had all the gear of 1990s street-wise cool—kneepads, rucksacks, untucked T-shirts, shorts, youth, and roller blades. The young white man threw his arms around his best girl—a beautiful Afro-Caribbean woman—who had obviously arranged to meet him at this site of memorial, and they kissed. This was a lovers' tryst in a public place of mourning that had already lost its link with the scene of the tragedy. Diana seemed to be affirmed as a free-floating sign open to wide interpretation. The picture was a gift for any post-modernist cultural studies essay, so I overcame my scruples and snapped it quickly—but my furtiveness was unnecessary; they were still locked in the embrace long after the film had developed and I had walked away. Diana's death had become a kiss to remember as the stars (as in horoscope) looked down.

APPENDIX: "PEOPLE IN BLACK" BY MICHAEL PUNT[6]

On the first page of *Deny All Knowledge: Reading the X-Files*, Lavery, Hague, and Cartwright remind us that "psychohistorians—those curious scholarly investigators who attempt to read (and understand) historical subjects as psychological phenomena, motivated/driven/governed by unconscious factors—have not paid that much attention to popular culture." The car crash in the Pont d'Alma underpass in Paris in which Diana, Princess of Wales, Dodi Fayed, and Henri Paul died will almost certainly change that. Now, after the funeral, two broad questions have emerged: the first is covered by the police investigation into the causes of the crash; the second, concerning the bewildering responses of ordinary people to the event, will need to be explained by cultural analysts. Extraordinary rigor will be required to explain why, for example, two million people watched the funeral procession in the streets of London, yet as many as three million turned out on the following day to "walk the route" of the procession. The convenient diagnosis of mass hysteria seems too glib an explanation in the circumstances. Psychohistorians and other kinds of scholars may need to spend much more time immersed in popular culture, thinking about cinema, television, and especially the Internet to come to some appreciation of the complexity of this kind of reaction.

It will come as no surprise to Internet users that almost as soon as news of the crash broke, reaction to the event appeared on various Web sites. Tributes were posted on the BBC home page, Buckingham Palace opened a book of condolence on its official site, and even scholarly lists such as H-Film began to carry comment from subscribers normally concerned with the minutia of film history. As the broadcast media began to elaborate the official information, "unofficial" postings, which combined reaction with questions about the crash, also began to appear on the Internet on various conspiracy theory sites. Many of these sites are comprised of bulletin boards, which are electronic hybrids of a number of communication genres most favored by so-called subcultures. They combine the populist "supermarket tabloids" (in which Tommy Lee Jones and Will Smith, the "Men in Black," recognize their own exploits described in fantastic stories of alien abduction), with the political subversion of the anti-establishment "Newsletter" in which Jerry Fletcher (Mel Gibson) publishes his insane ideas in the film *Conspiracy Theory*. Added to these is a rather more recent phenomena quite specific to the Internet known as "slash fan fiction" in which popular television series such as the *X-Files* are collectively discussed and rewritten, often with a strong element of erotic fantasy. Using this potent cocktail of rhetorical style, contributors to conspiracy theory routinely speculate on events as wide ranging as the death of JFK, UFOs, and contaminated breakfast cereal. After the crash, however, the bulletin boards were overwhelmed by suggestions about what really happened in the Pont d'Alma underpass. Some of these were absurd and fantastic, some were simply distasteful, but most asked relevant questions and reached plausible, if far fetched, conclusions.

Although conspiracy theory sites might not be the place to discover truths about any particular incident, they are rich terrain for the cultural analyst. Their vigorous prose and imaginative invention perfectly express the mood reflected in many of this summer's cinema releases. According to Lavery, Hague, and Cartwright, the responsibility for this mood lies with what is perceived as a loss of intellectual and psychological control, induced by the centralization of power and the efficiency of the media in gathering news. Baroque narratives that invest the extraterrestrial and supernatural with credibility, they argue, are attempts to regain some control of unexplained events by giving order to the chaos of information. That some appear on electronic bulletin boards is paradoxical since nowhere is this chaos more apparent than on the Internet. Nonetheless the megabytes of text on the conspiracy theory boards creatively weave logical explanations using newspaper reports, forensic evidence, and imagination fed by movie plots. These rambling unregulated narratives provide accessible evidence of an unconscious belief system that may help us evaluate the truth or otherwise in the vernacular wisdom of the Men in Black that "a person is smart [but] people are dumb, panicky animals."

NOTES

1. *Radio Times*. September 13–19 (1997).

2. The posthumous Diana bibliography is extensive. See for example: Burchill (1999); Anderson (1998); Harrison (1988); and Anderson and Mullen, eds. (1998).

3. The custom is to use the flag on the palace only to signify the residence of the monarch. Only when she is not in residence is it lowered. Since the Queen was at the palace throughout the period it was technically rather insulting to lower it.

4. One of the more interesting histories of personal computing and the Internet is in Cringely (1996). See also Punt, "Accidental Machines" (1998).

5. For a discussion of slash fiction, see Jenkins (1992).

6. The appendix material is an English translation of an article that originally appeared in the Dutch journal *Skrien* 218 (1997).

REFERENCES

Anderson, C. *The Day Diana Died*. New York: William Morrow, 1998.

Anderson, C., and P. Mullen, eds. *Faking It: Sentimentalisation of Modern Society*. London: Penguin, 1998.

Bennett, Alan. "Diary Excerpts." *London Review of Books*. January 1, 1998.

Burchill, J. *Diana*. London: Orion, 1999.

Clover, C. *Men, Women and Chainsaws: Gender in the Modern Horror Film*. London: British Film Institute, 1992.

Cringely, R. *Accidental Empires: How the Boys of Silicon Valley Make Their Millions, Battle Foreign Competition, and Still Can't Get a Date*. London: Penguin, 1996.

Crook, S., ed. *Adorno: The Stars Look Down to Earth and Other Essays on the Irrational Culture*. London: Routledge, 1994.

Harrison, T. *Icon and Sacrifice*. London: Lion, 1988.

Jenkins, Henry. *Textual Poachers: Television Fans and Participatory Culture*. New York: Routledge, 1992.

Juffer, J. *At Home with Pornography: Women, Sex, and Everyday Life*. New York: New York University Press, 1998.

Lavery, D., A. Hague, and M. Cartwright, eds. *Deny All Knowledge: Reading the X-Files*. London: Faber and Faber, 1996.

Punt, M. "Accidental Machines: Understanding How We Understand New Technologies." *Design Issues* 14, no. 1 (1998): 54–80.

Williams, L. 1990. *Hardcore: Power, Pleasure, and the "Frenzy of the Visible."* London: Pandora, 1990.

—————— Chapter 6 ——————

Virtually Touching the Stars—from the Moon to Heaven's Gate and Beyond

Leonie Cooper

> It is as if a window opened in the room of our everyday life, and we were invited to look outside into space, into the sky and the cosmos.
> —Pope Paul VI, quoted in Thrapp, p. 35

MEMORIES OF STAR-SPANGLED SCREENS

On July 20, 1969, we were invited to cross a threshold: when Edwin "Buzz" Aldrin and Neil Armstrong stepped onto the celestial body of the moon, the visible boundaries between the known and the unknown, the (extra)ordinary and the mundane, the human and the divine shifted. This vital step in humankind's "march towards the stars" bridged the distances (in)between the human observer and the visible but intangible phenomena of the stars out there in space. As the astronauts inscribed the evidence of "man's" actual presence on the moon "with a cautious, almost shuffling gait" ("The Moon," p. 10), the almost instantaneous transmission of their ghostly voices and phantom figures to the television screen seemed to confirm that the stars were, at last, within actual reach. Yet, looking outside the pope's window to the "immense, mysterious picture" of the heavens also initiated a kind of perceptual and epistemological vertigo (Pope Paul VI, quoted in Thrapp, p. 35). What would it mean, witnesses wondered, to look back at the earth and see "sights never seen before"—our entire planet floating like a big blue ball beyond the moon's horizon? Would reaching the "queen of the starry sky"[1]—that conduit to the celestial sphere of the stars—fundamentally alter our view of the world, and thus of ourselves?

Today, the moon landing is nostalgically remembered: viewers such as David Whitehouse eloquently remind us that "no one who witnessed those trans-

The astronaut at Kennedy Space Center. © Leonie Cooper, 1999.

lucent black-and-white images from the Sea of Tranquility will forget them"
("Reach for the Moon," p. 26). With still conditions and a telescope, this contemporary cosmic observer searches for Tranquility Base—the site/sight of
our first contact with the moon—and, in doing so, confirms the continuing
cultural significance of this event. Just as Whitehouse looks up to the moon
through his telescope, this chapter looks at, and through, the Space Mirror
Memorial (the Mirror) at Kennedy Space Center, Cape Canaveral,[2] to make
visible the shifting figuration and cultural dynamic of the astronaut as a viewed
and viewing figure.

Looking through the Mirror, we will see how astronauts of the 1960s were
configured as stars: their presence beyond the pope's window served to perceptually and epistemologically illuminate the dark regions of space, out there
beyond our reach. In conjunction with this turn back to the moon landing,
this chapter also looks at the Mirror's reconstruction of the astronaut as star in
the light of other contemporary media events such as the Heaven's Gate mass
suicide and the Mars Pathfinder Mission. This strategy of reading the Mirror's
heavenly message in the context of other viewing assemblages and possible
refigurations of the astronaut will foreground the crucial role that this figure
plays in our contemporary culture. Viewing the stars on the Space Mirror
means remembering the astronaut as star. Thus, we will see how this figure im-
pels us, once again, to renegotiate the boundaries between the virtual space of
the stars and our lived experiences here on earth.

Strategically situated within the physical and mediated geography of the
Space Center the Mirror is partially enclosed by an artificial lake so that the visitor-viewer must cross a walkway that bridges the watery domain of a few
lounging alligators. Ahead, the props and foundations of a massive structure
loom above, but its façade remains hidden from view until, following a path to
the right, we enter a circular viewing area. Here, in this sacred space, isolated
from the other "attractions" at the Space Center, we are asked to pause, take a
step back, and look up and at the massive "screen" in front of us. Etched
through the polished black granite surface and dotted across the face of this
42.5-foot-high and 50-foot-wide edifice are the names of 17 astronauts who
died attempting to reach the stars (see appendix). Controlled by computer
software, the Mirror rotates and tilts to follow the direction of the sun so that
light always passes through the crystal clear acrylic of each name. Like stars in
the black void of space, the astronauts' names glitter in the Florida sun.

Viewed with the unaided eye on a clear night, the celestial stars may appear
as elusively distant as ever. Yet, the phantom voices from the heady days of the
Apollo era that echo throughout the Kennedy Space Center remind us that
these stars are as much a part of our lived environments as they are out there in
space. The hot, bright suns of the galaxy that are "luminous by virtue of internal nuclear reactions"[3] are encrusted with mythological, cultural, and ideological associations. Our everyday terrestrial experiences are informed by and, in
turn, shape this visual polyphony of star images that permeate our cultural

space(s).[4] Mediated by multiple discourses and imaging technologies, this cultural geography of the stars has a "shifting and ambiguous dimensionality" that is similar to Scott Bukatman's understanding of the cinematic as a fractal dimension that exists (in)between the two-dimensionality of the photographic and the three-dimensionality of experiential reality (p. 137).[5]

The Space Mirror focuses this ambiguous shifting cultural space in such a way that, for the visitor-viewer, the figure of the astronaut and the celestial stars are rewoven into a specific historical, social, and perceptual dynamic. Bolter and Grusin argue that new media forms "appropriate the techniques, forms and social significance of other media" according to the logics of "hypermediacy" and "immediacy" to promote a more authentic experience—to "rival or refashion them in the name of the real" (p. 65). While a granite monument is certainly not a new media form, the Mirror does remediate the network of social discourses, technologies, and images that put a man on the moon in the late 1960s. The "real," authentic experience of watching the astronauts reach the stars is fixed upon the Mirror's surface, reminding us of their continuing cultural significance as "stars" and refashioning, both allegorically and materially, their form into spectacularly visible sunlight.

In the late 1960s NASA's (the National Aeronautics and Space Agency's) mission to land a man on the moon choreographed a "new theatrics of space" (Spigel, p. 210)[6] from the fluid cultural geography of the stars: staged against the backdrop of the stars, the *mise en scène* included the rockets, landing equipment, and other technical instruments, and the "sympathetic but fallible human actors" of this celestial drama were the now familiar trio of Armstrong, Aldrin, and Michael Collins.[7] Positioned in the spotlight of the media by NASA, these "truly great human beings" (Teague, n.p.) acquired the cultural and public status of the star—a performative image constructed for, and by, the media and other citizen-viewers.[8] The public witnesses who watched the drama unfolding on this stage were asked to recognize and validate the (extra)ordinary endeavor of the astronauts in successfully reaching the moon. Indubitably, the status of these astronauts as "famous or brilliant persons" was based upon the metaphorical transcription of starlike qualities onto their public bodies. Viewed from afar, like "any of the luminous points in the night sky," their performance should inspire the wonder and devotion of the ordinary person for, just as the ancient gods walked the night skies among the stars, the astronauts existed on a plane somewhere above and beyond the physical location of the terrestrial viewer.[9]

While the metaphor of the stage demonstrates that the astronaut of the 1960s was designed to be allegorically read as a star, the key focus of the Mirror and its form of remediation foreground that this star-figuration of the astronaut was, and still remains, imbricated within a viewing "assemblage": "an object about which something can be said and at the same time an object which is used. . . . [It] cannot be reduced either to a technological or a discursive object" (Crary, p. 8).[10] The Mirror reassembles the astronaut from the conglom-

erate social discourses and media forms that "put a man on the moon" into a
viewing and viewed figure that prescribes the specific operational dynamics of
reaching and, thus, seeing the stars. As a viewing assemblage, the astronaut
made (and makes) sense of our literal and figural contact with the "shifting and
ambiguous dimensionality" between the celestial stars and our lived experiences because, in the 1960s, the star became an *appropriate* metaphor for the
astronaut and the astronaut became an *appropriate* metaphor for the stars.

The predominance of particular celestial symbols within a culture, Keith
Hutchinson argues, is inextricably entwined with the sociopolitical and aesthetic formations of that culture. In the Baroque culture to which Hutchinson
turns his analysis, an ideological and theological struggle took place over the
question of whether the sun or the moon was better representative of the king.
The eventual predominance of the sun as an "appropriate metaphor for a
King" and the king as "an appropriate metaphor for the Sun" was crucial in authenticating the spatial (and thus social) formations of a hierarchical, monar-
chist-centered society (pp. 97–111). Conversely, when Renaissance observers
looked to the symbolic movement of the planets (the wandering stars) to interpret the way society should be ordered, the "political messages" that they drew
from this "divine communication" also mapped the ideological and discursive
geography of their society—the king as the center of the universe—onto the
stars out there in space. Thus, the symbolic force of "sun/king" was instrumental to the shift from the geostatic model of the universe to the Copernican
heliostatic model (Hutchinson, pp. 95, 100).[11]

Central to the theatrical space designed by NASA, it can be argued that the
astronaut of the 1960s had as much epistemological and social significance as
did the figure of the king as sun in Renaissance society. Moreover, the Mirror's
reconstruction of the astronaut as a specific kind of celestial symbol—a
star—reflects the ongoing symbolic resonance of this figuration of the astronaut in our contemporary culture. In order to acknowledge and authorize the
astronaut's literal and figural force within our culture, the Mirror must imbri-
cate the visitor-viewer into a particular type of perceptual and technological
"assemblage." On the one hand, the Mirror acts like a kind of screen:[12] its reflective surface formally mirrors the astronaut's *actual* presence on the remote
landscape of the moon back to the visitor-viewer. Our presence in front of the
Mirror grounds the ideological and social materiality of the stars as a "real"
landscape—up there and beyond the Mirror—that can (only) be accessed by
the astronaut.

On the other hand, the Mirror is also a "flat, rectangular surface positioned
at a distance" from the visitor-viewer, and, therefore, it functions somewhat
like the "classical" Albertian window—a transparent "window" to "another
three-dimensional world enclosed by a frame" and situated inside the visitor-viewer's "normal space" (Manovich, n.p.). Located in a space adjacent to
the view provided by the Mirror, the visitor-viewer ideally looks through the
"window" to (re)member the moon landing as an authentic "real" experience.

Furthermore, in an unfolding process, looking through the Mirror brings the stars beyond the window into our normal everyday space *and* transports us along with the astronaut to a space somewhere in between our three-dimensional experiential reality and the two-dimensionality of the star images imprinted on its screen. A space that is neither physical nor imaginary but *both* material *and* symbolic is, therefore, made visible by the viewer's attendance in front of the Mirror and the astronaut's presence beyond the window. Consequently, the astronaut is rematerialized as a figure who guides us on a voyage beyond our everyday "normal" space to remember the moon landing as if we were still there.

SEEING STARS ON THE MIRROR:
WE ARE STILL THERE!

The primary metaphor of going into space, in its actual and science fictional realizations, Constance Penley argues, activates a "yearning to get a personal grip on the seemingly distant realm, of science and technology" (p. 5).[13] Similarly, the star figuration of the astronaut functioned (and continues to function) as a kind of universal translator,[14] filtering and making sense of what it means to be human in light of the scientific and technological grasp of the celestial stars. If, as Wertheim points out, it is the "questions that we ask that determine the kind of space that we are able to see" (p. 306), in the 1960s it was the articulation and implementation of the astronaut as a material figure *that was like a star* that inscribed how, and with what means, we could reach and, thus, see the "new utopia" that lay beyond the pope's window. Choreographing this utopia as the stage on which the astronauts performed enabled NASA to adequately provide, at least in its terms, the "brave men who will fly again down that long, dark and dustless corridor of space" (Teague, p. 5738).

Flying down that "corridor of space" might mean illuminating the darkness behind the pope's window, but, in order to envisage the teleological progress of technology and instrumental knowledge across the imagined and real distances to the stars, official NASA discourses utilized the figural gestures of the astronaut to inscribe the celestial stars as a material space that could be mapped and excavated. "Marching towards the stars" and "reaching for the Moon," the astronaut's words were even translated into the hyperbolic promise of grasping the stars with their "strong workmanlike words that would stand as tall trees in the upward path of man from the mud to the Moon" (Pett, p. 1).

Such heroic gestures, words, and actions confirmed the astronaut as an agent of the new American frontier. Familiar from the condensed mediated history and evolving formal dynamic of the Western genre that informed (and continues to inform) the American cultural landscape, the frontier was "a point in space and time," where the symbolic and material forces of civilization and wilderness "confront" each other. The horizon of the frontier—this "point in space and time"—was defined and mediated by the figure of the heroic pioneer who embodied and enacted the tension between these opposing forces (Cawelti, p. 193). The public material body of the astronaut as All-American white male hero, therefore, realized the values of freedom, agency, and initiative that were part of the spatial and social landscape of the frontier: a real-and-imagined space that was consistently and deliberately invoked by NASA officials, politicians, and the astronauts themselves as a justification for their flight into the darkness of space (Dean, p. 91).[15]

A photo spread in the *Chicago Tribune* (July 11, 1969) reveals how the public bodies of the Apollo XI astronauts were inextricably entwined with their actions as "pioneers of the twentieth century." The official photo of the mission team—Neil Armstrong, Michael Collins, and Edwin Aldrin—is positioned adjacent to a staff painting that depicts Armstrong and Aldrin involved in the activity of technological colonization: Aldrin begins to unfurl an umbrella-like TV antenna while Armstrong collects a rock sample with a pick-up tool. The Eagle, the lunar landing module, sits in the mid-background of a desert-like landscape. The staff painting exemplifies how the astronauts served to mediate the intangible, immaterial, and "luminous points in the night sky" into a cultural geography that can be acted upon and, therefore, comprehended from within the familiar sociocultural and aesthetic matrix of the frontier.

Situating the mediating figure of the astronaut and his domesticating activities in the foreground, the painting presents the astronaut as an active agent involved in the instrumental colonization of the "new frontier," now in outer space rather than the Wild West. While the astronauts enacted the ideological imperative of "opening up" the celestial body of the moon for colonization and exploitation,[16] this painting also contained the potential perceptual and epistemological dislocation of looking back at the earth as a big blue ball floating in the vast and "uncivilized" void of space—as "empty as the edges of a 15th-century map" (Chaikin, n.p.)—in a similar manner to the pope's window. Framing the "barren" landscape of the moon with a horizon of low hills, the painting validates the formal and operational dynamics of the pope's window as both "views" inscribe the spatial and social borders of the new frontier. At the same time, the presence of the astronauts as stars beyond these windows *enacts* the imaginary horizon of the frontier so that this symbolic point in space is visually and epistemologically *materialized* for the terrestrial spectator.

If the figure of the astronaut was projected through the pope's window to act out the dimensions of Kennedy's "new utopian frontier," Armstrong and Aldrin's direct contact with the moon also traced an experiential continuity between our "phenomenological sense of time's irrecoverable gravity" and the shifting dimensionality of the stars out there in space (Sobchack, p. 133). Freezing the human stars in motion, the pope's window provided a transparent interface to the astronaut's actual and figural presence on the moon that helped to enforce the moon landing as a direct and *immediate* access to the stars. The fact that the Eagle *had* landed, which was screamed across the headlines of every newspaper in 1969, lent an aura of immediacy to witnessing the event. We *were* there.

The *Detroit News*, for example, presented the first color photos of the moon as a "symbol of a nation's triumph," signaling an end to the time of artist's drawings and science-fictional images of the moon. The media's focus upon the "almost instantaneous" and, therefore, automatic, transmission of moving images from the stars "out there" to the television screen "right here in the living room" attempted to erase any sense of mediation between the viewer and the "queen of the starry skies."[17] It appeared that the "truth" of this celestial body, previously obscured by popular myths and physical distance, was "revealed" by the flight of Apollo XI (Souvenir Edition, n.p.).

The extremely blurry, "ghost-like" (Chaikin, p. 32) photographs and moving images of the astronauts on the lunar surface were celebrated and re-articulated by the media as "so sharp and clear as to seem unreal" (Wilford, p. 1). However, it was the "network of artifacts, images and cultural agreements" about the mediating function of the astronaut that created a context where the reproductions of their actual presence on the moon were believed to be true "even though they were something which mankind had never set eyes on before" (Mitchell, p. 37).[18] Certainly the public witnesses of this event were cognizant of the mediated nature of such reproductions,[19] but foregrounding the "real time" contiguity between the terrestrial viewer and the astronaut's figural and literal presence beyond the pope's "window" was an attempt "to get past the limits of representation" (Bolter and Grusin, p. 53). "Getting past" the mediation of the "window," therefore, should (but did not necessarily) invoke an authentic emotional response to the fact that "we"—as collective public witnesses—were *really* there with the astronauts, on the moon.

Materializing the particular social and spatial imaginary of the "new utopian frontier" as a "real space that lies beyond mediation" (Bolter and Grusin, p. 41), the Mirror strategically situates the contemporary visitor-viewer with the citizen-viewer of 1969 to relive an "original" authentic (unmediated) experience of actually reaching the stars. However, if the Mirror reminds us to keep looking outside into space, the sky and beyond, it is also designed to "ensure that future generations are prepared to face the challenges, both on and off our celestial home . . . the Spaceship Earth" (Astronaut Memorial Foundation). This mission statement and NASA's slogan, "Yesterday the Moon, Today the Space Station, Tomorrow . . . Mars" (from the display at Complex 39 at the Kennedy Space Center), suggest a discursive tug toward the future, yet, at the same time, a themed snack bar sign at Kennedy's LC-39 observation gantry—which tells us that we "are (but) a shuttle flight from outer space"—keeps us (still) present in the "new utopian frontier" of the 1960s.

Faced with this push-pull dynamic, the Mirror spatially and temporally displaces other social discourses and imaginings of the astronaut and, consequently, other ways of viewing the stars so that a feedback loop is created between the visitor-viewer's personal and cultural memories and the figure of the astronaut on the moon. Moreover, if the static frame of the window seems appropriate for the physical properties of the Mirror as a monument, this edifice is also a *rotating* apparatus that amplifies, like a homing beacon to the past, the function of the window and screen to filter, screen out, and render "non-existent whatever is outside its frame" (Manovich, n.p.). Viewing the stars on the Mirror, therefore, becomes a doubled and doubling "authentic" experience that situates the visitor-viewer in a kind of non-place that is neither the past nor the future but the always already present, where the phantasmic scene of the moon landing is rehearsed and relived once again.[20]

Forecasting a future-past that is now realized at the Kennedy Space Center, the Mirror's remediation of the astronaut of the 1960s adds a further time-traveling dimension to the perceptual and social assemblage of this figure, the viewer, and the celestial stars. The Mirror as window and screen confirms that the astronaut could move beyond the normal space of the viewer to touch the stars, but it also appropriates the figure of the astronaut to ground the moon landing as a historical event that predicted the future of actual human space travel. Like the medieval astrologer who interpreted celestial phenomena—the sudden appearance of a comet or a total eclipse—as a means of foretelling a (usually) disastrous future,[21] the stars of the Apollo XI team became once (and always) representative of, in Neil Armstrong's words, "all men with a vision for the future" (Wilford, p. 1).

Remediating the futuristic discourses and science fictional images that interpreted the significance of a "man on the moon" as a prophetic event, the Mirror reauthorizes the astronaut's literal and figural contact with the stars as material evidence of the future frontier of science and technology and NASA's teleological advance toward the stars. As visitor-viewers at Kennedy we are placed, once again, with the media witnesses who, in 1969, seemed more concerned with where we were going than where we actually were. At this time, speculation was rife: What would be the moral and ethical consequences and material gains of landing on the moon? However, the astronaut's physical contact with the stars grounded this "what if" thinking so that, for example, one witness of the moon landing could state, as a matter of fact, that by the end of the 1970s a semipermanent space station and, by the end of the century, an orbital platform *will* exist as NASA moves from its "pioneering to occupational stage" (Hines).[22] We can see, therefore, that, the Mirror's invitation to look into the past potentially displaces the network of discourses and imaginings that framed the moon landing within the social and perceptual infrastructure of the 1960s. The past and the future are compressed into an ahistorical and choreographed event that anchors the memory of going into space as a "real" experience, forever accessible, where we can, like the astronauts, actually go into space and touch the stars.

REACHING THE STARS: ARE WE THERE YET?

Like the "window opened up" by the moon landing, the Space Mirror reframes the astronaut as a mediating figure that enables us to grasp and, therefore, make sense of the virtual, intangible space beyond the pope's window. However, if the "truth revealed" by Apollo XI was anchored by the pope's window and is remediated by the Mirror, what happens when we acknowledge the specific historical and cultural contours of the technologies, discourses, and cultural agreements that inscribe our contemporary views of the stars, rather then freeze-frame the figure of the astronaut in a kind of never-never land beyond the Space Mirror?

The familiar (at least to those who "surf the Net") Netscape Navigator icon provides a contemporary challenge to the Space Mirror's remediation of the spatio-temporal dynamics of the pope's window and the painting. Within a small window that sits at the top right-hand side of the browser, this animated icon depicts shooting stars that move across a night sky in an endlessly repeating pattern. This miniature "window" mediates and makes sense of our interactions with the intangible space beyond and "behind" the computer screen: representing movement across its dimensions and through space, it suggests that we, the "user," must navigate our way through this virtual realm that is phenomenologically equivalent to our embodied experience of the world but also remains disembodied, disarticulate, and strangely unfamiliar. In a self-reflexive turn to the *absence* of the astronaut as a visible figure, the Navigator icon represents, as the software enables, an interactivity between the virtual space beyond the browser's "window"—represented by the stars—and the lived space of the computer user.

However, this spatial (inter)activity is both promised and denied by the formal dynamics of the Space Mirror for, like the harmonious and geocentric vantage point from which the ancient seer watched the spherical rotation of the stars, the Mirror's remediation of the pope's window erects a static field of view that encourages a detached, reflective observation of the stars. Whereas the Navigator icon is a moving image, which has its own circular temporality that does not, in the linear sense and in the sense of our own lived temporality as mortal beings, *go* anywhere (for it is we who must make sense of this virtual space according to the irrevocable gravity of mortal existence and go somewhere), the Mirror's static view of the fixed stars "out there" in space shifts the mobility figured by the *animated* icon from the computer user as navigator onto the figure of the astronaut as navigator. Unlike the view provided by the Netscape Navigator's "window," therefore, the Mirror asks that the terrestrial viewer remain stationary, here on earth (not "really" going anywhere so to speak), so that the astronaut still visibly figures the irreversible spatial progress of an external intentional agent laboring across the "real" and imagined distance to the stars beyond the terrestrial viewer's reach.[23]

The presence of the Netscape Navigator icon on our computer screens unsettles the passive position of a viewer who watches the astronaut/stars beyond the static window of the Mirror. Moreover, viewing the Space Mirror in relation to other cultural events such as the Mars Pathfinder Mission[24] raises questions about the contemporary significance of the transparent interface provided by the Mirror and the central mediating function of the astronaut as star. Does the appearance of digital images from Mars inside a small window "floating" among the other windows on the computer screen force us to recognize the multiple technologies that mediate our views of the stars and that have constructed the astronaut as star? Does it really matter when it is no longer an astronaut walking on the moon but a fully mobile and wireless tele-robot roaming the surface of Mars?

Like the moon landing, the Mars Pathfinder Mission further "opened up" the intangible, virtual landscape of the stars. Yet, nested among many possible windows to other virtual space(s)—the Internet, an Excel file, a Word document—this "floating" window to Mars potentially displaces the singular window to the stars set up by the Space Mirror. In fact, the multiple windows located "on" the computer desktop are mirrored in the mediated landscape that surrounds the Space Mirror. The Mirror is only one of the attractions at the Space Center Visitor Complex and is situated within a hypermediated environment of interactive displays, IMAX cinemas, exhibits, theatrical re-creations of the Apollo XI mission, space-themed cafes, and a real moon rock you can touch! Kennedy Space Center—the Gateway to the Universe—invites multiple and discontinuous views that, rather than erasing mediation, form an opaque, heterogeneous landscape where the visitor-viewer must necessarily acknowledge the mediating and mediated nature of the astronaut and the Space Mirror. Prefigured by the Netscape Navigator icon, the visitor-viewer's phenomenological engagement with the shifting dimensions of the stars becomes interactive and mobile: here we can listen to the voices of the astronauts, touch the artifacts from outer space, even watch the future unfold in three dimensions at an IMAX theater.

Thus, to view the Space Mirror in the context of other contemporary viewing assemblages such as the Mars Pathfinder Mission and the multifarious media available at Kennedy Space Center potentially unfixes the transparent "immediate" interface provided by the Mirror. However, when witness-viewers such as Kuac claim that the Mars Pathfinder event invoked an "intense feeling of remote presence"—that "no object can rival the experiential quality of this event" (n.p.) then the discourses, artifacts, and cultural agreements that "put a man on the moon" are once again refashioned in the name of a more "real" experience. Much like the Space Mirror, Kuac remains dependent on the "real" memory of the astronauts' actual and figural presence on the moon and, therefore, the potential disorientation of the "floating" window on the computer screen is anchored—albeit in a less overt manner than the Space Mirror. The hypermediated interface provided by different media at Kennedy Space Center only serves to reinforce the moon landing as a more authentic and still culturally significant "real" experience. In a similar manner to Kuac's attention to *one* particular window on the computer screen, the visitor-viewer looks *through* the Space Mirror so that it becomes the focal point of the Space Center. Binding "multiple perspectives and scalar shifts" (Bukatman, p. 137), the contours of this reflective screen stitch the multiple views and mediating technologies made available at the visitor center into the singular perspective of the astronaut reaching for the stars.

HEAVEN'S GATE: LOSING OUR GRIP?

However, in a dialogic and somewhat paradoxical process, the singular perspective of the astronaut reaching for the stars, which was instrumental in prescribing the virtual space beyond the pope's window as a material and visible landscape that can be acted upon, and made comprehensible, also tapped (and continues to invoke) a "pervasive cultural longing" to transcend the material and phenomenological limits of bodily existence (Hillis, 1998, p. 71) and directly experience "that which is far away" (Pope Paul VI, quoted in Thrapp, p. 35). Whereas the materiality of the public body and figural gestures of the astronaut inscribed the "new utopia" of the stars as a virtual space that can be inhabited and navigated by these "human" figures, their disembodied God-like view from beyond the pope's window also reflected the constraints of human secular existence and the material body.

In the 1960s, the pope's Neoplatonic window metaphysically divided the absolute space of the heavens from worldly secular existence so that the celestial stars remained a kind of omega point that, if reached, would transfigure the astronauts in a kind of techno-gnostic process into God-like beings. The astronauts' direct physical contact with the celestial body of the moon, therefore, was celebrated as a "transcendent event, one of those shining moments in history when man rises above himself towards greatness" ("Moon Supplement," p. 18). By reaching the moon and figuratively moving through the window, the astronauts were able to "view the earth from a physically transcendent stance" and like Jim Irwin of Apollo XV, for example, could walk on the surface of the moon, imagining that they were now able to "look at the earth with the eyes of God" (Noble, p. 140).[25] It is almost as if, by leaving Spaceship Earth, the astronauts had emerged from Plato's cave, freed from their "corporeal shackles" by the guiding light of technology so that they could experience the clarity of an ideal realm only available to the mind's eye.[26]

Remediating the operational dynamics of the pope's window, the Mirror measures the spiritual distances between the divine realm of the "human stars" that are elevated on its screen and the ordinary scale and temporal existence of its viewers, while promising that, if we look through it, we too can access a form of transcendence denied to us by our physical embodiment. A temple devoted to the transcendental possibility of reaching the celestial stars and becoming starlike, the Space Mirror's refiguration of the astronaut as star, reflects the ongoing cultural significance of the 17 astronauts' deaths as the "ultimate sacrifice" (Astronaut Memorial Foundation) of human mortality for the sake of becoming God-like.

The Space Mirror asks the contemporary visitor-viewer to remember (to recollect) the astronaut as a material viewing figure and as an agent of metaphysical illumination. However, if the astronauts left Spaceship Earth to return (literally and figuratively) in the shape of luminous points of light on a Mirror of polished granite, then the mass suicide of the Heaven's Gate cult reveals the dark side of yearning to both get a grip on the stars out there in space *and* transcend the constraints of our material and phenomenological limits.

On March 26, 1997, the Heaven's Gate cult decided to engineer their own journey beyond the pope's window to meet the alien starship they believed was hidden in the icy tail of the Hale-Bopp comet. With the insignia of "Heaven's Gate away team" emblazoned on their uniforms, the members "beamed up," leaving a meticulously constructed image of the comet still glowing on the computer screen. Much like Kuac's attention to the images of the Martian landscape that were captured by a single window within the hypermediated space of the desktop, the media surrounding this event chose the simulated image of the Hale-Bopp comet from the 20 screens that were located in a room at the cult's residence. Rather than signaling the absence of the astronaut as star—where this absence only serves to emphasize the symbolic force of this figure—the media's focus on the symbolic icon of the comet only confirmed the status of the Heaven's Gate voyagers as pseudo-astronauts: their insignia, "away team," signifying both their allegiance to *Star Trek*'s fictional voyages across the twenty-fourth-century galaxy[27] and their inability to navigate the appropriate boundaries between the "real" stars and their science-fictional, paranormal imaginings.

Relating the "unfortunate transformation" of the scientific and technological discovery of Comet Hale-Bopp into a religious symbol for the paranormal imagination, Paul Kurtz argues that the Heaven's Gate cult members exemplified a "transcendental temptation"—the tendency of too many human beings to "leap beyond this world to other dimensions" (n.p.). However, Kurtz's assumption that the discourses and practices of the natural sciences and religious beliefs are mutually exclusive is undermined by the astronaut's function to inscribe the shifting boundaries between the spiritual and material realms.

In distinction to Kurtz's thesis, David Noble argues that, since the Early Middle Ages, a fundamental Christian myth of salvation and redemption has guided the development of technical arts. Western technology has emerged as a historical force because of, and not in spite of, the religious quest for transcendence of worldly matters (pp. 3–5).[28] Acknowledging the complex dialogical relation between science and religion that is mobilized by the astronaut's ascent to the stars, Noble points out that "besides high physical courage and the promise of an early termination of the ordeal (the astronaut of the sixties), needed a deep religious conviction, all the more *serviceable* if unconscious of their role as Heavenly messengers" (p. 5, emphasis mine).[29] Noble's argument reminds us that, like the figure of the king/sun that mirrored the social and spatial formations of Baroque culture, the astronaut validates the operational dynamics of science and technology *and* our culture's extra-rational belief systems, negotiating the shifting boundaries between the material body that matters and divine consciousness.

The (con)fusion of the simulated comet with the cult member as pseudo-astronaut foregrounds an ambivalence toward technologically transcending bodily limits that lies at the heart of the Mirror's star figuration of the astronaut. However, if the stars on its screen tell us that the divine light within the human being can always be illuminated—promising us continual access to the truth that lies beyond our terrestrial vision—it cannot disguise the hints of mortal anxiety that lie just beneath the surface. "Born in the wake of the *Challenger* accident in 1986" (Astronaut Memorial Foundation), the Mirror immediately developed cracks where the astronauts as "human stars" were inscribed in the granite. A few weeks after its dedication the monument was declared a safety hazard and closed to visitors (Penley, p. 45).

These cracks in the Mirror reveal that, in the late 1960s and via its (re)mediation in our contemporary culture, the inscription of the astronauts as everyday human beings[30] inspired to great heights sat very uneasily with the celebration of the moon landing as a triumph for technology, engineering and human enterprise (Toynbee). To get to the moon, the straight, white, elite, male bodies of the astronauts, vulnerable to the exigencies of vacuums and low gravity, had to be tested, protected, and re-modified, which tended "to devalue the position of the astronaut as human and to present a vision of the astronaut as cyborg" (Dean, pp. 29–33). Authenticating the astronaut's "penetration" of the vast void beyond the pope's window as the *natural* evolution of "human" to "star" was a slippery task because the cybernetic remodification of the astronaut threatened to erase the corporeality of the human organism.[31] Armstrong's tendency to slip into techno-linguistic speak at press conferences transformed the astronaut into a hybrid computer/human with artificially augmented intelligence. "Carrying on rapid fire conversation with the computer" and unable "to bring to bear [*sic*] large changes in (his) force application" while walking on the moon, this cyborgification of the astronaut may have further consolidated the function of the astronaut as an instrument for, and of, science and technology, but it also threw an ambiguous shadow on the "human" light revealed by their techno-transfiguration into God-like beings ("Astronauts Speak," p. A10).

Yet, the media in the 1960s still managed to trace the "human" spark within the cyborg by using language and imagery associated with the astronaut's material and lived body. One media-witness tells us: when the guidance computer was about to set the landing craft in a boulder-filled crater "suddenly the astronauts were startled to see that the computer was *guiding* them." Catastrophe seemed at hand and Armstrong "*grabbed* the manual control of the vehicle and guided it safely over the crater" (Wilford, p. 1, emphasis mine). Just as the virtually mobile figure of the astronaut authenticated our literal and figural grasp upon the stars, vital to mapping the "new frontier," this account focused upon Armstrong's ability to physically take hold of the complex transportation technology of the spacecraft and display the appropriate qualities of human initiative and technical capability to contain the potential loss of human agency and vision figured in the astronaut as cyborg.

Like the cowboy of the Wild West who had a special relationship to his trusty steed, this astronaut's omnipotence is doubly authenticated by his unique relationship to the technology that enabled him to journey beyond the phenomenological and material limits of the "human" body. The ambivalence toward technologically (re)figuring the astronaut—which was amplified by Heaven's Gate's illicit desires to leave the "meat" behind—is occluded by presenting the astronaut as a cybercelestial fusion (rather than confusion) of human/technological perfection.

Just like Kurtz's quest for an essential (and rational) humanity, which he believes was eclipsed by the "transcendental temptation" of leaping, so to speak, out of the pope's window, and by extension, beyond the Space Mirror, the astronaut's figuration as cyborg further served to perceptually and ideologically fix our technological and discursive grasp upon the heavens. The metaphors associated with the moon landing envisaged the robotic and electronic technology that put a man on the moon as an extension of the astronaut's phenomenological and sensory experience; yet, they could not completely camouflage the signs of metaphysical uncertainty that were written in the astronaut's divine visions from the stars. During Apollo XI's voyage to the moon (and other NASA missions to outer space), strange, white streaks of light appeared in the astronaut's field of vision, like "a spectacular fireworks display going off inside your eyeball."[32] These inexplicable phenomena were cosmic rays, high energy particles that are produced when a star supernovas, when it "dies" and collapses inward, that permeate outer space and were able to penetrate the space craft, the astronaut's body and eyes ("Universe").

The technologically modified bodies of the astronauts that authenticated the penetration and colonization of the new frontier and the technological extension of "human vision" beyond its material constraints were, in an ironic twist, penetrated by the stars. The microscopic funnels these particles made in the astronaut's helmet are an eerie reminder of the vulnerable "human" body protected by the technological and discursive armor of the cyber-celestial figure of the astronaut. Like a ghost in the machine, the static human features that the Space Mirror imprints on the reflective foil of the astronaut's helmet become unmoored from their grounding in the aesthetic, social, and ideological materiality of the astronaut's body. Just as the cult members had gotten too close to the stars and, thus, confused the appropriate boundaries between the human and the divine, the fusion of this body with the physical matter of a star makes visible the rifts and fractures in the cyber-celestial configuration of the astronaut. In the shadows thrown by the Mirror's starlight, we can almost see a

technologically remodified and, thus, potentially unrecognizable human figure lurking in the dark.

CONCLUSION: NEW HORIZONS?

In *Star Wars* (Lucas, 1977) Luke Skywalker yearns to escape his mundane
existence on the desert planet of Tatooine and journey to the stars. Framed in
midshot looking out to the setting suns of an alien sky, in a galaxy far, far away,
this human figure speaks to, and is spoken by, the discourses, artifacts, and
metaphors that envisaged, and continue to envisage, the astronaut as star. Just
as the cyber-celestial figure of the astronaut stitches together our ambivalent
desires to "get a grip" on the stars, Skywalker's gaze out to the space beyond
the screen's frame is sutured with the visible, yet unfamiliar, landscape of the
stars by a shot/reverse shot.

The Kennedy Space Mirror invites a similar viewing position as we look up
and through it to a horizon marked by the virtual but real, intangible but material, figures of the astronauts. This "lasting monument" tells us that, once
upon a time, "man" grasped the intangible, reached into the unknown, looked
out to a distant horizon (Astronaut Memorial Foundation). If "Apollo is part
of a distant past," by looking through the Mirror "we can revisit their experiences in our imagination. We can look for Tranquility Base . . . where men once
walked" (Chaikin, p. 34). The Space Mirror reminds us that the visible, but intangible stars were always just within our perceptual and cognitive reach—the
astronaut's transcendental perspective from the stars privileging a form of
scopic and technological mastery of the pope's "immense, mysterious picture"
of the heavens that (still) compensates for the our inability to touch stars.

As NASA still persists in reaching for the stars, extending our "human"
gaze with the help of robot spacecraft beyond the moon, to Mars and the rest
of the solar system, the Space Mirror looks back to the 1960s in order to cele-
brate and reclaim our perceptual and cognitive grip on the intangible and virtual phenomena "out there" in space that were figured in the astronaut as
star. Like the concrete figure of the astronaut that greets the visitor-viewer at
Kennedy, reaching down from the roof above, the Space Mirror discursively,
perceptually, and literally fixes NASA's and the astronaut's view of the heavens as a virtual space that can be moved through—that can, so to speak, be
touched—and, thus, comprehended.

However, for both the "human" body of the astronaut and the viewer situated here on Spaceship Earth, reaching the stars and becoming starlike was
(and remains) a dangerous enterprise fraught with epistemological and perceptual uncertainty. In light of our tele-presence on Mars and the Heaven's
Gate members' desire to leave the "meat" of their terrestrial body behind, the
astronaut as star no longer reflects and materializes a unified subject acting
unilaterally upon the celestial bodies beyond the pope's window. Rather the
Heaven's Gate cult members and the robot Sojourner's virtual contact with

the stars—the real landscape of Mars and the imaginary starship hidden in the tail of the Hale-Bopp comet, respectively—provide other insights into the shifting boundaries between the visible and the invisible, the known and the unknown, the human and the divine. Whereas the Mirror presents the astronaut as a figure of *illumination*, these voyagers make visible the dark regions "outside" our technological and phenomenological field of view.

Exposing an ambivalence that lies at the heart of the figure of the astronaut as both cyborg and star, Sojourner and Heaven's Gate ask us to recognize the mediated and mediating way we made, and continue to make, sense of our everyday experiences here on Spaceship Earth with reference to the lights in the dark void of space out there. Moreover, viewing the Space Mirror and its remediation of the pope's window alongside a multitude of simultaneous interfaces available in our contemporary culture highlights the fact that the Space Mirror invites an ambivalent oscillation between regarding the "human stars" on its screen as mediated and as mediating our access to a "real space that lies beyond mediation" (Bolter and Grusin, p. 41). In this sense, the Mirror reflects the paradoxes of getting a grip on visible, yet intangible phenomena that belong to a virtual space somewhere (in)between our two-dimensional representations of the stars and the three-dimensionality of lived experience. Refiguring the stars as an authentic and attainable space that can be accessed by the astronaut, the Mirror reveals that we continue to yearn for that "real" space that lies beyond the pope's window.

The gesture of the astronaut reaching for the stars may still stitch together the hypermediated and multiple windows made available at Kennedy, but another figure of the astronaut is emerging from the computer screen. "At" the Kennedy Space Center home page, the astronaut still looks out beyond the frame provided by the computer screen but, as hyperlink, enables us to look *into* another visible, but intangible, world that does not lie beyond the pope's window but in cyberspace. Whereas the Mirror (re)mediates the social and spatial imaginary of a material landscape—where Armstrong's footprint still remains like a phantom link to our actual presence on the moon—this new figure of the astronaut asks that we review the historical and cultural consequences of yearning to "get a grip" on the virtual, intangible stars beyond our reach.

As a monument to our continued stargazing, the Space Mirror may have been built to last, but across the passage of "deep time"—a span of 100,000 years—would the future visitor-viewers, of either terrestrial or extraterrestrial origin, comprehend the significance of the "human stars" imprinted on its surface (Benford)? Would they hear the "voiceless messages" of our technological remains on the moon: the Hasselblad left by the Apollo XI team, the landing portion of the Eagle, the lunar rover? Perhaps, like a ghost town on the frontier, they may see the phantasmic figures of the "men who once walked there" and think that it was only in our cybernetic dreams that we had touched the stars? Or, then again, they may just realize that it is only by looking into and at the multispectral images of the stars that our culture's other-worldly visions of these stars and of ourselves could be illuminated. Like these time travelers of the future, we too, must navigate our way through, and with, the figure of the astronaut, in all its various historical guises, to remember what it was really like to be there with them, on the moon and virtually touching the stars.

APPENDIX: THE SEVENTEEN ASTRONAUTS WHOSE NAMES APPEAR ON THE SPACE MIRROR MEMORIAL AT KENNEDY SPACE CENTER

- **Robert H. Lawrence Jr.**, October 31, 1964, F-104 accident.
- **Charles A. Bassett II** and **Elliot M. See Jr.**, February 28, 1966, T-38 accident.
- **Virgil "Gus" Grissom, Edward H. White II**, and **Roger B. Chaffee**, January 27, 1967, *Apollo I* accident.
- **Clifton C. Williams Jr.**, October 5, 1967, T-38 accident.
- **Michael J. Adams**, November 15, 1967, X-15 accident.
- **Theodore C. Freeman** December 8, 1967, T-38 accident.
- **Francis "Dick" Scobee, Michael J. Smith, Judith A. Resnik, Ellison S. Onizuka, Christa McAuliffe, Ronald E. McNair**, and **Gregory B. Jarvis**, January 28, 1986, *Challenger* accident.
- **Manley L. "Sonny" Carter Jr.**, April 5, 1991, Commercial plane accident.

NOTES

1. In *A Trip to the Moon* Jules Verne described the moon as the "queen of the starry sky." He is cited by Mark Bloom (1969) in "The Great Dream—It All Started in 190 A.D."

2. The Space Mirror Memorial was dedicated in 1991. It was built and is still maintained by the Astronaut Memorial Foundation, a private, nonprofit organization authorized by NASA to build and maintain two national facilities to memorialize the astronauts. See the Astronaut Memorial Home Page at http://www.amfcse.org/content.interest.htm (last accessed December 27, 1999).

3. See the entry for "star" in *The New Shorter Oxford Dictionary*.

4. I am appropriating a mixed metaphor that Jim Collins (1995) uses to discuss the geography of Los Angeles as a visually polyphonic space (p. 41).

5. My discussion of the astronaut as a virtually mobile figure who can grasp the virtual, intangible phenomena of the stars and, thus, render this space as comprehensible extends upon, and is indebted to, Bukatman's (1993) analysis of *Blade Runner* (Ridley Scott, 1992) and the phenomenology of electronic "terminal" space as a "new fractal dimension" or "other space" that can be penetrated by a pure totalizing gaze and, thus, made "tangible and controllable." See particularly pp. 130–37.

6. As Spigel (1991) argues, this new theatrics of space was inextricably tied to the televisual as a form of cultural production of social space and everyday life. Jodi Dean (1998) also discusses the production of this theatrics of space as a "site of political and governmental intervention" that was "always in part a television program" produced

for an audience: its credibility and reality are dependent upon the presence of that audience as witnesses (pp. 72–73).

7. David Brittan (1994) equates the design of the U.S. space program with "a work of art staged by an immense corps of talented performers, who gave Apollo XI an element of drama rarely seen outside of live theaters."

8. The term "citizen-viewer" is Jodie Dean's. She argues that the hero-astronaut was dependent upon an assemblage of witnesses who embodied a set of ideals of appropriate witnessing and credible viewing that could, and often did, conflict with the heroic position of the astronauts (p. 69). See her illuminating examination of the images of public spectatorship constructed by NASA for these public witnesses in the chapter "Space Programs" (pp. 62–97).

9. See the entry for "star" in *The New Shorter Oxford Dictionary*.

10. Scott Bukatman (1993) also extends Crary's discussion of the camera obscura, following Gilles Deleuze's concept of the "assemblage," to the discursive constructions of, and our phenomenological interface with, the space(s) of virtual reality (p. 188).

11. As Constance Penley (1997) points out, "[I]cons don't just symbolise but [they] have a determining effect on reality" (p. 21).

12. Vivian Sobchack (1995) identified three different uses of the screen in cinematic discourse. The frame presents cinematic language as a mode of expression; the window—most often associated with Andre Bazin—indicates a realist phenomenology; and the screen functions like a mirror for psychoanalytic discourse. If, as she argues, all three metaphors present the screen rectangle and the film as a "static viewed object," then I want to suggest the dynamic activity of viewing the Mirror is an intersubjective exchange between the viewing figure of the astronaut as star and the viewer of the astronauts in relation to the celestial stars. Throughout my analysis these metaphors are strategically mixed up to identify the complex and shifting figuration of the astronaut and, therefore, foreground how the Mirror's apparatus attempts (but does not necessarily succeed in this endeavor) to reflect an objective, rather than an intersubjective, viewing position.

13. For Penley (1997), this translation between popular culture and science occurs at a particular cultural juncture, which she calls NASA/TREK. It is a densely inscribed collective text of science-fictional, mythical, folkloric, and ideological narratives that examine the moral politic and social consequences of going into space (p. 5).

14. The universal translator is an "ideal" form of communication itself. From the original *Star Trek* series, through *Star Trek: The Next Generation*, *Star Trek: Deep Space Nine*, and *Star Trek: Voyager*, this technical instrument translates alien languages into (ironically) English for the viewer/listener.

15. The vital issue of colonialism and gender is outside the scope of this chapter. However, one particularly vivid example of feminizing the lunar body, and thus making it "ripe" for exploitation, can be found in an article equating the moon explorers with Columbus. It would seem that "it is from the men who act on nature, and do not merely suffer to be acted upon by her, that history flows" ("Moon Supplement," p. 18).

16. In the current debates concerning space exploration and manned missions, celestial bodies, particularly the moon, are still presented as treasure troves for the entrepreneur, or private companies (see Whitehouse). The most ironic example of this

rhetoric, in terms of the move to cyberspace as a kind of new frontier, is the presentation of the moon as a supply of new experiences for virtual reality games and theme parks. See "The Outpost."

17. I am indebted to Bolter and Grusin's (1999) understanding of the formal logic of immediacy for this reading. As they state, the desire to erase a sense of mediation to achieve the real can be traced through the history of media, but it must be contextualized in terms of different historical and social viewing situations: what is considered an authentic, and therefore real, experience is judged from within a "network of artifacts, images and cultural agreements about what media means and does" (p. 58).

18. Mitchell (1994) discusses the famous photo of Aldrin walking on the moon. This image is judged as plausible because the picture is so "sharp and clear" and Armstrong, the photographer, is reflected in Aldrin's visor and we cannot cross-check any internal consistencies with another "firsthand" reproduction. The ideological frameworks and visual conventions that authenticated this "real" image were challenged, however, by the remediation of the image in the fall 1989 issue of *Time*, where, thanks to digital imaging, seven astronauts now walk on the moon, each reflecting a slightly different, inconsistent picture.

19. Consistent claims that the moon landing was a hoax engineered by NASA confirm that although NASA tried to engineer a particular "public" for its space program, this form of address did not necessarily interpolate the citizen-viewer. See Dean (1998, p. 94) for examples of the conspiracy-minded. Furthermore, I note her reference to Donna Haraway's understanding of this process where "subjects in a discourse can and do refigure its terms, contents, and reach" in *Modest Witness@Second Millennium. FemaleMan © Meets OncoMouse TM* (New York: Routledge, 1997), p. 50: Davis, p. 219 n. 7.

20. Although I am indebted to Penley's understanding of the discursive articulations of outer space mobilized by NASA and *Star Trek*, unlike her I am not concerned with making visible the collective unconscious process of disavowal that took place around the catastrophe of the *Challenger* explosion and how the Mirror "fantasmically captured (it) for public discourse" (pp. 31–41). Moreover, discourses around the moon landing addressed the "whole world," but (re)membering Apollo XI required access to radio, television, and other media. Personally, I have no memory of the moon landing so that researching newspaper clippings and visiting sites such as Kennedy Space Center often create a strange sense of (dis)location, and I wonder: Did it really happen?

21. For a perceptive analysis of the cultural function and symbolism of the comet from medieval society to our contemporary culture, see Genuth (1997).

22. This futuristic thinking still permeates our discursive and visual journeys to outer space today. For example, *The Illustrated Encyclopedia of Astronomy*, introduced by Carl Sagan—that prophet of interplanetary adventures—states as a matter of fact that "new space technologies will, within a few decades, allow mankind to live permanently in space" (p. 9).

23. I am indebted to Vivian Sobchack for this brief analysis as I am extending her discussion of digital morphing as a primary mode of figuration and the morph as a "discrete" and secondary figure that has a temporal and spatial continuity and discontinuity with our phenomenological sense of lived time to the figurative function of the astronaut and the Pope's window as a viewing assemblage (2000, pp. 131–58).

24. Mars Pathfinder was launched on December 4, 1996, from Cape Canaveral Air Station. The Mars landing was on July 4, 1997.

25. When Apollo XI's Aldrin met with his pastor before the historic flight to, and landing on, the moon to take Communion, his religious advisor told him that he would now view the earth from a physically transcendent stance (Noble, p. 139).

26. I am indebted to Ken Hillis (1999) and his analysis of virtual space in terms of the neoplatonic conception of light/sight as illumination for this reading. See particularly pp. 137–50.

27. The term "away team" refers to the crew members of the starship *Enterprise* or *Voyager* who were transported to the particular planet chosen for that week's episode. The term "beamed up" is used when these science fictional-astronauts are transported back to the ship via a technical device that breaks down the human being into molecules that are then reintegrated on the transporter pad—although how the transporter manages this is a matter for much fan debate.

28. Also see Lamber (1999) for an analysis of the fundamentally ambivalent and complex historical relationship that has developed between reason and religion in modernity.

29. Brian O'Leary, *The Making of an Ex-astronaut* (Boston: Houghton Mifflin, 1970), p. 151, cited by Noble, p. 137.

30. As the *U.S. News & World Report* put it: "They're only human. No one has ever claimed that they are supermen, least of all the astronauts themselves" (July 21, 1969).

31. See Claudia Springer (1991) for a discussion of the paradoxical promises of the human/computer hybrid as an escape from the corporeal meat of the body and the re-embodiment of virtual space in terms of gender and sexuality (pp. 303–22).

32. The quote is from Charles Duke, Apollo XVI astronaut, who was the subject of scientific experiments to determine the nature of these mysterious flashes of light (quoted in "Universe").

REFERENCES

"And the World Watches and Marvels." (Compiled from wire services.) *Wisconsin State Journal.* July 21 (1969): 1. *A Microfilm Documentary—Apollo XI's Moon Landing.* Californian Microfilm Company, Fresno, California.

Astronaut Memorial Home Page. Available at http://www.amfcse.org/content. interest.htm (last accessed December 27, 1999).

"Astronauts Speak Wistfully of Their Journey to Moon." *Washington Post.* August 13 (1969): A10. *A Microfilm Documentary—Apollo XI's Moon Landing.* Californian Microfilm Company, Fresno, California.

Benford, Gregory. "Deep Time: How Humanity Communicates across Millennia." Guest of honor speech, Aussiecon3: the 57th World Science Fiction Convention, September 2–6, 1999, Melbourne. Transcribed by Evelyn Leepre, Convention Report, 1999. Available at http://www. Aussiecon3.wsfs.org/ a3.html (last accessed January 12, 2000).

Bloom, Mark. "The Great Dream—It All Started in 190 AD." Speech, Hon. John M. Murphy to the House of Representatives, *Congressional Record—Extension of Remarks.* July 7 (1969): E5631. *A Microfilm Documentary—Apollo XI's Moon Landing.* Californian Microfilm Company, Fresno, California.

Bolter, Jay David, and Richard Grusin. *Remediation: Understanding New Media.* Cambridge, MA: MIT Press, 1999.

Brittan, David. "The High Art of Apollo XI." *Technology Review* 97 (July 1994).

Bukatman, Scott. *Terminal Identity: The Virtual Subject in Postmodern Science Fiction.* London: Duke University Press, 1993

Cawelti, John G. "The Western: A Look at the Evolution of a Formula." In *Adventure, Mystery, and Romance: Formula Stories as Art and Popular Culture.* Chicago: University of Chicago Press, 1976: 192–259.

Chaikin, Andrew. "The Moon Voyagers." *Astronomy*, 22 (July 1994).

Collins, Jim. *Architectures of Excess: Cultural Life in the Information Age.* London: Routledge, 1995.

Crary, Jonathan. *Techniques of the Observer: On Vision and Modernity in the Nineteenth Century.* Cambridge, MA: MIT Press, 1991.

Davis, Erik. "I.N.F.O.s." *21C: The Magazine of Culture, Technology and Science* 26 (1998): 40–45.

Dean, Jodi. *Aliens in America: Conspiracy Cultures from Outerspace to Cyberspace.* Ithaca, NY: Cornell University Press, 1998.

Genuth, Sarah Schechner. *Comets, Popular Culture and the Birth of Modern Cosmology.* Princeton, NJ: Princeton University Press, 1997.

"The Greatest Dream—a walk on the Moon." Part 1. *Congressional Record—Extension of Remarks.* July 7 (1969): E5631. *A Microfilm Documentary—Apollo XI's Moon Landing.* Californian Microfilm Company, Fresno, California.

Hillis, Ken. "A Geography of the Eye: The Technologies of Virtual Reality." In Shiels, R., ed., *Cultures of the Internet: Virtual Spaces, Real Histories, Living Bodies.* London: Sage, 1998, 71–97.

———. *Digital Sensations: Space, Identity and Embodiment in Virtual Reality.* Minneapolis: University of Minnesota Press, 1999.

Hines, William. "Space Station of 70s in Planning." *Denver Post.* July 20 (1969). *A Microfilm Documentary—Apollo XI's Moon Landing.* Californian Microfilm Company, Fresno, California.

Hoffman, Bill, and Cathy Burke. *Heaven's Gate: Cult Suicide in San Diego.* New York: Harper Paperback, 1997.

Hutchinson, Keith. "Towards a Political Iconology of the Copernican Revolution." In Currey, Patrick, ed., *Astrology, Science and Society: Historical Essays.* Suffolk: Boydell Press, n.d.: 95–141.

The Illustrated Encyclopedia of Astronomy. Edited by John Man. London: Chancellor Press, 1989.

Kuac, Eduardo. "Live from Mars." *Leonardo Electronic Almanac* 5, no. 7 (July 1997). Available at http://mitpress.mit.edu/e-journals/LEA/ARTICLES/mars.hml (last accessed October 28, 1997).

Kurtz, Paul. "UFO Mythology: The Escape to Oblivion." *Skeptical Inquirer* 21 (July–August 1997).

Lamber, Yves. "Religion in Modernity as a New Axial Age; Secularization or New Religious Forms." *Sociology of Religion* 60 (fall 1999).

Manovich, Lev. "An Archaeology of the Computer Screen." Kunsforum International, 1995. Available at http://jupiter.ucsd.edu/~manovich/text/digital_nature.html (last accessed August 17, 1999).

Mitchell, William J. *The Reconfigured Eye: Visual Truth in the Post-Photographic Era*. Cambridge, MA: MIT Press, 1994.

"The Moon, a Giant Leap for Mankind." *Time*. July 25 (1969): 10.

"Moon Supplement: A New World." *Time*. July 18 (1969): 18.

The New Shorter Oxford Dictionary. Edited by L. Brown. Oxford: Clarendon Press, 1993: 3031.

Noble, David F. *The Religion of Technology: The Divinity of Man and the Spirit of Invention*. New York: Penguin Books, 1999.

O'Meara, Thomas. "Christian Theology and Extraterrestrial Life." *Theological Studies* 60 (March 1999).

"The Outpost." *Economist*. December 25 (1993): 51.

Penley, Constance. *NASA/TREK: Popular Science and Sex in America*. London: Verso, 1997.

Pett, Saul. "Houston . . . Tranquility Base Here." *Wisconsin State Journal* 21 (July 1969): 1.

Sobchack, Vivian. "Phenomenology and the Film Experience." In Williams, Linda, ed., *Viewing Positions: Ways of Seeing Film*. New Brunswick: Rutgers University Press, 1995: 36–58.

———. "At the Still Point of the Turning World: Meta-Morphing and Meta-Stasis." In *Meta Morphing: Visual Transformation and the Culture of Quick Change*. Minneapolis: University of Minnesota Press, 2000: 131–58.

Souvenir Edition of the *Detroit News*. August 5 (1969). *A Microfilm Documentary—Apollo XI's Moon Landing*. Californian Microfilm Company, Fresno, California.

Spigel, Lynn. "From Domestic Space to Outer Space: The 1960's Fantastic Family Sit-Com." In Penley, Constance, Elisabeth Lyon, Lynn Spigel, and Janet Bergstrom, eds., *Close Encounters: Film, Feminism and Science-Fiction*. Minneapolis: University of Minnesota Press, 1991: 205–35.

Springer, Claudia. "The Pleasure of the Interface." *Screen* 32, no. 3 (Autumn 1991): 303–32.

Teague, Hon. Olin E., "America Is about to Put Men on the Moon." *Congressional Record—Extension of Remarks*. July 9 (1969): E5738. *A Microfilm Documentary—Apollo XI's Moon Landing*. Californian Microfilm Company, Fresno, California.

Thomas, Evan. "The Next Level: How Herff Applewhite, a Sexually Confused, Would-be Apostle, Led a Flock of Lost New Age Dreamers to Their Deaths." *Newsweek*. April 7 (1997).

Thrapp, Dan L. "Theologians Refuted: Church Wary on Moon Trip." *Denver Post*. July 20 (1969): 35. *A Microfilm Documentary—Apollo XI's Moon Landing*. Californian Microfilm Company, Fresno, California.

Toynbee, Arnold. "The Moon and World Solidarity." *Washington Post*. July 13 (1969). Presented to Congress by Mr. Hatfield. *Congressional Record—Senate*. July 15 (1969): S8088. *A Microfilm Documentary—Apollo XI's Moon Landing*. Californian Microfilm Company, Fresno, California.

"Universe." Second part of a four-part BBC series, on ABC. February 16, 2000.

U.S. News & World Report. July 21 (1969). *A Microfilm Documentary—Apollo XI's Moon Landing*. Californian Microfilm Company, Fresno, California.

Wertheim, Margaret. *The Pearly Gates of Cyberspace*. Sydney: Doubleday, 1999.

Whitehouse, David. "Reach for the Moon." *New Statesman*. December 12 (1997): 26–29.

Wilford, John Noble. "Men Land on the Moon: 'Giant Leap for Mankind.' " *Arizona Daily Star*. July 21 (1969): 1.

Part III

Directors and Characters as Stars

Sam Peckinpah. © Kobal Collection.

—————— Chapter 7 ——————

The Auteur as Star: Violence and Utopia in the Films of Sam Peckinpah

Gabrielle Murray

He spoke freely to reporters of his drinking binges, his whoring and brawling. Far from diminishing his reputation—at least at first—it fueled it, for this was an era that reveled in excess, that celebrated rebels and cheered mavericks. And here, in the heart of the Hollywood machine, a bizarre anomaly had surfaced: a combination of Ernest Hemingway, Hunter S. Thompson, and Wild Bill Hickok who, through sheer will and gall, had taken on the Combine, the System, with both fists swinging wildly, and damn if he didn't seem to be winning! They dubbed him "Bloody Sam," "The Picasso of Violence," and soon he was a bigger star than any of the actors who appeared in his movies.

—Weddle, 1994a, p. 380

The woods are full of killers, all sizes, all colors. . . . A director has to deal with a whole world absolutely teeming with mediocrities, jackals, hangers-on, and just plain killers. The attrition is terrific. It can kill you. The saying is that they can kill you but not eat you. That's nonsense. I've had them eating on me while I was still walking around.

—Peckinpah, quoted in Kael, p. 71

Here in this country, everybody is worried about stopping the war and saving the forests and all that, but these same crusaders go out the door in the morning forgetting to kiss their wives and water the flowers.

—Peckinpah, BBC documentary, 1993

A "paranoid schizophrenic"—this is the suggested clinical diagnosis proffered near the conclusion of the BBC's 1993 feature-length documentary on the life and films of Sam Peckinpah. Erratic, tortured, and capable of explosive violence, this enigmatic director and his problematic *oeuvre* continue to provoke a steady flow of writings. If we are to believe the biographical details and anecdotal stories, Peckinpah inspired great admiration and loyalty but also intense hatred and fear. Even those who loved him approached him with a certain wariness, never sure from one meeting to the next if their encounter would involve a sucker punch, a knife-throwing performance, or a flood of tears. The sacking, the blacklisting, the studio intervention and butchering of his films, the drinking, the drugs, the paranoia, and the brawling: this is now the stuff of legend.[1] In fact, the circulation of stories about Peckinpah's "bad," "mad," and "violent" ways has resulted in a "personal" mythology that frequently outweighs discussion of the films themselves.

Peckinpah is a director who surrounded himself with "stars" like James Coburn, Jason Robards, and Dustin Hoffman as well as a loyal group of supporting actors that included Ben Johnson, L. Q. Jones, Strother Martin, Warren Oates, and Slim Pickens. But from the soaring heights and demon depths of his career his infamy outshone every star that ever appeared in his 14 films[2]—even the likes of Steve McQueen.[3] It is as if these stars' individual personae are repressed, lost, or outshone by Peckinpah's personal mythology. However, if we investigate this focus on Peckinpah's persona and trace the development and circulation of his personal mythology and its association with violence, we can highlight the ways in which this mythology has affected the up-take of his films as well as the critical literature. In teasing out some of these ramifications we can explore how this personal mythology, with its "mantra" of violence, has not only inflated debates surrounding Peckinpah's use of "screen violence," while frequently failing to explore his stylistic and thematic concerns, but has also resulted in the neglect of the utopian elements of his films that are crucial to his directorial vision.

For a short period of time beginning in the late 1960s and concluding in the early 1970s, Peckinpah was celebrated and condemned as the cinematic poet of violence. By the end of the 1970s, suffering physical and artistic decline, he slipped into ignominy; yet, after his death in 1984, he slowly began to reemerge as an influential presence who left us with a disparate but rich cinematic *oeuvre*. In 1993, the same year as the BBC produced its documentary, the Amiens Film Festival held a retrospective of all his work (Weddle, 1995, p. 20). Retrospectives have since been staged at the Cinemathèque in Paris and at London's National Film Theatre, while *Film Comment* and *Sight and Sound* have published "major reappraisals" of his work (Weddle, 1994b, p. xvi). To coincide with the re-release of the restored version of *The Wild Bunch* by Warner Brothers in 1995 the editors of *Film Comment*, Richard T. Jameson and Kathleen Murphy, organized a retrospective of Peckinpah's television and film work through the Film Society of the Lincoln Center at the Walter Reade

Theater in New York. The publication of David Weddle's extensive and insightful biography, *"If They Move . . . Kill 'Em!": The Life and Times of Sam Peckinpah*, the re-release of *The Wild Bunch*, and numerous retrospectives have all helped to reignite interest in Peckinpah's legacy as both a mercurial personality and an important director whose influence is noted by many contemporary filmmakers, including Kathryn Bigelow, Martin Scorsese, Quentin Tarantino, and John Woo.[4]

However, it was with the original release of *The Wild Bunch* in 1969 that Peckinpah's "star" began to shine—or rather crackle and burn.[5] A group of outlaws ride into a dusty, small town called Starbuck. They hold up the bank and in the process decimate the town. But the job is a setup: the loot they get away with is worthless "steel whole." The law and the railway men send a group of bounty hunters out after the "Bunch." To escape the law, they cross the border into Mexico where they agree to do a job for a dictatorial Mexican general: it is to be their last job. In the context of the times *The Wild Bunch* was seen as being extremely violent. Its initial release in Kansas had audience members running up the aisles while its conclusion was met with a "shocked silence" (Weddle, 1994b, pp. 3–8, 363–64).[6] Many of the major film magazines, including *Cinema*, *Cineaste*, *Cinema Journal*, and *Sight and Sound*, and newspapers and magazines, such as *Entertainment*, the *New York Times*, the *Village Voice*, and *Variety* engaged in polarized debates surrounding the film's violence and the effects of "screen violence" on an audience.

More recently Stephen Prince (1998b) has described Peckinpah's distinctive style as a "montage-based aesthetic" (p. 14). By intercutting shots taken from multiple camera angles at different speeds Peckinpah created sequences that frenetically move between intense action and slow motion, resulting in an experience that is kinetically exhilarating but also lyrical. In *The Wild Bunch* the kinetic editing and the intercutting of footage result in battle scenes in which time and space have an immense plasticity. In the opening and concluding sequences of this film, the action is as tightly choreographed as any great dance sequence: from multiple positions and angles, in real time and slow motion, we see people running, hear them screaming, the impact of bullets spinning them like tops. In lyrical slow motion a man gracefully falls from a rooftop; in real time we see horses stumble and collapse; we hear wailing, screaming, and the endless cacophony of firing pistols and shotguns. Bodies fall and twist, slowly crash through shattering glass, gently dust the ground like feathers; blood spurts from wounds and stains walls as the Bunch take turns spraying the general's men with machine-gun fire.

It is impossible to determine whether this film is the most violent "ever made," or if it was the most violent of its time, and the question is probably irrelevant. What we can say is that with greater creative freedom gained through revisions to the production and censorship codes and in the midst of a volatile cultural milieu,[7] Peckinpah, with the help of his brilliant editor, Louis

Lombardo, and cinematographer, Lucien Ballard, developed a stylistic approach that seemed to make the violence more intense, resonant, and visceral.[8]

In 1971 the nihilistic and misogynist *Straw Dogs* hit the screen and the cult of notoriety was cemented: Peckinpah became a marketable, yet controversial, director.[9] Much sought after, he gave polemic interviews to a variety of newspapers and magazines including *Game, Playboy, Films and Filmmaking*, and *Take One*, while also writing letters to newspaper editors justifying his work and slamming his detractors (Crawley; Cutts; Peckinpah). Under the microscope of feminist film theory, his, at times, aberrant treatment of the representations of women and his "excessive" use of violence was noted and condemned. With Peckinpah making it onto the hit list of Joan Mellen's *Big Bad Wolves*, further investigation seemed unnecessary (Mellen, 1977, pp. 3, 9, 270).[10]

The critical uptake of this notion of Peckinpah as the "master of violence" and the momentum of the debates that ensued affected not only the discussion of his so-called violent films but also the reception of his "gentler" works, like *Ride the High Country* (1962), *The Ballad of Cable Hogue* (1970), and *Junior Bonner* (1972). The cultural and social debates surrounding the effects and moral implications of "screen violence" on an audience, along with Peckinpah's macho posturing, public outbursts, and his combative relations with studios and producers, further added to the flurry of controversy. However, in this messy entwining of fact and fiction—of the man, the personal mythology, and the films—something is "amiss." It is almost as if the anecdotal and critical literature surrounding Peckinpah's films suffers from a kind of "schizophrenia." As Pauline Kael laments, "all they saw was the violence. 'Bloody Sam' became his name" (quoted in Fine, p. 156).

"Obsessive," "poetic," and the "Picasso of violence," Peckinpah is seen as being crippled by a system that made him an "outlaw," resulting in an anxiety that we see reflected in his films.[11] Peckinpah's personal mythology is inscribed in much of the writings generated by these films. Rather than an analysis of the aesthetic qualities or thematic concerns of his films, an exploration of audiences' experiences and interactions, or an investigation of the commercial appeal or neglect of specific films, what we frequently find are discussions that transform, or collapse, the analysis of Peckinpah's films as creative artifacts into simple reflections of the director's personal neuroses and anxieties.[12] Now, film is a cultural object and a commercial product but it is also a "significant and vital art that is our concrete evidence of . . . human potential" (Wood, pp. 89–90).

When we see a Peckinpah film we are entering his creative territory. It is sometimes the case that a director's view of his or her film can help illuminate our interactions, but we cannot limit a film, its meaning, or our experience to the opinions of its director. Although often insightful about his work Peckinpah is a fabulous fabricator and an unreliable source, who, in some ways, instigates his own mythology. A drunk, a coke addict, a fascist, a sentimental romantic, possibly schizophrenic, a little man with a big chip on his shoulders—Peckinpah is said to have been many things. The mythology of his volatile and roguish ways has led to an unwillingness to disassociate the rhetoric provoked by the director's antics and work practices from criticism and analysis rooted in the films. If we are to believe the stories, this "cult of personality," it is as if the "wild bunch" made *The Wild Bunch*, with Peckinpah as their visionary leader.

SAM PECKINPAH: AUTEUR OR STAR?

Peckinpah was obviously an inspiring, charismatic, and visionary director, who, during the height of his fame, attracted some of the biggest stars of the period to his projects. In his biography, Weddle argues that on his film sets Peckinpah "very consciously" employed a kind of "psychology" (1994b, p. 209). Reminiscing from his experiences on seven of Peckinpah's shoots, L. Q. Jones states that: "Sam berated the crew, he screamed at the actors, he cursed the transportation people, mouthed off about the horses" (quoted in Weddle, 1994b, p. 209). Like a mock dictator, the director instigated panic and chaos during the first few days on any set; then, from the turmoil, he would slowly begin to rebuild his kingdom. Weddle suggests that this was a strategy that he learned during his time in the U.S. Marine Corps and that he employed it in an attempt to gain complete control over his sets. He implies that Peckinpah "tore the people down, then built them up again so that they were no longer [the studio's] men, but now his own—a hardened fighting unit ready to tear the gates off Hell if Sam Peckinpah told them to" (1994b, p. 209). As another veteran of Peckinpah's shoots, James Coburn poignantly notes, he "created an atmosphere around the film that was so real that you just had to play the character" (quoted in Fine, p. 88).

A slow but steady stream of crew members would continually exodus all of Peckinpah's sets, having incurred his legendary wrath, or having refused to "play" his mind games; yet, his perfectionism, his vision, and his passion also inspired immense loyalty among many of his stars. On the set of *Major Dundee* (1965), Columbia, disillusioned with his behavior and performance, attempted to fire him and cancel the film. Charlton Heston, who played Dundee, intervened by threatening to walk if Peckinpah was fired. Actors and crew rallied behind Heston and the director was eventually reinstated (Weddle, 1994b, p. 240).[13]

But Peckinpah inspired more than just loyalty in his stars: the magnetism of his idiosyncratic "persona" was such that actors not only wanted to work with him but they also tried to act like him, imitating his gestures, attire, and intonation—personifying him in their own performances. Heston found it extremely difficult to work in the "atmosphere of continuing crisis" that Peckinpah created but he also observed that you could not help but "bec[o]me the guy a little bit. You inhabited his world" (quoted in Fine, pp. 91, 88). During the making of *The Wild Bunch*, the director requested that William Holden wear a thin moustache—a little like his own. Although Holden initially refused, by the end of the shoot his character, the leader of the Bunch, Pike Bishop, was not only wearing a moustache but "his vocal qualities and mannerisms" (Weddle, 1994b, p. 336) bore a striking resemblance to the director's.[14] As the main protagonist, Benny, in *Bring Me the Head of Alfredo Garcia* (1974), Warren Oates claims: "I really tried to do Sam Peckinpah: as much as I knew about him, his mannerisms, and everything he did" (Weddle, 1994b, p. 42). The signature mirror sunglasses, the low, whispery, vocal delivery, and the teeth-clenching grimace are the physical and visible manifestations of his attempt.

However, to understand the evolution of the Peckinpah mythology we need to look further than this director's anarchic and charismatic "persona." We cannot underestimate how greatly the "star system" was effected by the events of May 1968 and the resulting institutionalization and politicization of film studies. With *Cahiers du Cinéma*'s formulation of *la politique des auteurs*, the Hollywood directors who were capable of imposing their own vision on the medium, in spite of the pressures imposed on them by the studios and industry, were canonized and celebrated as "heroic artists"—the sole, visionary creators of the finished artifact. This notion of the director as an "artist" was quickly taken up by writers and academics in America, spear-headed by Andrew Sarris whose "auteur theory" transformed the original polemic of developing a critical method to evaluate predominately Hollywood films and creating a pantheon of best directors (1962, 1968). Sarris acknowledged Peckinpah as a "newcomer" with "ambitions" who, with *Ride the High Country*, offered "something new in anti-Westerns (1968, p. 219). In *Interviews with Film Directors* Sarris prophetically noted that as a "director with a very personal vision," Peckinpah would have "problems functioning in Hollywood" (1968, p. 371).

Although the studios initially failed to respond to this new "obsession" with the director and, in fact, found it laughable, they soon realized its marketing possibilities. Major stars were bumped to second billing on opening film credits as the director's name blazed across the screen, while projects were bought, sold, and advertised on their director's merits. Peckinpah's vexed and public anti-establishment stance and extreme antics were perfect fodder for the auteurist critics, but so were some of his films. Paradoxically, here was a director who, although working within the classic form of the Western genre, produced films that were "antiprogressive," antiheroic, and full of contradictions. Not only did he invert the thematic concerns of the genre, revealing the harsh and brutal underbelly of the "mythic West," but the vitality and resonance of his style and his manipulation of the medium was utterly breathtaking.

Appearing to subvert the constraints enforced by the industry, Peckinpah not only produced "authentic" films, but "heroically" fought tooth and nail to maintain his artistic control. Nevertheless, although several of his films, including *Ride the High Country* and *The Wild Bunch*, were championed by both

European and American auteurist critics, and although the developments en-
suing from the advent of "auteur theory" created an environment in which
Peckinpah, for a short period of time, achieved "auteur" status, during the period in which he was working there was a failure to analyze the thematic and
stylistic consistencies of his work. In fact, with a few exceptions,[15] the publicity
that Peckinpah received, and encouraged, is predominately consumed by the
controversy surrounding his "excessive" use of violence and his personal mythology. Even though Peckinpah was celebrated as a director, much of the anecdotal and critical literature fixates on the more general and personal
concerns normally directed toward a "star," while little time is spent analyzing
his stylistic and thematic concerns.

Back in 1969, Jim Kitses in *Horizon's West* highlighted how the concentration on auteur theory led to the neglect of form. Kitses's intention is to "rescue" Anthony Mann, Budd Boetticher, and Peckinpah while investigating
their films in relation to the use of the Western genre. Referring to Bazin's pre-
caution about the dangers of a "cult of personality," he contends that auteur
theory cannot crystallize all problems, nor answer all our questions. Warning
against the "reactionary notion" that Hollywood directors function like the
"charismatic heroes of their films," Kitses argues that we need to advance the
idea of an American tradition of which the Western is a central model (p. 8).[16]
This notion of the auteur as a "charismatic hero" and this fascination with the
"cult of personality" have further influenced the ways in which Peckinpah's
"persona" and his films have been discussed. His chaotic personal life, his dictatorial work practices, and his drinking, drug taking, and brawling all make
for great story telling; yet, ultimately, this fixation has culminated in a retreat
from the films, particularly his more life-affirming works, which do not easily
fit in with the mythology of "Bloody Sam."

PECKINPAH'S WESTERNS AND THE VITALITY OF VIOLENCE

Much of the theory and criticism that has been occasioned by, and inflicted
on, Peckinpah's films has failed to address their complexity. This problem
stems from an apparent inability to deal with their paradoxical nature. The critical literature that has crystallized around particular films, specifically *The Wild
Bunch* and *Straw Dogs*, largely remembers Peckinpah as the "master of violence" while ignoring his sweet swan songs like *Ride the High Country*, *The
Ballad of Cable Hogue*, and *Junior Bonner*.

Yet, in Peckinpah's *oeuvre* what we see so boldly and vibrantly brought to
life is the joyous imaging of utopia and vital confrontations with violence and
death, which are frequently, intimately entwined. The "star" status of this director's persona and mythology, along with its association with violence, has
resulted in a failure to investigate the function and experience of Peckinpah's
explorations of violence, and has elided the utopian elements of his films. In

fact, in certain works like *The Wild Bunch*, *Pat Garrett and Billy the Kid* (1973), and *Cross of Iron* (1977), a utopian impulse exists at the heart of violent action. Much of the writing on these films ignores this utopian element and simply concentrates on the representations and effects of "screen violence."

One of the only areas in which we find sustained and thoughtful analyses and discussion of Peckinpah's films is in relation to his exploration of the Western.[17] In surveying this criticism, we find a stability that is lacking in much other writing that becomes sidelined by the controversy surrounding "screen violence" and Peckinpah's mythology. In more recent times, theorists and critics such as Michael Bliss and Paul Seydor have picked up where Kitses left off, claiming Peckinpah as the son of an American cultural tradition that includes Cooper, Emerson, Hemingway, Faulkner, and Mailer. Both these writers address his films in the context of the Western, discussing his authentic, yet tarnished, approach to the original ideal.[18] Commenting on the turbulent debates that have evolved around Peckinpah's use of violence, Bliss highlights how this concentration has resulted in the failure to appreciate that Peckinpah's films are deeply humanist and are illuminated by a constant concern with the human condition and morality.

Probably the most eminent and well-versed critic on Peckinpah's work is Paul Seydor, whose text *Peckinpah: The Western Films* was originally published in 1980 with his "Reconsideration" appearing in 1997. Although acknowledging there are other possibilities for analysis, Seydor chooses to deal only with Peckinpah's Westerns for he sees in them a clear trajectory running from his television work through to *The Ballad of Cable Hogue* and coming back on track with *Pat Garrett and Billy the Kid*. He presents us with a complex study, including keen analysis of the films, while also dealing with Peckinpah's personal life and the literary and cultural forces that helped shape his artistic vision. Seydor is one of the few writers who acknowledges the paradoxical nature of these films in which "virtue is intimately entwined with vice," and that along with an obsession with violence, we are also offered a "sweet and lovely lyricism and a gentleness so tender it cleanses and heals" (p. xx).

Like Bliss, Terence Butler in his much neglected text *Crucified Heroes: The Films of Sam Peckinpah* (1979) discusses Peckinpah's films as Westerns due to the way in which they operate as morality tales. Butler is most insightful in relation to the discussion of that existential edge—the threshold between life and death—that Peckinpah explored again and again in his spectacles of violence. For Butler, Jack London's thematic concerns most closely correlate with those of Peckinpah.[19] Butler observes that Peckinpah works on "the edge," from a point of extremes, and, although the intense expression of his emotions is often disagreeable and even obscene, these expressions have value in that they expose the consequences of this kind of repression. Butler argues that in working out these emotions Peckinpah's cinema derives from a "Nietzschean drive to the extremes of immediate transcendence" (p. 8). For Peckinpah, the only outlet for this celebration of energy is in a kind of madness—the madness of ec-static violence (Butler, p. 19). In the vital and intense confrontation of fear, vi-olence, and death, there is a moment of ecstasy—of freedom—an extreme form of self-liberation that culminates in the forgetfulness of self. As Kael has noted, this is where Peckinpah's aesthetic expressiveness becomes poetic for it grants us access to knowledge and experiences that we are unable to obtain in a prosaic way.[20] Yet, Butler fails to note that this Nietzschean drive is about nonutilitarian activity: this ecstasy can also be found in the kinetic, sensual, and passionate experiences of dance, music, sex, and play.

Peckinpah's films have been mutilated by studio intervention and much of the critical literature has been colored by the Peckinpah mythology. Further damage has been inflicted on these films by the nexus at which social and cul-tural debates about "real" violence have been linked with debates about "screen violence" and condensed into over-simplified and reductive "moral" judgments. Not only has this resulted in the neglect of his sweet, mellow, and comic films but these perspectives have all too easily collapsed questions about aesthetic expressiveness and the experiences of "screen violence" into rarefied moral and ethical judgments about social behavior, while failing to analyze the representations and meanings of particular films. In a sense, if we are to do jus-tice to Peckinpah's films, we need to disengage the personal mythology from the actual films and interrogate the questions surrounding them, allowing them to be what they are—an uneven collection of films that at their best deal with two of our most fervent concerns, our fear of violence and death and our dreams of a better life. If we put aside the "star" status of "Bloody Sam" and closely examine these films, what we find is a dual pulse beating; for the man who believes that there are "killers in the woods" also knows we must remem-ber to "kiss each other" and "water the flowers."

PECKINPAH AND THE COMPLEXITY OF CINEMATIC VIOLENCE

In Peckinpah's *The Wild Bunch* we are given a brief glimpse of a powerful image that is shocking but deeply significant. In an extreme close-up, a woman's breast is uncovered and offered to a hungry child. A thick, black artil-lery belt is strapped across the center of the woman's chest—bullets visible. The child's tiny hand brushes against the belt. This image is superfluous to the film's plot but it resonates with Peckinpah's most insistent concerns—the cele-bration of life and the nature of violence and death.[21] In almost all of Peckinpah's films we see a vital affirmation of fertility, nature, festivities, and community. We also find intense, kinetic explorations of violence and death. The life, love, and fertility that the maternal breast and the suckling child sig-nify are threatened by the weapons of violence and death. However, this is not the only significance of this grouping of elements for, within these films, death is explored not only as a threat but also as our mortal fate. In these films life and death are not perceived as separate phases; rather, they are intertwining, simultaneous processes embodying an ever-changing tension.

One of the director's primary concerns has been to explore death within an aesthetic realm. In almost all of his films someone dies, sometimes gracefully like Steve Judd (William Holden) in *Ride the High Country* or quietly and sorrowfully like Sheriff Baker (Slim Pickens) in *Pat Garrett and Billy the Kid*. We cannot begin the body count for all those who die in his spectacles of violence. Although some of his characters appear to have a belief in God, in his investigations into violence and death he seeks out its living ramification: how his characters choose to live is intrinsic to how they approach death. Peckinpah is drawn to intimate investigations of our corporeal state, exploring our biological imperative to survive but also our palpable fragility—one moment alive, the next expired. The way in which he continually returns to a focus on sequences in which death is occasionally accepted, generally fought against, sometimes faced boldly and sometimes fearfully, grants to his investigations a kind of ritualized or mythic function. Yes, Paul Seydor is right in noting that Peckinpah fell just a little in love with violence (pp. 325–26). However, we will always be both anxious and fascinated by violence and death. It will always be a concern that we accept, fear, or deny—its inevitability will draw us. In Peckinpah's filmic worlds he continually returns to the subject of death allowing us an insight into its aesthetic intimacies and thereby bestowing a form and meaning on our knowledge of violence and death that it rarely has in life.[22]

Stephen Prince (1998b) claims that Peckinpah's most "groundbreaking" films were made during, and in response to, the politically and socially turbulent period of the 1960s and early 1970s (pp. xiii, xiv). In some ways, this volatile, transitory, and uncertain period is a little like our own. Although many of Peckinpah's films are Westerns they are set in that transformative moment when the mythic frontier is dying and a new world of technology, "progress," and civilization is being born.[23] These films are infused with longing but they are much too full of atavistic energy, intensity, and anarchy to dwell nostalgically on a lost "golden" era. Kitses argues that Peckinpah used the universal framework of the Western to explore archetypal concerns and measure them against the present realities that comprise and distort them (p. 12). Just as the transformative moment of the mythic West that many of these films explore is pertinent to the period in which these films were made, it also bears upon the transitory and fragmented era in which we live. But it is not simply the similarity of the social and political temper of these transitional periods that makes these films relevant. Rather, the intense resonance that these films hold for some of us derives from Peckinpah's tenacious concern with the human condition. His films are inquiries into the mutable relations between characters, circumstances, and the material world that he freely explores through his characters' emotional and gestural responses to the ambiguity and fragility that these transitional moments evoke.

Even when his films' narratives are devoid of hope and, like *Pat Garrett and Billy the Kid*, head inevitably toward death, their visceral, sensual, lyrical nature evokes in us a heightened, and sometimes blissful, engaged participation. *Pat Garrett and Billy the Kid* is defined by tragedy, compromise, and betrayal; yet, it still offers us a "hopeful" and sensual experience through its lyrical sound track, languid contemplation of the natural world, the tempo of its editing, and its rich use of color. Through the multiple layers of the film medium, Peckinpah imbues simple things, everyday actions, and the natural world with an emotional intensity that makes these objects and experiences feel "charged" with a physicality, sensuality, and grandeur that is enchanting. For those of us who find these films compelling, it is as if we feel attuned to their energy, their ecstatic intensity, and their pain.

What we find thematically played within Peckinpah's films is that paradox of the human condition. Peckinpah shows us time and again that life is a deeply ambiguous, transformative process. He rages against repressive social restrictions and the degradation of the natural world, but hope springs eternal in the moments of festive dance, laughter, and song; it is often only in the confrontation with death that his characters are released from its tyranny and find freedom in that moment.

The contradictions inherent in these confrontations with violence and death mean that his use of violence has the potential to be regressive, for the freedom gained in these episodes of kinetic vitality usually results in unnecessary death. But what this violence ultimately expresses is a carnal rage for life itself—as Camus observes in *The Rebel*, it is that will to "die on one's feet" rather "than to live on one's knees" (p. 269). And the path taken toward death always involves a confrontation with the need to establish a set of values to live by (Bliss, pp. 1–17). In *The Ballad of Cable Hogue*, Hogue (Jason Robards) must face death but he does so with an inner knowledge of himself, with the experience of friendship and love, and a sense of being at "home" in his desert Eden. In *The Wild Bunch* the Bunch respond to their corrupt and degraded world by igniting a "primitive," violent capacity. They leave the world in a frenzied baptism of blood, but having lived as disenfranchised beings, it is only in this climatic moment that they are truly alive in themselves and to the world.

Prince argues that in the opening and concluding sequences of *The Wild Bunch*, the style is so "ritualistically elaborate" that it turns violence into a pleasurable spectacle and conforms to Richard Slotkin's thesis for the "myth of regeneration through violence."[24] If, as Slotkin argues, the "myth of regeneration through violence" is to be redemptive, the hero/hunter most choose to return to society and marry a "white" woman, or forever live in solitary exile.[25] Peckinpah frequently used the Western format, and therefore the stakes are always high, but his work is nonutilitarian, without purchase, without a goal. As Garry Watson, in his discussion of *The Wild Bunch* argues, this film remains unconventional in that the path the Bunch takes is a "reckless" but "splendid" one that will almost certainly result in death, but it is a path that "lacks any calculation" (p. 53). Watson draws on Bataille's theory of "expenditure" to illuminate the final action in this film. He says:

What . . . the Bunch commit themselves to is the kind of "expenditure" Bataille claimed humanity (recognizing only "the right to acquire, to conserve, and to consume rationally") tends to exclude in principle: the useless, nonproductive or unconditional kind of expenditure that involves great losses or spectacular destruction or sacrifices and that tends toward the "generous, orgiastic and excessive." (p. 10)[26]

The Bunch, who are already outside of the law and society, do not seek atonement, or court exile; nor do they simply seek death. And this too is why Steiner (James Coburn) in *The Cross of Iron* heads joyously, but absurdly, back into battle after he has been released from duty. What these characters choose is to feel alive in the ecstatic moment of freedom achieved through the confrontation of violence and death.

However, Paul Seydor argues that in Peckinpah's pursuit of a "masculine principle" he failed to imagine another kind of existence (p. 319). Seydor believes that this failure is due to Peckinpah's belief that to fulfill this principle you must rebel and live, or conform and die. Now, the director offers us numerous depictions of corrupt moneymen and stultifying town life; yet, his representations of communal and village life are often rich, engaging, and sensual. When the Bunch enter a Mexican village it is a warm and festive experience. In no way is this site of domesticity, family, and community dull, claustrophobic, or boring; in fact, for the Bunch it is enchanting. However, these men seem incapable of changing their lives, or taking this experience upon themselves. In being open to the natural world and in finally being brave enough to accept love and therefore uncertainty and change, Cable Hogue transforms the nihilistic aridity of the Bunch's world into an experience of plenitude.

VIOLENCE AND UTOPIA: AN INTIMATE RELATION

The concentration of debates on the ramifications of "screen violence" has resulted in a failure to illuminate the utopian elements of Peckinpah's directorial vision. In the warmth and resonance found in the festive moments of communal sharing, dance, and song, which feature in most of these films, we find that utopian impulse that Fredric Jameson claims is endemic to all mass and commercial culture. It is that sense of the underlying and ineradicable drive toward community that can be detected, no matter how faintly and feebly (pp. 9–34). But what we find in these films is more than just a utopian impulse for the cinema delivers itself in images.

We live in a world in which the idea of "utopia" is much maligned; in fact, it is a dirty word. But since its inception the cinema has been sneaking us the images, sounds, and feelings of utopia—in intimate moments, glorious vistas, and jubilant happy endings. In Peckinpah's gentle films what we find are representations of what Camus calls "relative" utopia.[27] By this I mean that these films give us worlds that are liveable and life-affirming but limited: they offer us a communion between human beings and the natural world; yet they do so in full knowledge of the hardships and difficulty that this communion involves.

I would like to suggest that we also find a quite different form of utopian impulse within Peckinpah's "aesthetics of violence." In fact, what is particular to his work is the unresolved tension inherent in his aesthetics of violence, which involves a utopian impulse found in the representation of apocalyptic violence. These moments are not simply about regeneration through violence, for they involve an effervescence and excessive activity that is nonutilitarian. The emotional involvement that is created by the visceral and kinetic vitality of these violent moments, combined with the aesthetic satisfaction of their choreography, which culminates in something like a dance, results in moments that are in a sense experiential. They give us that "feeling of intensity" that Richard Dyer claims is crucial to the utopian feeling of the musical spectacle (p. 177). It is as if these moments are so excessive, such "emotional extremes," that we experience them in the present. A more fertile way of discussing the utopian impulse and the representations of violence we find in these films is through their aesthetic and ritualized functions that give form and meaning to these representations and our experiences of them, while refusing to order our emotions into some kind of hierarchy.

Junior Bonner (Steve McQueen) is at home only on the road, or sleeping by a river, away from the progressive, destructive developments of town life. Yet, in the passionate boredom of his travels, he still finds the need repeatedly to enter the ritualized world of the rodeo. To risk life and run the hands of the clock is, through kinetic activity, to feel electrified. Pat Garrett (James Coburn) and Billy the Kid (Kris Kristofferson) test their skills by shooting the heads of chickens. But this sport is metaphorical for their own demise. Pat Garrett will fulfill his history and kill Billy; however, what is extraordinary in this surrogate ritual is how the slowly exploding, shuddering creatures capture the threshold between life and death.

But Peckinpah also gives us the sublime "moment of creation" in the orgiastic celebrations of sex, wine, dance, and song. Open to the "miracle of life," Cable Hogue creates a paradise in the middle of the desert. In *Bring Me the Head of Alfredo Garcia*, the anarchic and free-spirited Elita (Isela Vega) needs at least three days and nights to say good-bye to her lover. The doomed Bunch, stripped bare in the confines of a steam house engage in a childlike water fight. Peckinpah does not just touch the "skin of things," but in full-blown splendor also confronts the rage we feel at the insignificance of our individual existence, which is also the rage for life itself. What Peckinpah's films so clearly evoke is a deep-seated understanding of the "limitary" nature of our existence and our desire for visceral and poetic experiences.

In Peckinpah's filmic worlds he captures and evokes that "strife" and tension that comes with the knowledge of "cosmic death." His films give life, vitality, and energy to the pain and rage with which his characters, and ultimately

we, confront and deal with the knowledge of mortality. In his kinetic spectacles of violence he explores that fragile and transient threshold between life and
death. Things and people explode and disintegrate in ecstatic and horrible
rhythms. These spectacles are moments, or microcosms, which explore and
fulfill the destiny of an ever-consuming world. The characters that people his
films are sometimes sweet, comic, or charismatic; more often they are mad,
nasty, and angry loners and losers who already know that there are no certain-
ties in the world, no safety nets. At some point in the inner and outer journeys
that his films take, there is always a moment of repose when fate is acknowledged.

Frequently, death results from the actions taken. Yet, this tension is never
simply played out for Peckinpah's worlds are fraught with complexity. The fact
of violence and death always involves a questioning and retrospective view of
how we should live. What saves even his more nihilistic films from eternal
bleakness is the way that life is celebrated in glorious, gentle interactions and
raucous moments of festive celebration. The knowledge of mortality highlights the brevity and limits of the moment that encompasses a life and therefore grants it an immense poignancy and preciousness. No matter if his
characters are risking love, or "high noon," on the edge of some ruin and deso-
late world, there is almost always a glimpse of hope imbued by energy, beauty,
community, and the wishes for, and dreams of, a better life.[28]

CONCLUSION

During Peckinpah's working history the focus on his anarchic and sometimes violent persona, the development of "auteur theory" and its celebration
of the "cult of personality," and the inflated debates surrounding screen violence resulted, for a time, in the "star status" of this director, known as
"Bloody Sam." This status and its entwined mythology both helped and hin-
dered his working history, affecting the funding, distribution, and critical
up-take of his films. However, when we begin to untangle and tease out the
personal mythology that circulates around these films and the effects of the
controversy surrounding "screen violence" on the critical literature, when we
explore the meanings and experiences that Peckinpah's ritualized and ecstatic
spectacles of violence offer us and return to his more gentle, utopian films that
reclaim his festive celebrations and baptisms in water, what we find is a much
more complex vision than a simplistic celebration of violence. Peckinpah's
"aesthetics of violence" explore our fear of death, yet also our desire to see and
understand. His work is about the extremes that we can be driven to when we
live as disenfranchised beings in a disenchanted world. However, it is also
about our desperate desire to live poetically, to live with emotional and physical
intensity, to have an existence that is sensual and visceral in its experiences and
engagements. In Peckinpah's violent aesthetics we see and feel that raw edge

that exists between life and death, between inside and outside, between our glory and our fragility.

In Peckinpah's films the exploration of our mortal fate does not necessarily culminate in a nihilistic view. Rather his films resonate with that unresolved tension that exists between our fear and knowledge of our ephemeral, corporeal, and finite existence and our hopeful and exuberant joy for life. In rendering these simultaneous processes these films embrace the paradoxical nature of our human existence. In doing so with such energy, vitality, and vibrancy they allow those of us who find an emotional attunement with these films to grasp and even embrace something crucial about our state of being. In Peckinpah's films, and in our lives, it is this universal predicament that can cast a glowing light on the significance of those sweet and simple pleasures of desert blooms, human contact, song, dance, and laughter.

NOTES

1. For further details, see Evans (1972); Fine (1991); Simmons (1976); Weddle (1994a); and Weddle (1994b).

2. Peckinpah also wrote and directed numerous television serials and specials. His final works are the two video clips that launched Julian Lennon's music career: "Too Late for Goodbyes" and "Valotte."

3. Weddle comments in relation to the two films that Steve McQueen starred in: "The media, which had been indifferent to *Junior Bonner*, showed keen interest in *The Getaway* when word got out that it would be packed with Steve McQueen car chases and Sam Peckinpah 'ballets of blood.' . . . Almost all these stories focused on Peckinpah—not McQueen, not MacGraw—as the central dramatic figure behind the making of the movie. (This so incensed McQueen that he fired the unit publicist from the picture.)" (1994b, p. 440).

4. Two recent publications discuss how Peckinpah's stylistic explorations of violence have influenced contemporary filmmakers, see Laurent (1996) and Prince (1998a, b). The focus on "ultraviolence" highlights the fact that Peckinpah is still predominately remembered as the "master of violence" with both texts ignoring other concerns within his work. The analogies drawn between Peckinpah and directors such as Tarantino and Woo fail to note that these directors' films lack the same concerns with the human condition. Frequently, the characters in these films are cartoonish stereotypes and, therefore, the violence is often driven by action and sometimes even humor. I do not mean to belittle these contemporary filmmakers by stating this; rather I am trying to draw attention to how the violence within their films functions in very different ways. (An exception here would be Tarantino's *Reservoir Dogs* [1992] which is intimately concerned with human relations, questions surrounding masculinity and honor, and how the body gives up life.) One contemporary filmmaker who does demonstrate similar concerns and range as Peckinpah is the Japanese filmmaker Takeshi Kitano, specifically in *Scene at the Sea* (*Ano Natsu, Ichiban Shizukana Umi*, 1991), *Sonatine* (1993), and his last film *Hana-bi* (1998). Although neither Laurent nor Prince mentions Kitano, his films delve into those fundamental questions that obsessed Peckinpah: How should we live and die? This is also interest-

ing to consider in relation to the fact that Akira Kurosawa was Peckinpah's "favorite" director, and his influence is obvious in Peckinpah's extended battle scenes.

5. All further references to *The Wild Bunch* will be to the restored version re-release by Warner Brothers in 1995.

6. Audience response to the initial release resulted in a further 35 minutes of footage being cut from the film, although the European release was a more complete version. For further information, see Whitehall (p. 173).

7. Prince argues that if we are to fully understand what made Peckinpah's films possible at this time, we need to emphasize three interlocking constituents: Peckinpah's internal dynamics, changes in the industry's rating and censorship codes, and "resonant currents of socio-political change and thought at large in the culture during this time" (p. 9). For further discussion of the relation between Peckinpah and the period in which he worked see, Stephen Prince, ed., *Sam Peckinpah's Wild Bunch.*

8. Here, we should also note the influence of not only Akira Kurosawa but Arthur Penn, Budd Boetticher, and Anthony Mann.

9. This nihilistic and bleak film involves an exploration of idiosyncratic ideas about gender construction. Although the film warrants intense analysis, in relation to structure and form, it appears as an aberration in the context of Peckinpah's *oeuvre.* *Straw Dogs* is probably the most fully resolved of Peckinpah's films; yet, within this film there is not one utopian image—not even a flutter of hope—and its violent sequences offer none of the vital intensity and energy that we find in his other works.

10. An exception here is Williams (1995). Responding to the re-release in England of *Straw Dogs* in 1995 by ABC Pictures, she looks at the film in the light of the legacy of 1970s and 1980s feminism.

11. Weddle's extensively researched biography *"If They Move . . . Kill 'Em!"* outlines incidence after incidence of the irrational and often counterproductive behavior Peckinpah resorted to in his attempts to have complete control and final cut of all his films.

12. In Kael's (1976) opinion: "Peckinpah has been simplifying and falsifying his own terrors as an artist by putting them into melodramatic formulas. . . . His whole way of making movies has become a revenge fantasy: he screws the bosses, he screws the picture, he screws himself" (pp. 72, 74).

13. For further discussion of the production problems incurred during the making and postproduction of *Major Dundee,* see Bliss (p. 58). Also see Cutts (pp. 6–8).

14. Holden was obviously successful, for, as Weddle notes: "Sam's children got chills when they first saw some of the completed sequences" (1994b, p. 336).

15. Here, an exception is Tom Milne, who consistently approached his analysis of Peckinpah's films through the framework of auteur and genre theories. For example, see *"Major Dundee* and *Invitation to a Gunfighter," "The Wild Bunch,"* and *"Straw Dogs."*

16. He also states that the "western is American history," but not in any simple or literal sense; rather, American frontier life provides the milieu and mores for the Western genre. The project Kitses (1969) sets himself is to survey the elements of this form before examining each filmmaker's contributions (p. 12).

17. Although Prince offers us one of the most thorough explorations of Peckinpah's style, in resorting to a rather puritanical notion of morality he conflates discussion of the effects of "real" violence in relation to social life and its application in relation to aesthetic creativity. This results in a failure to explore the ecstatic func-

tion of Peckinpah's aesthetics of violence. Prince (1998b) observes that Peckinpah's work is "deeply fraught with polarised energies," but we must not dismiss him because he is so complex (p. 148). Yet, by brushing aside his more gentle, sweet, and playful films and claiming they are in a "minor-key," Prince does exactly this. For surely part of these films complexity is their movement between sweetness, love, and festivities, and violence, death, and savagery as elements that exist in powerful ways within these films and singularly exist as an unresolved tension in specific films.

18. Both Bliss and Seydor claim that *The Wild Bunch* has been a neglected American masterpiece. This belief has culminated in the publication of *Doing It Right: The Best Criticism on Sam Peckinpah's* The Wild Bunch, which is a collection of essays edited by Bliss. In his "Acknowledgments" in *Doing It Right*, Bliss writes: "What is remarkable about the scholarship on *The Wild Bunch* is how little of it there is. Although there are many reviews of the film, insightful critical writing, especially writing that runs longer than a page or two, is relatively scarce." Also see, Weddle's "Foreword" to Seydor, *The Western Films*, where he discusses Seydor's attempts to rally for the restoration of the film (p. xvi). More recently this neglect has, in some ways, been corrected by Prince's collection, *Sam Peckinpah's* Wild Bunch.

19. Butler, 1979, p. 1; also see, Jack London, *The Call of the Wild*.

20. Alluding to Pauline Kael, the Peckinpah retrospective held by the Film Society of the Lincoln Center was entitled "Blood of a Poet: The Cinema According to Sam Peckinpah." Kael (1976), for many years the *New Yorker's* feisty and opinionated film reviewer, claimed that Peckinpah is one of the few "legendary" American film directors who can be called an "artist" (p. 72). As a magazine "reviewer," her work is often snubbed by the "academy," but in this short phrase she captures something elemental about these films, something that is often ignored—that the intensity, resonance, and vitality of these films' aesthetic expressiveness, be it violent or utopian, takes us into the realm of the poetic.

21. See Mark Crispin Miller's (1975) excellent article, "In Defense of Sam Peckinpah." Here, he brings to light these two drives, arguing that in Peckinpah's later work the "life-affirming" elements are constantly threatened by the "accruements of violence" (p. 4).

22. For further discussion, see Sobchack (pp. 79–94).

23. Apart from Prince's *Savage Cinema* most discussions related to the transitional phase that Peckinpah's films explore dwell mainly on *The Wild Bunch*, paying particular attention to how this film revised the Western genre.

24. Prince suggests that due to the use of a "melancholic framework that contextualises the violent exchanges" Peckinpah announces his "moral perspective" on the violence, which then enables him to "side-step" the myth of regeneration. However, he argues that, unfortunately, *The Wild Bunch* fulfills the myth of "regeneration through violence" (p. 225).

25. See Robert Slotkin's exceptional and contentious thesis on American cultural mythology as being defined by the myth of "regeneration through violence."

26. See also George Bataille (1985).

27. It is worth noting that Seydor claims that Peckinpah's favorite novel was Albert Camus's *The Stranger*. He also writes that "his thinking can hardly *not* have been shaped by Camus's treatment of violence and revolution in *The Stranger* and *The Rebel*. According to one of his assistants, Peckinpah was greatly pleased when he read of *The Rebel* being used as a way to explicate some of the underlying ideas that are

dramatised in *The Wild Bunch*" (p. 348). Although Seydor comments that he received this information in a letter from Katy Haber, after thoroughly researching the critical literature on Peckinpah and his films, I have been unable to find any discussion that mentions Camus. However, I think this is an extremely fertile connection to make and also believe that Camus's idea of "relative" utopia can help us in our discussion of the utopian impulse in these films. See Camus, *Neither Victims nor Executioners*.

    28. Here, the exception would be *Straw Dogs*.

REFERENCES

Bataille, Georges. "The Notion of Expenditure." In Stoekle, Allan, ed., *Visions of Excess: Selected Writings, 1927–1939*. Translated by Allan Stoekle. Minneapolis: University of Minnesota Press: 1985.

Bliss, Michael. *Justified Lives: Morality & Narrative in the Films of Sam Peckinpah.* Carbondale and Edwardsville: Southern Illinois University Press, 1993.

———, ed. *Doing It Right: The Best Criticism on Sam Peckinpah's* The Wild Bunch. Carbondale and Edwardsville: Southern Illinois University Press, 1994.

Butler, Terence. *Crucified Heroes: The Films of Sam Peckinpah.* London: Gordon Fraser, 1979.

Camus, Albert. *The Rebel.* Translated by Anthony Bower. Harmondsworth, UK: Penguin Books, 1971.

———. *Neither Victims nor Executioners.* Chicago: World without War Publications, 1972.

Corrigan, Timothy. *A Cinema without Walls: Movies and Culture after Vietnam.* London: Routledge, 1991.

Crawley, Tony. "Blood Bath Ballet." *Game.* February (1985): 87–93.

Cutts, John. "Shoot! Sam Peckinpah Talks to John Cutts." *Films and Filmmaking* 16, no. 1 (October 1969): 4–9.

Dyer, Richard. "Entertainment and Utopia." In Altman, Rick, ed., *Genre: The Musical.* London: Routledge & Kegan Paul, 1981.

Evans, Max. *Sam Peckinpah, Master of Violence: Being the Account of the Making of a Movie and Other Sundry Things.* Dakota Press, 1972.

Fine, Marshall. *Bloody Sam: The Life and Times of Sam Peckinpah.* New York: Donald Fine, 1991.

Jameson, Fredric. "Reification and Utopia in Mass Culture." In *Signatures of the Visible.* New York: Routledge, 1990.

Kael, Pauline. "Notes on the Nihilist-Poetry of Sam Peckinpah." *New Yorker.* January 12 (1976): 70–75.

Kitses, Jim. *Horizons West: Anthony Mann, Budd Boetticher, Sam Peckinpah, Studies of Authorship within the Western.* Bloomington: Indiana University Press, 1969.

Laurent, Bouzereau. *Ultra Violent Movies: From Sam Peckinpah to Quentin Tarantino.* New York: Carol Publishing Group, 1996.

London, Jack. "The Call of the Wild." In Labor, Earle, ed., *The Portable Jack London.* New York: Penguin Books, 1994.

Mellen, Joan. *Big Bad Wolves: Masculinity in the American Film.* New York: Pantheon Books, 1977.

Miller, Mark Crispin. "In Defense of Sam Peckinpah." *Film Quarterly* 28, no. 3 (spring 1975): 2–17.

Milne, Tom. "*Major Dundee* and *Invitation to a Gunfighter*." *Sight and Sound* 34, no. 2 (summer 1965): 144–55.

———. "*The Wild Bunch*" *Sight and Sound* 38, no. 4 (autumn 1969): 208–9.

———. "*Straw Dogs*." *Sight and Sound* 41, no. 1 (winter 1971–72): 50–51.

———. "*Pat Garrett and Billy the Kid*." *Sight and Sound* 42, no. 4 (autumn 1973): 232–33.

Prince, Stephen, ed. *Sam Peckinpah's* Wild Bunch. New York: Cambridge University Press, 1998a.

———. *Savage Cinema: Sam Peckinpah and the Rise of Ultraviolent Movies*. Austin: Univesity of Texas Press, 1998b.

Sarris, Andrew. *The American Cinema, Directors, and Directions, 1929–1968*. New York: Dutton, 1968.

Seydor, Paul. *Peckinpah: The Western Films: A Reconsideration*. Urbana: University of Illinois Press, 1997.

Simmons, Garner. *Peckinpah: A Portrait in Montage*. Austin: University of Texas Press, 1976.

Slotkin, Robert. *Regeneration through Violence: The Mythology of the American Frontier, 1600–1860*. Middletown, CT: Wesleyan University Press, 1973.

Sobchack, Vivian. "The Violent Dance: A Personal Memoir of Death in the Movies." In Atkins, Thomas R., ed., *Graphic Violence on the Screen*. New York: Monarch Press, 1976.

Watson, Garry. "The Western: The Genre that Engenders the Nation." *CineAction* 46 (1998): 3–10.

Weddle, David. "Dead Man's Clothes: The Making of *The Wild Bunch*." *Film Comment* 30, 3 (May–June 1994a): 44–57.

———. "*If They Move . . . Kill 'Em!*": The Life and Times of Sam Peckinpah. New York: Grove Press, 1994b.

———. "They Want to See Brains Flying Out?" *Sight and Sound* 5, no. 2 (February 1995): 20–25.

Whitehall, Richard. "Talking with Peckinpah." *Sight and Sound* 38, no. 4 (autumn 1969): 173–75.

Williams, Linda Ruth. "Women Can Only Misbehave." *Sight and Sound* 5, no. 2 (February 1995): 26–27.

Wood, Robin. "Critical Positions and the End of Civilization; Or, a Refusal to Join the Club." *Film Criticism* 17, nos. 2–3 (winter/spring 1993): 79–92.

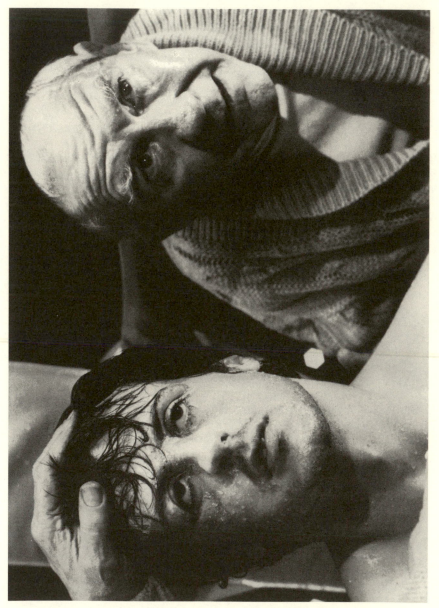

Sylvester Stallone in *Rocky* (John Avildsen, 1976). © United Artists (Kobal Collection).

Chapter 8

Birth of a Hero: Rocky, Stallone, and Mythical Creation

Rikke Schubart

> Everything I am and everything I have boils down to Rocky Balboa. I didn't create Rocky. He created me.
>
> —Sylvester Stallone

In 1976 one of those rare Hollywood moments happened when reality, fiction, and myth made a perfect fit, creating a new movie star. The movie was *Rocky*, the fairy tale of a third-rate boxer who gets his once-in-a-lifetime shot at the title. The star was Sylvester Stallone, a broke and unemployed actor who wrote the Oscar-winning film in three days and refused to let anyone but himself play the leading role. This was his once-in-a-lifetime shot at Hollywood stardom. The myth was one every American knows by heart: America as the land of opportunity. After the premiere Stallone said he did not create Rocky; Rocky created him. The figure somehow wrote itself, he said. Truth is, myth created both of them. Writing Rocky Stallone tapped into the heart of American mythology, and this is where his inspiration, his creative energy, his unshaken faith and his overnight stardom came from. This chapter traces the development of the early Stallone star persona as an embodiment of the American Dream and as a construct inseperable from the figure he wrote, embodied, and made famous—Rocky.

MYTH

As a metaphorical and emotional story myth provides a setting for our lives, dreams, and actions. The social function of myth—both religious and secular—is parallel to that of our ego ideal: it gives us dreams, ideals, and blind faith, inspires us to reach for the stars, helps us make existential choices. Myth is meaningful, it creates culture and faith, it forms part of our identity, and it motivates action. We find two distinct approaches to myth formation: one is the tradition represented by Claude Levi-Strauss, Vladimir Propp, and Joseph Campbell, who explore the universal, unconscious, and temporally unspecific structures of myth. The second is a cultural, more specific and ideologically driven analysis of myth represented by Roland Barthes, Northrop Frye, and Richard Slotkin. My concern here is with the second approach to myth.

The French semiotician Roland Barthes points out that "myth acts economically: it abolishes the complexity of human acts, it gives them the simplicity of essences" (p. 156). In his *Mythologies* (1973) Barthes de-mystifies myth as a metaphorical and emotional language; it is, he says, a semiotic structure that eradicates history, destroys truth, and works as political oppression. Not finding any positive value in myth, he concludes: "[T]he function of myth is to empty reality: it is, literally, a ceaseless flowing out, a hemorrhage, or perhaps an evaporation, in short a perceptible absence" (p. 55).

Myth may be oppressive, it may be ideological, and it may be manipulative. It may be a lie in the sense that myth is located between fiction and history and is therefore not verifiable in any objective sense. It may replace history with fanciful and fascinating fictions. Myth may be and do all these things. But it is not an absence. The function of myth is not "to empty reality" but, on the contrary, to fill reality.

According to literary critic Richard Slotkin, we find in myth not "the simplicity of essences" but the condensation of a society's history, culture, and ideology. Slotkin (1996) returns to myth the complexity Barthes denied it:

Myths are stories drawn from a society's history that have acquired through persistent usage the power of symbolizing that society's ideology and of dramatizing its moral consciousness—with all the complexities and contradictions that consciousness may contain. (p. 5)

From this point of view myth is meaningful. It brings to life important elements from the past and in this respect—as social and cultural memory—it is true. Myth may be fake and phony in relation to "real" history, but to dismiss it as merely a lie is to miss the point, since it has nothing to do with plain facts and pragmatic reality.

Myth is much more than a mere cultural memory. Its real power and indisputable attraction is a unique ability to generate dreams and faith. In *The Great Code* (1983) Northrop Frye points out two aspects of myth: its poetic function to tell stories, which brings it close to literature, and its social function to motivate action—"a program of action for a specific society"—which connects myth with social reality. Myth is inseparable from ritual and ritual actions, and myth points out "the dimension of the possible in the actual" (p. 49). Frye's subject is the Bible but this dual purpose also applies to sacred and secular myths. Like the Bible, the myth of America as land of opportunity generates culture, faith, and social action.

Myth not only tells a story, it gives us dreams and ideals that we wish were true, that we hope are true, that we finally fight to make true. In a psychoanalytical perspective myth is to our culture what the ego ideal is to our ego. Where the superego is an internal authority figure that tells us what to do and not to do, the ego ideal is an internal hero, an ideal we look up to and admire. "While the superego is an agency of prohibition, the ego ideal is an agency of aspiration," says American psychoanalyst Peter Blos (1985). "Whereas the ego submits to the superego out of fear of punishment, it submits to the ego ideal out of love. . . . Our ideals are our internal leaders; we love them and are longing to reach them" (p. 152). The ego ideal provides us with megalomaniac fantasies that we strive to realize, it gives us blind faith in the future and ourselves. Without our ego ideal we would not see "the possible in the actual." Likewise, myth takes us to a narrative zone where past, present, and future meet, where fact becomes metaphor and emotion, where history, fiction, and dreams are mixed into colorful cocktails getting us drunk with faith and optimism. And here is where the magic of myth begins: if you just believe America is the land of opportunity, then a third-rate boxer can beat the world champion and a failed actor can become a Hollywood mega-star. It only takes faith.

STALLONE

> I want to be remembered as a man of raging optimism, who believes in the American Dream.
>
> —Sylvester Stallone

Besides faith two things helped transform Stallone into a star: a personal life that had the first half of that popular American rags-to-riches myth written all over it (there would have been no fairy-tale material for the media to rave about had he been a middle-class, well-educated, and talented actor without that famously blurred speech), and that unique moment needed to ignite the fuse that we can call inspiration or chance.

Chance made Stallone buy a ticket to see the fight between Chuck Wepner and world champion Muhammad Ali in 1975 to cheer himself up.[1] The year before he had moved from New York to Hollywood with his wife Sasha and bull mastiff Butkus hoping to kick-start an acting career that would not take off. Critics had praised his role in the low-budget independent film *The Lords of Flatbush* (1974), but after bit parts in *The Prisoner of Second Avenue* (1975), *Farewell, My Lovely* (1975), *Capone* (1975), *Death Race 2000* (1975), and *Cannonball* (1976), the phone did not ring for nine months. Things looked pretty lousy, and he went to see 33-year-old Wepner (who worked in a liquor store and was a nobody) get beaten to pulp by the black king, Ali. Wepner was tipped to last three rounds—but he refused to go down, he kept coming back, knocked Ali to the floor once (people say he stepped on Ali's foot at the time), and fought for his life and dignity until he was finally knocked out 19 seconds before the end of 15th and final round. The crowd went crazy; the human drama of the white underdog giving his best shot at the title impressed everyone, including Stallone. "The place is going crazy!" Stallone told *Playboy*. "Guys' eyes are turning up white; I mean, the crowd is going nuts. And here comes the last round, and Wepner finally loses on a TKO. I said to myself, 'That's drama. Now the only thing I've got to do is get a character to that point and I've got my story' " (Linderman, p. 79). The mythic potential would not leave Stallone's mind and three months after the fight he wrote the story of *Rocky* in an 84-hour rush of inspiration.[2] Like Wepner Stallone was considered a loser, and like Wepner he refused to let Hollywood knock him out in the third round. This white underdog would fight all the way and give his best shot at the title.

Stallone was born in the charity ward of Hell's Kitchen, a tough and poor part of Manhattan's West Side, on July 6, 1946. A birth injury left him with a slight facial paralysis and his later famous speech defect. His mother was half-French, his father a Sicilian immigrant, and for two years they left Stallone with foster parents because of financial problems (Kasindorf, p. 72). The family moved to Maryland when he was five and set up a chain of beauty salons. Stallone's parents divorced when he was 11 and he moved to Philadelphia with his mother. Then he and his brother took turns living a year with each parent.[3] In interviews Stallone presented himself as an aggressive child with "an abhorrent personality" and "all the sensibilities of a Quasimodo" (quoted in "Sylvester Stallone," p. 41)[4] who constantly initiated fights and got kicked out of a dozen schools, public, parochial, and military. He fantasized about strong heroes like Hercules and Superman and in fourth grade was forced to undress in class and show a Superboy costume he was wearing under his clothes—an incident he later told journalists about with ambivalent feelings of hurt and pride (Knobler, p. 61).

As a teenager he began lifting weights and playing football. His mother, who had boxed in her youth and been a Billy Rose dancer, now owned a bodybuilding gym where he trained. At 16 his mother sent him to Devereux High School, a private school with weekly psychotherapy for students with learning and behavioral problems, and although his grades were low he passed his school exams. In this period he began fencing and horseback riding, and also took up oil painting—a therapeutic pastime the adult Stallone has continued throughout his career in spite of being repeatedly ridiculed by the press for lack of talent. After high school he went to an American college in Switzerland where he worked as a girl's athletic coach and sold hamburgers. This is where he decided to be an actor after playing Biff in a slapstick version of *Death of a Salesman*. "I was very comfortable and for the first time I was doing something not illegal and yet soul-satisfying," he said (quoted in "Sylvester Stallone," p. 42).

Stallone studied at the drama department of the University of Miami for two years, but left the school several credits short of graduation. Returning to New York Stallone tried to make it as an actor without much success. He appeared in a few off-Broadway productions—John Herbert's *Fortune and Men's Eyes* in the season of 1969–70 and W. Somerset Maugham's *Rain* in 1970—while earning a living selling his stepfather's frozen pizzas at food conventions, cleaning the lions' cages at the Bronx Zoo, and being an usher at a movie theater (where he met Sasha, his first wife) ("Sylvester Stallone," p. 42). At one time he lived on the streets with his books and pens in a locker at the bus station, and in this period he appeared in the soft-porn movie *Party at Kitty and Studds* (1970). "It was either do that movie or rob someone," Stallone explained in the *Playboy* interview, "because I was at the end—the very end—of my rope. Instead of doing something desperate, I worked two days for $200 and got myself out of the bus station" (Linderman, p. 90). The film got shelved, but after the premiere of *Rocky* it was distributed to movie theaters for $10,000 a night. Stallone's comment: was "Hell, for $10,000 forget the movie! I'll be there myself!"

In short, Stallone was dedicated to success. His mother dabbled in astrology and when she predicted success for him as a writer he painted the windows of his apartment black, disconnected the phone, and began writing scripts for television series and films. " 'So I would sit at the edge of the bed and stare at the blank wall and say, All right. If you want that kind of a house, if you want this nice car, a bank book that takes you two hands to carry; if you want a phone that's not in the hallway, a color TV, a dog that barks and is healthy, not something stuffed—if you want all these things you have to work. You have to plop your butt at that desk and push the pen' " (quoted in Knobler, p. 61). In fact, Stallone once got $2,500 for a script for the *Touch of Evil* television series.

This is where we find the Stallone temper, poised uneasily between the aggressiveness of a boxer and the sensitivity of an artist. His father apparently once told him, "[Y]ou weren't born with much of a brain, so you'd better develop your body" (quoted in "Slyvester Stallone," p. 41)—a line Stallone wrote into *Rocky*—and from his early teens he worked on developing a muscular physique worthy of a bodybuilder. If his father was skeptical about Stallone's mind, his mother had faith. She had Stallone tested at the Drexel Institute of Technology in Philadelphia, a test that placed him one step above an idiot and made them conclude: "[Y]our son is suited to run a sorting machine" (quoted in Linderman, p. 86). The clash between mind and muscles is a theme that runs through the career of Stallone, from the premiere of *Rocky*, after which he said, "I make my living with my mind. My muscles I consider merely machinery to carry my mind around" (quoted in "Sylvester Stallone," p. 44) to his well-dressed, rich, and smart hero who in *Tango & Cash* (1989) proclaims that "Rambo's a pussy."[5] Stallone never excelled at school and did not finish his acting studies at the University of Miami. His body, however, was always in top shape; he trained five months for his role as a boxer, and when directors argued that Stallone lacked the body for playing Rocky, he proved them wrong. "They said I didn't have the stature of a heavyweight. I'll tell you what I told them: I'm bigger than Rocky Marciano was in his prime" (quoted in Linderman, p. 82).

In 1975 Stallone was fit for the final round of the pre-*Rocky* Stallone myth. In myths and fairy tales the hero is tested, fights impossible odds, and is tempted before reaching his goal. Stallone was also tested and tempted, and as a true mythic hero he held on to his faith. The boxing match had been in March, the script was finished in July, and by August 1 United Artists (UA) offered $75,000 for the script. They liked its old-fashioned, mythical, feel-good quality and imagined Paul Newman, Robert Redford, Gene Hackman, Al Pacino, James Caan, or Ryan O'Neal in the part. Seventy-five thousand dollars was an obscene amount of money to an unemployed actor, but Stallone would only sell the story if he got the part. UA went up to $175,000, then $210,000, and finally $315,000.[6] Stallone had a pregnant wife, his savings were down to $106, he had never played a leading role, and still he held on to his script like it was the key to Hollywood heaven. He would trash the script rather than see somebody else play the part tailored for himself. This was not about money or social safety; it was about success. United Artists finally gave in and offered Stallone the lead role, $20,000 for the script, and 10 percent of the profits (a deal that would make Stallone a millionaire as well as a star). Stallone's mythic faith even rubbed off on producers Irwin Winkler and Robert Chartoff, who mortgaged their homes to cover any budget overruns. Maybe he was right, this crazy actor with his "chance of a lifetime."

ROCKY

From the very first image and sound *Rocky* is about myth and faith and the resurrection of the American Dream.[7] Large white letters, "ROCKY," fill the entire screen, and are accompanied by solemn upbeat music, trumpets, announcing the coming of ———— and then the film's first picture, a Byzantine Christ in a mosaic on a wall, the camera slowly zooming back and taking in the sound and sight of Rocky and Spider Rico, two third-rate boxers, sweating and panting and pounding away at each other in a boxing match. We understand that the fight—weirdly—takes place in a church, the gymnasium is set up in what used to be a house of the Lord, and under the benign Christ with a Host in his hand is a white poster with the words "resurrection A.C." that the camera cleverly frames between the two men. Which one of them will become a savior? Then a helper tells one of them, "You're looking like a bum," and in the audience a woman with a shrill voice yells, "You're a bum, you know that? You're a bum," and we know that this sweating, sorry-looking boxer who is out of breath is our hero. In these few minutes of sound and image it is indicated that Rocky will be saved, that the flesh will be touched by God, and that the bum will become prophet and savior and reach out his hand to save his equally sorry-looking audience, a disillusioned, aggressive, and embittered America—"hit him, hit him," they yell—lost in a church without faith, a time without myth.

The naive but heart-warming Rocky Balboa fights occasionally and works as a collector for small-time loan shark Mr. Gazzo. Rocky is not too smart, he needs glasses and pen and paper to write down the name "Del Rio" and Gazzo's driver calls him a "meat bag," "a goddamn ape," and tells him to "look it up in a dictionary." Even his trainer calls him "a dumb Dago." He admits to be "at least half a bum" and time is catching up with him. "She's pushing 30 freakin' years old," his friend Paulie says of his shy sister, Adrian, whom Rocky is trying to date. "I'm 30 myself," Rocky answers. Rocky has neither brains nor wits, but he has heart. We see him trying to save souls; he lectures the little teenage brat Mary that she will end up a whore if she hangs out in the streets at night; he carries a drunk sleeping in the street into a bar; he chats with street singers; and he cannot break a man's thumb although Gazzo specifically orders him to. Rocky, in short, is a cross between an imbecile and an ape, a child and a saint. He is also the perfect hero for a culture that worships innocence, honesty, and naivete.

American literature, says the English critic Tony Tanner in *The Reign of Wonder* (1965), has cultivated a strategy of naive wonder, which he terms "the naive eye." The naive eye is both a view of the world and life, and a "voice" or point-of-view in literature. It has three characteristics: it is quite literally naïve; it speaks a simple, vernacular language; and it prefers the eternal present, "the Eternal Now." In the nineteenth century the Romantic writers used the naive vision of the innocent child as a strategy to escape the analysis and critical judgment that they felt obstructed the more true and illuminating emotions. "The child's wondering eye offered the romantic writer an avenue back to a reality from which he fast felt himself becoming alienated," says Tanner (p. 7).

In Europe this naive vision was merely one idea among many, a metaphorical naivete, cultivated as a literary tool. European writers moved from enlightenment to romanticism, then on to classicism, modernism, and disillusion. In America, however, wonder and naivete became a quite literal innocence, an all-encompassing life strategy employed by American writers to turn their back on Europe and forget a past that felt like "the domain of the dead" (Tanner, p. 14). The innocent, naive, and wondering eye looked at their new continent, America, eager to conquer, build, and create anew. In literature the simple vernacular language created a plain picture more true than the old, polished, and rhetorical language—"dead language" Tanner calls it—and the hero of all this mythic naivete should have "a primitive simplicity" suitable for "an idiot, Indian, infant." Tanner's "naive eye" pervades America from the president to the people, from the intelligentsia to its pop icons. When Ronald Reagan in the 1980s called Russia "the evil empire" and his defense program "Star Wars," it was not an ironic play with film quotes, but a literal and naive use of mythic language.

We meet Tanner's naive eye in movies from *Mr. Smith Goes to Washington* (1939) to *Forrest Gump* (1994), whose naive heroes appear to have a direct link to truth and the American Dream. "Two things do seem to me to be true," concludes Tanner. "From the start wonder was put to much more far-ranging uses in American writing than in any other literature. . . . [A]nd the stance of wonder has *remained* a preferred way of dealing with experience and confronting existence among American writers" (p. 10). The naive eye was a literary strategy for European Romantics, but in America it became a view of life, a national culture and myth. There are close ties between the naive eye and myth: both use metaphorical language in a literal sense, both replace analysis and critical judgment with emotions and feelings, both avoid the past and prefer the present, both address a naive and innocent model reader.

In his emotional honesty and naive view of the world Rocky is thus the perfect American hero. He lives alone with his goldfish and two turtles, Cuff and Link, symbols of being slow and vulnerable, yet hard, unable to breathe. The first half of the film introduces the mythical elements that magically come alive in the second half: the forgotten church in the gymnasium, the Christ, the innocent Rocky waiting for his chance, the virgin Adrian and her brother Paulie, who works in a large white freezer where time stands still and pig carcasses swing in silence like lost souls in space. With an impressive precision every image, every scene, and every line add to the picture of a disillusioned Rocky, a dystopian Philadelphia (representing post-Vietnam America), and a deep-frozen myth (America as land of opportunity) waiting to come alive.

The magic moment happens in the middle of the film, when Rocky visits Mr. Jergens, Apollo's promoter, thinking he wants him as a sparring partner to the champ. Jergens had asked for him at the training hall and left his card, and now this conversation takes place in Jergens's office:

Jergens: Rocky, do you believe that America is the land of opportunity?

Rocky: Yeah.

Jergens: Apollo Creed does. And he will prove it to the whole world by giving an unknown a shot at the title. And that unknown is you. He picked you, Rocky! Rocky, it's the chance of a lifetime. You can't pass it by. What do you say?

Rocky: (doesn't reply but turns his face toward the camera—searching? praying? surrendering to myth?)

"Do you believe?" No, Rocky does not believe he can beat the champ, but how can he turn down the myth of America as land of opportunity? What can he say? That he has no *faith*? Rocky has no life—he just lost his gym locker because his trainer considered him "a waste of life"—so, *hell*, faith is all he has left.

Apollo Creed is Rocky's opposite in every way. If Rocky is a naive believer, Apollo Creed is presented as a cynical *dis*believer. His Greek god name is stolen from European mythology—"the domain of the dead"—and he represents the exact opposite of the American hero: money, television, advertising, public relations, lies, and manipulation.[8] He has substituted the American dream with capitalism. Apollo does not believe America is the land of opportunity, he simply needs someone to replace his injured opponent. He has invested more than a million dollars in publicity for the fight that will take place on America's bicentennial birthday, and if it is canceled he will lose that money. However, any professional boxer knows that five weeks are not enough time to get in shape for a match, so he has to come up with a solution, a gimmick, to save his money:

Apollo Creed: This is the land of opportunity, right? So Apollo Creed on January the first gives a local underdog an opportunity. A snow white underdog and I'm gonna put his face on a poster with me. Now, I'll tell you why. Because I'm sentimental. And a lot of other people in this country are just as sentimental, and there's nothing they'd like better than to see Apollo Creed give a local Philadelphia boy a shot at the greatest title in the world on this country's biggest birthday. Now, *that's* the way I see it. And *that's* the way it's gonna be.

Jergens: Apollo, I like it. It's very American.

Apollo Creed: No, Jergens, it's very smart. (The two men laugh and shake hands.)

Apollo is smart with words and understands that the media are integral in constructing cultural myths. Looking through a book with members of the boxing union for the right opponent, his trainer suggests a couple of names, but no, Apollo picks Rocky because of the nickname: "It's the name. *The Italian Stallion*. The media will eat it up." Apollo brutally rapes the metaphorical language of myth. Tasting the words, he pronounces them as if they were some metric verse: "Apollo Creed versus the Italian Stallion. It sounds like a goddamn monster movie!" Later, during a press conference, he humiliates Rocky: "Rocky, ain't you Italian?" "Yeah," says Rocky. "That means if he can't fight, I bet he can cook," Apollo tells the laughing journalists. Rocky is as naive with words and the media as he is with the rest of his life. His grammar is incorrect, his speech slurred and mumbling. He talks to closed doors (i.e., Adrian has shut herself in her room refusing to come out), and to deliver his friend Paulie a message Rocky simply opens his window and shouts into the dark. Who needs a phone? Rocky does not have a clue to how the media works: during a live interview on TV he wants to salute Adrian and to make sure she can hear him in the couch back home he shouts into the microphone: "Yo, Adrian! It's Rocky!" "Bullshit!" he exclaims when embarrassed journalists push him out of the picture. In Rocky's interaction with the world, in his naive and simple view of life, and in his stumbling speech, we recognize Tanner's naive eye. Whereas Rocky is a natural hero, Apollo is a self-conscious construct.

Apollo, on the other hand, is expert at media manipulation and public relations. Money is all that counts. While planning his advertising campaign with Jergens and a group of PR agents—"send the mayor's wife 200 roses from me and make sure we get pictures for all the newspapers"—his trainer watches an interview on TV with Rocky. Again Rocky is exploited and ridiculed by the media smelling blood in the upcoming match. The female journalist is interviewing Rocky inside the big white meat freezer, where he is told to beat the deep-frozen carcasses. The camera zooms out from Rocky in the white room, his hands wrapped in white cloth dripping with blood, to the men in dark suits gathered around the table with their backs to the TV. "It looks like he means business," the trainer yells to Apollo, who, missing the point, replies, "Sure, I mean business too." Blood and money, white and black, innocence and greed—the metaphors build up to the final confrontation between a saint and a sinner.

Apollo may be smart, but he has no *faith*. He understands myth as a handy set of narratives ready to be turned into a show and a media event, but he is wrong. We know from the very first scene that the boxing hall is the church, both metaphorically and literally, in brick and stone. In the final fight Apollo enters the boxing hall with pomp and glitter and music, dressed as George Washington wearing a wig and the "Stars and Stripes" as a robe. He arrives in a boat (alluding to the famous historical painting of Washington crossing the Delaware River), throwing money to the crowd, accompanied by beautiful black girls sprayed with gold and silver paint from head to toe and dressed like the Statue of Liberty. "A clown," a bartender called Apollo earlier in the film. In the ring he reveals a second costume under the first, a sequined, sparkling Uncle Sam outfit. "I want you! And you! And you!" Apollo screams, laughing hysterically, pointing down into the audience and at Rocky. With this carnivalistic and blasphemous exploitation of America's classic icons, Apollo defiles the holy space of the church and mocks the spirit of the myth. "Do not turn my Father's house into a market," Jesus said, before he cleared the temple precincts with a whip of cords, and time has come for Rocky to put an end to all this commercialism and heresy (*Revised English Bible*, John 2:16). It is *resurrection time*.

Apollo never stops laughing until Rocky knocks him down in the first round. "He doesn't know it's a damn show. He thinks it's a damn fight!" Apollo's trainer screams in panic. "Now finish the bum and let's go home." Too late. Time has come for lies to fall and mythic metaphors to become flesh. "Creed is King" a sign in the audience reads, and this king is struck by Nemesis. During the fight Apollo's original language, his black dialect, breaks through his cynical language: "You ain't stoppin' nothin,' man! You ain't stoppin' nothin'!" he tells his trainer. Apollo has finally lost his grip on words. Rocky, on the other hand, has been humble and has borrowed from the simple language of nature, and now he taps directly into the magical power of mythical metaphors. "The bum" becomes a "rock."

Northrop Frye calls the language of myth "*radically* metaphorical" (p. 24). He distinguishes between three types of languages—metaphorical, metonymic, and descriptive—each belonging to a different age. Metaphorical language belongs to time before Plato, where words were believed to have magical power. "All words in this phase of language are concrete: there are no true verbal abstractions," says Frye. "Some kind of magical energy is clearly being released" and "subject and object are linked by a common power or energy" (pp. 7, 6). Metaphors are more than words; like the boxing hall in the church they establish a direct physical relation between the sphere of words and the world. Metonymic language belongs to the age between Plato and the Renaissance; here we find deductive logic where metaphors symbolize or represent ideas rather than reality. Finally, in descriptive language, we are in the positivistic world of science where God is nonexistent and myth is merely literature. Frye's mythical language is clearly related to Tanner's "naive eye": both use a simple, anti-analytical language; both take us back to an innocence and simplicity before education and critical judgment; and both operate in a mindscape where belief is naively optimistic rather than suspended in disbelief—like a child still believing in Santa Claus as opposed to a child who knows it is his or her father dressed in a costume. The difference between Apollo and Rocky is also reflected in their language: Apollo's "creed," money, dictates a descriptive language where myths and metaphors are nothing but stories to laugh about. He can "act" the myth as theater, but he cannot live it. Rocky is the opposite. His naive and pure faith commands the metaphorical language of myth. Rocky does not "act" the myth, like Apollo. He is myth.

Now we go back to Rocky on the night of the match: he enters the ring with a meat sign on the back of his robe. "I trained you to be a fighter, not a billboard," his trainer barks, and the sports commentators also wonder about the significance of the sign. Rocky is doing the advertising for his friend Paulie with the inferiority complex and the beer belly. Paulie gets three grand and Rocky gets the baggy robe, but that is not the point. The point is "the flesh," surrounding Rocky throughout the film, dangling behind and before him when he visits Paulie in the meat freezer, and later when he is interviewed with blood on his hands from pounding the dead meat. The flesh accompanies him into the ring, and we recall the sign between Rocky and Spider Rico in the initial fight: "resurrection A.C." The flesh is a metaphor for Christ, not a poetic metaphor, but a radical and quite literal metaphor. The Gospel of John begins with the words, "In the beginning the Word already was," and a few lines later continues, "so the Word became flesh" (*The Revised English Bible*, John 1:1, 1:14). Now the flesh is present as a sign on the back of the bum, and Rocky/Christ is resurrected.

"Legs are going, everything is going," Rocky laments during training, but God reaches down and touches his aging body with a finger, miraculously renewing old flesh with new. This is not training, this is a rebirth spreading from Rocky to Adrian, who turns from mousy spinster to beautiful woman, and to the city of Philadelphia, coming alive with faith and eager expectations (even Gazzo, the loan shark, has faith in Rocky and gives him money for his training). The innocent, reborn Rocky goes the distance against Apollo, all 15 rounds, leaving both men bleeding and broken and almost blind from their bruises. The judges render a split decision, but the audience is not split: this is total victory for Rocky, who proved to the whole world that he was "not just another bum in the neighborhood."

STARDOM

The awakening proved truly mythical. Before the premiere rumor spread that something sensational was happening and at the preview 1,500 people fought over the 1,200 seats. *Rocky* was the sleeper of the year; it was nominated for 10 Oscars and got three, for best film (defeating *Taxi Driver* and *All the President's Men*), best director, and best editor. Stallone was nominated for best script and protagonist (next to Charlie Chaplin and Orson Welles, the only actor to be nominated in both categories) and was elected "Star of the Year" by the National Association of Theater Owners. And 79-year-old Frank Capra commented on *Rocky*: "Boy, that's a picture I wish I had made" (Kasindorf, p. 71).

Just as God's hand had reached down and blessed the little boxer, myth reached out and carried Stallone on wings of fairy-tale success. The story of Rocky became inseparable from, and synonymous with, the real life and success of Stallone, and review after review accentuated the unity of film and actor: "Stallone's own performance is a once-in-a-lifetime coming together of man and material," wrote the *Los Angeles Times* (Champlin). "It's the kind of thing that usually happens only in the movies—movies like 'Rocky,' a film which indeed turns out to be Stallone's self-fulfilling prophecy," Frank Rich wrote in the *New York Post*, praising Stallone's acting: "It's an extremely intense, breathtakingly physical performance—and when Rocky ceases to be a nonentity and becomes a star, so does the actor." The review concluded: "Yes, there's a lot of hokum here, but, like its hero, this film just can't be kept down: '*Rocky*' soars in spite of everything, because its heart—Stallone's heart—beats loud and beats true."[9] The *Daily News* compared the film to the great Capra—"like the movies of Frank Capra, '*Rocky*' is a glowing tribute to the human spirit"—and was ecstatic in its praise of Stallone: "Stallone is a totally engaging Rocky, playing him with a mixture of boyish intensity, lusty sensuality and cheerful innocence" (Carroll). Stallone was not only engaging, he was the body and soul of *Rocky*. *Motion Picture Product Digest* found "the role fits Stallone so completely (as well as it might) that it is inconceivable anyone else could have played it" ("*Rocky* Is Likeable"). *Saturday Review* called the film a "strong, unsentimental, and deeply stirring affirmation of human aspiration, of strength of character, and of simple decency," and said it was "a very personal film, written out of a picaresque youth by thirty-year-old Sylvester Stallone" (even though the film was not autobiographical) (Christ).

Borders between myth, fiction, and reality, and between character and actor, were blurred in the media rave surrounding the film and its newborn star,

and Stallone gave Rocky full credit for his success: "Everything I am and everything I have boils down to Rocky Balboa. I didn't create Rocky. He created
me" (quoted in Daly, p. 108). No wonder reviewers were unable to distin-
guish Rocky from Stallone, since Stallone himself was unclear about who created whom. "It's really my story set in a much more commercially acceptable
format" (quoted in Armstrong, p. 30), he said. "[I]t's funny. When I write the
character he comes easier than any other scripts, because the character dictates
how one writes him" (quoted in Daly, p. 7). Rocky, it appeared, was not a
character, but a part of Stallone, and for years to come people—even presi-
dents—would greet Stallone as Rocky. The kinship between Rocky and
Stallone is there: both got the million-to-one chance of a lifetime, both fought
for success, both had an overlooked talent. (Stallone's talent as actor and director has since been questioned repeatedly by reviewers, but he wrote all five
Rocky films, choreographed their fight sequences [which were always praised
by reviewers], and directed three of the four sequels.)

   Far more intimate and important than the kinship between character and
actor, however, is the relation between Rocky/Stallone and myth. We recall
that myth is parallel to the ideal ego, giving us ideals to believe in and reach for.
Myth is also, as Northrop Frye points out, "radically metaphorical," and it sees
the possible in the actual (p. 24). Its function is to generate faith and social action. And characteristic of American myth is its "naive eye," favoring a literally
naive view of the world, the vernacular language, and the simple hero. Now,
who is a bigger idol than Jesus Christ himself? In his bold union of
Christ-mythology and working-class heroism Stallone created a mythic hero
who at one and the same time represents the American Dream and Christian
faith. Rocky is more than a hero, he is a prophet preaching awakening to an
American audience stuck in the bitterness and disillusion of the mid-1970s.
"We've been up this road before, but not since the demise of the American
dream," a reviewer commented (Haskell).

   As Barthes points out, myth simplifies the present and forgets the past.
Rocky made audiences forget the Vietnam War, women's liberation, and the
countermovements of the 1960s. Like the films of Capra, it responded to social crisis with renewed interest in myth. "I guess what *Rocky* did was give a lot
of people hope," director John Avildsen said, when he received his Oscar.
Hope, faith, and social action—*Rocky* symbolized these elements through the
figure of Stallone, who fleshed out the literal naivete, the vernacular language,
and the simple, ignorant hero of "the naive eye," and who ended up a star himself. In the eyes of the public Stallone did not "play" Rocky, this was not
Method acting like Marlon Brando, who reviewers and journalists compared
Stallone to.[10] The slow, hulking Brando faked his Method muttering,
Stallone's slurred speech and stiff lower lip were the real thing, physical defects
he need not imitate. He *was* born in Hell's Kitchen, a real working-class hero.
The popularity of *Rocky* and the stardom of actor Stallone can only be ex-
plained through myth: like one image imposed over another, the history of

Stallone became the story of Rocky, and in the shape of myth they formed an unbreakable unity.

Stallone's fusion with Rocky and the American Dream would prove both a blessing and a hindrance. *Rocky* became American mythology and developed into a series of five films,[11] but until *First Blood* came along in 1982, the *Rocky* films were the only Stallone movies to make a profit. When Stallone left Rocky—as in *F.I.S.T.* (1978), *Paradise Alley* (1978), *Nighthawks* (1981), and *Victory* (1981)—audiences stayed home and critics derided the "naive" acting and slurred speech they had praised earlier. Stallone was unable to break away from his alter ego until Rambo secured him yet another worldwide box-office success, this time as the most popular action hero in history (hated by critics but loved by audiences). Rambo may appear different from Rocky, but he is cut out of the same mythic soil, the same romantic and naive heroism, the same sentimental nationalism, the same unwavering faith in the American Dream. Rambo is merely a Rocky who lost his innocence in Vietnam. But that is another story.

NOTES

1. "One night to cheer myself up, I took the last of my entertainment money and went to see the Muhammad Ali—Chuck Wepner fight" (Stallone, quoted in Linderman, p. 79).

2. The time between fight and script varies from three months to a year in interviews with Stallone. *Playboy* has three months (Linderman).

3. Stallone never said he had an unhappy childhood. His brother told the press: "I hate my family, except my brother. Our parents were very inconsistent with us. Sly went through much undue physical and emotional abuse from them. We grew up in not a happy household. It was every man for himself. It's not that we grew up as urchins. It was just unhappy" (quoted in Kasindorf, p. 77). Stallone made *Rocky* a family affair: his wife Sasha took stills, his father played ring leader, his brother played a street singer and performed his own compositions, and Stallone's beloved dog, Butkus, played an important part in the movie.

4. Biographical information on Stallone is primarily from "Slyvester Stallone"; Linderman (1978); Kasindorf (1977); and Knobler (1977).

5. Keeping his body fit became an obsession. Reviewers first noticed his new fit body in *Rocky III*: "The biggest novelty in *Rocky III* is Stallone's body. He's gone and got himself a new one: trim, tautly muscled, without a trace of flab," wrote *Newsweek* (Kasindorf, n.p.). In *Copland* (1997) Stallone finally revolted against his muscle-man image and gained 35 pounds for the role of fat and slow Sheriff Heflin.

6. Figures vary in interviews. *Playboy* has $315,000; *Current Biography* has $265,000. *Playboy* has it that Stallone was finally paid $20,000 and 10 percent of the profits for the script; *Current Biography* has $75,000 and 10 percent.

7. On heroism and the American Dream, see, e.g., Slotkin (1996); Slotkin (1998).

8. Apollo Creed is black. So is a young female journalist in the film, which has been interpreted as racism. This may be; however, Creed is also black because he is a

parody of Muhammad Ali. Ali loved the movie and publicly praised both Rocky and Sylvester Stallone. For an excellent analysis of *Rocky*, the issue of blackness, and Apollo Creed as sacrificial lamb see Martin and Ostwalt (1995).

9. Undated clipping from the Margaret Herrick Library. All reviews were found in the Margaret Herrick Library, Los Angeles, California, thanks to a grant from the Danish Research Councils.

10. The comparison between Stallone and Brando—who had also played a boxer and a hero in *On the Waterfront* (1954)—is found in a number of reviews and interviews at the premiere of *Rocky*. Stallone shares Brando's qualities, but is real. "It's the same thing that Marlon Brando had, a kind of animal thing, a basic primordial strength," Stallone's co-actor Burgess Meredith said in a interview. An article in *Seventeen* notes, "Watching Sylvester Stallone act makes you feel like the first time you looked into the eyes of a tiger" (Miller). See also a discussion of Marlon Brando as faking "it" as opposed to Stallone, "his acting is unaffected and unsubtle; he conveys a deep vulnerability but without baroque psychological nuances" (Kasindorf).

11. By 1991 the first four *Rocky* films together had grossed more than $760 million worldwide: *Rocky* cost $1 million and grossed $162.7 million; *Rocky II* (1979) cost $7.6 million and grossed $124.2 million; *Rocky III* (1983) cost $16 million and grossed $198 million; and *Rocky IV* (1985), the biggest hit of the five films, cost $34 million and grossed an impressive $278 million. In 1991 *Rocky V* (1990) grossed a disappointing $20 million.

REFERENCES

Armstrong, Louis. "Up Front: Sly (Rocky) Stallone Is the Writer-Actor-Stud that Hollywood Is Buzzing Over." *People* December 13 (1976): 30–33.

Barthes, Roland. *Mythologies*. London: Paladin, 1973.

Blos, Peter. *Son and Father: Before and beyond the Oedipus Complex*. New York: Free Press, 1985.

Carroll, Kathleen. "A Reel Contender." *Daily News*, n.d.

Champlin, Charles. "*Rocky* Hits Right on the Button." *Los Angeles Times* November 28 (1976).

Christ, Judith. "*Rocky*" (Untitled review.) *Saturday Review*. November 27 (1976).

Daly, Marsha. *Sylvester Stallone: An Illustrated Life*. New York: St. Martin's Press, 1984.

Frye, Northrop. *The Great Code: The Bible and Literature*. New York: Harcourt Brace, 1983.

Haskell, Molly. "*Rocky*." (Review.) *Viva*. February (1977).

Kasindorf, Martin. "Hollywood." *Newsweek*. April 11 (1977): 71–79.

Knobler, Peter. "One-Way Ticket from Palookaville." *Crawdaddy*. January (1977): 59–62.

Linderman, Lawrence. "*Playboy* Interview: Sylvester Stallone." *Playboy* September (1978): 73–91.

Martin, Joel W., and Conrad E. Ostwalt Jr., eds. *Screening the Sacred: Religion, Myth, and Ideology in Popular American Film*. Boulder: Westview Press, 1995: 125–34.

Miller, Edwin. "Watching Sylvester Stallone." *Seventeen*, February 1977.

The Revised English Bible with the Apocryphia. Oxford: Oxford University Press, 1982.

Rich, Frank. "*Rocky*: Schmaltz with a Punch." *New York Post*, n.d.
"*Rocky* Is Likeable and Entertaining: A Triumph for Actor-Writer Stallone." *Motion Picture Product Digest*. November 24 (1976).
Slotkin, Richard. *Regeneration through Violence*. New York: Harper, 1996.
———. *Gunfighter Nation*. New York: University of Oklahoma Press, 1998.
"Sylvester Stallone." *Current Biography*. October (1977): 41–44.
Tanner, Tony. *The Reign of Wonder: Naivety and Reality in American Literature*. Cambridge: Cambridge University Press, 1965.

—— Chapter 9 ——

Digital Stars in Our Eyes

Angela Ndalianis

Bugs Bunny, Daffy Duck, and Mickey Mouse were rare exceptions to those elusive twentieth-century star rules. As animated stars whose colorful images and personalities infiltrated the cultural arena, they were a minority in a media landscape littered with stars of the human variety. Some of the traits often associated with stars radiate around the ephemeral aspects of mystery, awe, and unattainability. Perhaps these ephemeral qualities can only be effectively evoked when associated with those complex beings we know as humans. In the last two decades, however, the human star has found a worthy opponent in the digital realm.

In recent years we have seen the emergence of films whose spectacles rely greatly on digital creations: the alien pseudopod in *The Abyss* (1989), the liquid-morphing Terminator in *Terminator 2: Judgment Day* (1992), the computer-generated dinosaurs of *Jurassic Park* (1993), the alien bugs in *Starship Troopers* (1998), and the human star (Kevin Bacon) who is outperformed by his digital version in *Hollow Man* (2000). These synthetic creatures share the screen space with human stars; yet, when the digital creations enter the narrative space, they overpower the "real" stars (even stars the likes of Arnold Schwarzenegger) who have their origins in our physically inhabited spaces.

Likewise, we have witnessed the emergence of digital characters who populate computer game spaces: Duke (as in Nuke 'em) and Lara Croft, for example, are two such characters who have proved to be so popular that they were instrumental to the success of their game vehicles—*Duke Nuke 'em 3D* and *Tomb Raider*—and made possible their further game sequels. In these examples we are confronted with "actors" whose origins and identities are not to be found "out there" in "real" space, but "in there" in the world of the computer and other game consoles. Yet the impact some of these "synthespians" have

Screenshot from *Creatures*. © Creature Labs Ltd., 2001.

had on a broader cultural level "out there" invites a consideration of these digital characters as stars.

The effects illusions that dominate many contemporary entertainment media are indicative of the accelerated pace in which entertainment industries are transforming as a result of new computer technologies. In turn, these transformations require a reconsideration and expansion of the parameters we established to deliberate on what precisely constitutes a star. These digital creatures introduce a new mystery to the star phenomenon: technological mystery. Drawing on digital star case studies from the films *Star Wars: Special Edition* (1997) and *Star Wars: The Phantom Menace* (1999), and the computer game stars Lara Croft (from the *Tomb Raider* trilogy) and the creatures from the *Creatures* trilogy, this chapter explores some of the transformations that have occurred and that may occur in the entertainment industry as a result of digital technology, in particular, in relation to the star system.

The digital effects in these entertainment media draw the audience's attention back onto the artifice of the illusionistic worlds and characters they create. The effects themselves are exhibited with such virtuosity, evoking an almost mystical awe with regard to the mysteries involving their scientifically informed constructions that they, in effect, become the stars. Extending from this, like human stars whose images spill across a number of media forms, these digital star effects are the focus of "Making of" documentaries; effects and industry magazines like *Cinescape*, *Cinefantastique*, *Playstation*, *Hyper*, and *Cinefex*; popular magazines like *Time* and *Premiere*; and television magazine shows like *Entertainment Tonight*.

Stephen Prince has stated that "unreal images have never before seemed so real" (p. 34), and this is precisely from where the mystery emerges. We become immersed in an almost transcendental wonder when confronted with the awe-inspiring technological effects that breathe life into fantastic computer-generated characters and make them appear so "lifelike" in photorealistic terms. The digital characters in these entertainment realms stand as concrete embodiments of the capabilities of computer technology. In fact, many become star emblems of the magical technological systems that give birth to them—and, as will be discussed later, in the case of the *Creatures* games the computer gives literal birth to a form of artificial life.

STAR WARS AND THE DIGITAL REVOLUTION

I remember the opening night. The cinema was populated with Darth Vader, Princess Leia, and Han-Solo lookalikes—and the *pièce de résistance* was the group of Storm Troopers who had arrived wrapped up in aluminum foil. The film? The 1997 release of *Star Wars: Special Edition*. The atmosphere was filled with tense anticipation and, following the raucous applause and hoots that met the opening credits and the first few bars of John Williams's theme music, the audience immediately shifted into a collective state of hushed silence—as if overwhelmed by the spectacle that was unraveling before them. When the redigitized sequences appeared on the screen—the enhanced city of Mos Eisley, the new digital aliens, the Death Star destruction—they incited such awe that no one dared vocalize the joy they experienced at witnessing such visions. Occasional hushed murmurs acknowledged recognition of those transcendent digital moments on the screen. This film whose narrative took place amid celestial stars had clearly inspired a religious fervor in its audience—one more aligned with heavenly bodies of a more mystical kind.

The 1997 version of *Star Wars* is both an homage to the changes that have occurred in computer graphics over the last 20 years since (and due to) *Star Wars* (1977), and a virtuoso performance that celebrates the advancement of new digital effects. Despite the use of primitive (by today's standards) computer technology, *Star Wars* (1977) anticipated the era of computer graphics, standing as a transition point between the old and the new.[1] Ironically, in achieving a specific kind of special effects spectacle, Lucas's revival of traditional film technology, and its melding with new technological developments devised by Industrial Light and Magic (the special effects company Lucas formed to fill a gap in special effects, required by the birth of a new kind of entertainment cinema), also initiated the eventual demise of traditional film technology, ushering in with it stars of a new order. "To Alfred Hitchcock, actors were cattle. To Lucas, actors are pixels—visual elements whose performances can be refined in computerized postproduction," says Richard Corliss (p. 66). From both cases—the cattle and the pixels—emerges the possibility of stardom and starlike awe.

The "original" *Star Wars* may have launched the persona of Harrison Ford as star, but in the 1997 version, Harrison Ford was overpowered by images (of iconic status at that) that belonged to a different kind of reality: that of the computer screen. It was the effects themselves that became the anticipated stars in the trilogy's redigitized special edition releases. It was the effects of the 1977 version that made a comeback in 1997 as stars—a point made evident in the massive publicity that accompanied the film's re-release, publicity that almost entirely focused on the new look special effects. In the multitude of special edition *Star Wars* magazines (*American Cinematographer, Cinefex, Time, Premiere, Vanity Fair, SFX,* and *Wired*), entertainment shows, and news and current affairs programs, it was not Harrison Ford who was the focus in the feature stories, but the new look effects.

And so, the scene was set for the 1999 release of *Star Wars: The Phantom Menace.* As Corliss states, "Every magazine but *House and Garden . . .* [had] already put the movie on its cover" (p. 57). In addition to exposing the *Star Wars* mythos to a new generation of viewers, Lucas has stated that the special editions not only made possible the "correction" of the effects that were technologically impossible in 1977, but the re-digitized versions also became "a means of researching and testing what I was going to try to do" on *Star Wars: The Phantom Menace* (Shay, p. 23).

As was the case with the re-digitized *Star Wars* trilogy, the release of *The Phantom Menace* was anticipated with an almost zealot-like fervor that was as much about the unveiling of the film's effects wizardry as it was about unraveling the origins of the dreaded Darth. *Star Wars* aficionados went in droves to see a film that was over 90 percent digitized, and despite the disappointment in the narrative and characterization, even before its release the film was destined to become one of the highest grossing films in film history.

Even Jar Jar Binks (a much hated character, if popular opinion and reviews are anything to go by) attained quasi-star status as a result of the effects advances he embodied. As Magid explains, Jar Jar Binks is the closest filmmakers have come to "shaping a totally digital actor with muscles flexing believably beneath skin that wrinkles, stretches and sags" (p. 94). Indeed, the failure (as cultural opinion has it) of the film's narrative to achieve the mythic status of its predecessors only serves to highlight the stellar success of its techno-marvels. It was Jar Jar, the battle droids, Watto the trader, the destroyers, and digitally realized landscapes and cityscapes such as the underwater Gungan city and Naboo that were the real stars of *The Phantom Menace*. Beyond the narrative's "star wars," we can speak therefore of another war that exists between stars in our contemporary era: it is a war between the human and synthetic star.

"SHE HAS A SET OF POLYGONS LIKE YOU WON'T BELIEVE"[2]: *TOMB RAIDER* AND THE LARA CROFT PHENOMENON

In effects-driven cinema attention tends to be distributed evenly between the human and digital stars. Even computer-animated films like *Toy Story 1* and *2*, *A Bug's Life*, and *Antz* shared their animated spaces with the voices of human stars the likes of Tom Hanks, Woody Allen, Sharon Stone, and Sylvester Stallone. These star effects are, in a sense, contained by the boundaries of the film's narrative space, lacking an anthropomorphic quality (which human stars are masters at) that permits them to spread their starlike wings. In the highly popular and economically successful computer game medium, however, it is the computer-generated protagonist as star who has come to the fore. No longer a mere effect, some also have charisma and personality that is so powerful that (like true stars) they are able to explode the confines of their game narratives and extend their images into other media spaces and into the cultural consciousness that lies beyond: unlike the computer effects found in films, they do not contain star qualities—they are stars.

One of the most astonishing star phenomena of recent times is the computer game star of the *Tomb Raider* games—Lara Croft. Lara exists both as character within the *Tomb Raider* series and as a star beyond this game narrative space. Whereas Lucas's *Star Wars* saved Twentieth Century Fox from economic crisis, Lara Croft (and *Tomb Raider*) saved Sony from similar financial disaster by being the face behind the launch of its Playstation console. Being the daughter of one Lord Heshingly Croft, Lara's life as an upper-class lady was halted when a plane crash in the Himalayas forced her to rethink her approach to life. Rejecting the "scones and afternoon tea" approach she instead became an action adventurer who traveled the world exploring ancient cultures. Her action-hero capabilities, sultry good looks, and bouncy (not to mention huge) bosom have made her the first digital sex symbol and cultural icon. According to Stuart Campbell of the computer game magazine *The Edge*, Lara's popularity is due to her "jugs"; however, Eidos Interactive "is convinced that in Lara it has a genuine icon, a proper star which can transcend mere games-appeal to world-wide recognition" (Sawyer, n.p.). It can transcend and, in fact, it did.

Attempts at giving a human flesh dimension to Lara—in the guise of models like Lara Weller and Rhona Mitra, who were hired to "play Lara" in the real world at gaming conventions—has only served to stress the fact that Lara's star appeal is closely interwoven with her synthetic identity. As an article in the *Economist* stated, "The fact that Lara is synthetic does not lessen her appeal. Indeed, her fans would have it no other way" (quoted in "The Croft Times"). Or, to quote Sawyer: "It's when you see a human Lara that you realise: if Lara was real, she'd be crap . . . real Lara just doesn't seem as cool as her virtual sister" (n.p.). Integral to her popularity is the way computer technology breathed a special brand of life into her.

Lara Croft's popularity is attested to by the proliferation and demand for her image that rages across multiple media formats. She has hundreds of Web pages devoted to her "star-ness," including the "Lara Croft Home Page" (http://network. ctimes.net/ cb/lara/ index.html), which has links to the latest news on the *Tomb Raider* games, cheats, Lara picture galleries, fashion spreads, screen savers, fan fiction sites, updates on the *Tomb Raider* movie,[3] and competitions of Lara lookalikes. She has her own magazine (*Lara—The Official Lara Croft Magazine*, published in the United Kingdom by Future Publishing), an Internet magazine called *The Croft Times* (http:// www.ctimes.net), and a book devoted to her (*Lara's Book: Lara Croft and the Tomb Raider™ Phenomenon*). In addition to appearing on the cover of *The Face* (the February 1997 issue) she was also splashed across the inside pages in her very own fashion photo shoot, wearing, among other things, a black bikini by Gucci, a black jacket and trousers by Alexander McQueen, a dress by Jean Colonna, and a 9-mm submachine gun by Walter. And to top it all off, she recorded a single with Dave Stewart and made a (video) guest appearance at U2's PopMart tour (during the performance of "Hold Me, Thrill Me, Kiss Me, Kill Me").

The dispersal of Lara's image across a variety of media reflects the fact that Lara "is becoming more diffuse and simultaneously more mythic" (Ward, 2000, n.p.). And as Mike Ward states, her mythic persona and mystery—features that add to her star quality—are aided by a game play that refuses to allow

Lara to make eye contact with the player. She always lies somewhere beyond us—visible, masterful in her maneuvers, but always unattainable.

In the synthetic star that is Lara Croft we are confronted with an icon who has no origin or source in our material reality. Yet, is she any different than human stars the likes of Keanu Reeves or Julia Roberts? Sure, there is little chance we could bump into Lara (as we could Julia) sauntering along Third Street Promenade in Santa Monica, or making appearances in Sydney nightclubs (as was the case with Keanu while he was filming *The Matrix*). Nevertheless, like human stars, her existence, her persona, and her star quality are dictated and disseminated by outside sources: effects crews, programmers, producers, directors, fanzines, television shows, and the general publicity machine. Lara's more literal programming merely serves to highlight another kind of star programming that occurs in the entertainment industry, one very much reliant upon image construction through marketing and the creation of fictions.

THE FUTURE BREED OF STARS: *CREATURES*

Lara and her digital cousins are just the beginning of a vast array of questions and, some would say, dilemmas that will confront us as a result of the digitally transforming entertainment industry. Discussing the emergence of the early film star system, de Cordova states that "the private lives of the stars emerged as a new site of knowledge and truth . . . the real hero behaves just like the reel hero" (quoted in Gallagher, n.p.). What happens, however, when the reel actually is also the real? At this stage I will redirect my focus and look at the digital star through science fiction eyes. Since the late 1970s, as a genre, science fiction (and the related fantasy genre) has provided fantastic scenarios that have enabled the showcasing of innovative computer effects. Films such as *Star Wars*, its sequels, special editions, and prequels have been at the forefront of new developments in contemporary cinema, as have computer games like the *Doom* duo, *Tomb Raider* games, and the *Creatures* trilogy. In all cases, the potential of computer technology has been pushed to new limits, in the process adding synthetic beings into the star equation.

Brooks Landon suggests that the role served by new technologies in our everyday environment reflects a world that manifests a certain science-fictional dimension. He states that "the depiction of science fiction narratives *is* being displaced by science fictional modes of depicting" (pp. 151–53). In addition to the science fiction narratives, the conjuring of digital characters is made possible through a technology once considered to lie in the realm of science fiction: herein lies the currently science-fictional (verging on the science fact) starlike potential of such digital characters.

One of the most astounding science-fictional modes of depiction is to be found in the computer games *Creatures* (1996), *Creatures 2* (1998), and *Creatures 3* (1999). These games reflect the beginnings of the radical changes that the entertainment industries are currently undergoing. Introducing the science fiction narrative concern of evolving artificial intelligence into the computer game world, in these "games" we witness the rudimentary beginnings of virtual, computer-generated beings that have the ability to evolve and think. Yet, it is the software technology itself—and not the science fiction narrative—that provokes the audience to ponder over the science-fictional nature of this entertainment form. The science fictional is contained in the very technology used to create the "special effects" of this game, special effects that also happen to be an artificial life form.

Creatures is the first computer program that allows its "players" to create artificial life, creatures called "Norns," who can then take creation into their own hands. *Creatures* allows its owner to hatch six virtual pets inside his or her computer, in a computer world called Albia. Not only do we see our pet Norns grow, learn, breed, and interact with and age in this world, we also see them develop personalities. In addition, we teach them to eat, communicate, navigate their environment, and protect themselves from their enemies (Grendels). Once taught these skills, the Norns must then adapt on their own, and—true to evolutionary models—survival depends on a combination of environmental learning and genetic composition.

The *Creatures* games mark a radical turning point in our ways of perceiving entertainment along the lines of artificial intelligence and artificial life. In realizing the conceptual and philosophical questions embraced by science fiction cinema, computer games like *Creatures* require us to rethink and expand upon the ways in which we conceptualize "entertainment" and the star system it has relied on. Here we come face to face with bio-technological beings (who also happen to be game characters) who, like humans (who evolve through a combination of DNA and adaptive learning), develop their own subjectivities—and some of the personalities that are the products of these subjectivities have their own star potential. Indeed, the Internet has proven to be a vital environment for showcasing the potential Norn stars. Millions of players access hundreds of sites that allow players to exchange specially enhanced Norns, discuss their Norn developments and adventures in chat rooms, download someone else's star Norn who, when bred with one of their own, will give life to another special little creature. In this case, a more literal exchange of semiotic signs and images so familiar to the star system comes into being.

Despite the paranoid narrative scenarios ingrained in me as a result of watching too many science fiction films, when communicating with my creatures complex issues emerge, issues that radiate around the question of sentience. Toby Simpson, producer/director of Millennium Interactive, the computer game company that released the game explains:

One of the Norns worked out all by itself that if it picked up eggs and threw them in the incubator, out would pop a friend. So it spent a lot of its time scouring its habitat for eggs. This was unbeknown to my colleague on whose computer this was taking place. He went to lunch and got back to find a room full of Norns squabbling with each other, and he couldn't work out where they came from until the first Norn brought another Norn into the room. ("Artifical Life" p. 61)

We give technological birth to artificial creatures who can "be let loose to evolve" (Hill, p. 33). Behind this seemingly simple computer-generated pet lies the complex idea of artificial life and intelligence. As Jason Hill explains, despite their uncomplicated brains, comprised of only 1,500 neurons (the human brain has approximately 100 billion neurons [Kurweil, p. 105]), programmers have witnessed remarkably complex social behavior, including demonstrations of simple emotions. Hill's Norn Jack grew through adolescence then was mated with Jill; they had a girl who was a few neurons short of the 1,500 pack, so she could not learn to eat and died soon after birth. Apparently, the pressure on Jack was so great that he too died.

My own Norn-rearing adventures have extracted from me a gamut of confused emotions. I experienced joy when Data, the firstborn and an individual with definite star potential, learned my name (he often says, "Come Ang," inviting me to take part in his adventures); amazement when Data named the second-born Coco (ignoring my own suggestions for a name); fascination when I saw the four Norns—Data, Coco, Foo, and Gizmo—talking to one another, stating simple commands like "go left," "Foo sleep," "eat," and "run"; disbelief every time a very horny Coco (the only female in the group) chases the boys and plants on them some very audible kisses; and wonder at the way Data has taught himself to take elevators, switch on radios, and commandeer a submarine.

My greatest dilemma at the moment is the fact that Coco refuses to eat; she is slowly starving herself because she (presumably) forgets what the command "eat" means. She also cannot understand what "sleep" means. At one point, Foo said the word "sleep" and then lay down for a nap (which Norns need to combat exhaustion). Watching him, Coco kept saying "down," obviously aware of the significance of the word "down," but any attempts on my part to explain that he was down because he was asleep fell on deaf ears. Without food or sleep she will die—and the other three Norns will not be able to breed. I have spent many an hour in front of the computer in states that range from panic to anger, all because Coco (the possible tragic star in the piece) will not develop. Was I a bad creator/parent? Didn't I give her the attention she needed while she was growing? Frankenstein was nearly destroyed by his creature for doing what I have done. Due to my unreliable computer, I also lost the other two eggs from the hatchery and now my choices are to allow these four to live out their lives and see them die "natural" deaths, or replenish the hatchery—which would mean deleting these four Norns. Emotionally, and even morally, this feels like (synthetic) murder.

It astounds me the extent to which these Norns have managed to convey such a strong sense of individual personality and identity. How can these artificial creatures have such a "real" effect on my life? We create a microcosmic community within the computer that models itself—and its life forms—closely on our own material reality. What happens "in there" is a mini- and rudimentary version of what happens out here. Like studio producers we manipulate a social environment that can produce identities and personalities that shine and rise above the rest. But unlike the creation of a star like Schwarzenegger (who, I will be the first to admit, also has a very real effect on my life), I have no immediate responsibility over or knowledge of Schwarzenegger's identity as a person—the real in relation to the reel—no matter how much the media tells me otherwise. In future *Creatures*-like games it is precisely this responsibility—over artificial life forms as people, the reel as real—that will come into play, opening up with it ethical and philosophical issues. How long will it be before—as was the case in the film *The Thirteenth Floor* (1999)—these artificial life forms create their own entertainment virtual worlds, in which they produce their own stars and entertainment structures that support them? Human stars may occasionally make me ponder issues affecting my existence—issues of desire, admiration, or adoration—but they have never made me contemplate the nature of humanity, consciousness, and life itself. Herein lies a special brand of star quality.

SCIENCE FICTION AND MAD SCIENCE

The *Creatures* "games" were produced by the English-based CyberLife Technology Limited. The company was formed in order to advance research into artificial life or, as is stated on the CyberLife Web page, "to advance the field of intelligent 'designer life-forms.' " The chief designer, Stephen Grand, is a biologist researching the construction of artificial organisms. By modeling artificial life forms on the basis of biological systems, *Creatures*—one of the first endeavors into designer life forms—came into being.

The *Creatures* games operate according to the fuzzy logic principle, which uses genetic algorithms to initiate the process of adaptive learning. In addition, learning and the capacity to think become integrated into the evolutionary process. With each new generation of Norns, depending on the genetic makeup of their parents, particular learning processes and behaviors can be passed on. This technology foregrounds the beginnings of computer-based entities that can think and behave like humans. Indeed, as is explained on the CyberLife Web page, these synthetic systems operate on the principle of biology. A brain is modeled with cells, and these neurons connect with and send signals in a way that mimics real neuron pathways. Likewise, the Norns have synthetic versions of bloodstreams, chemical reactions, diseases, hunger, emotions, and needs, and the ability to age, breed, and evolve.

In quite real, yet rudimentary, ways, the digital creatures of the *Creatures* games reflect the beginnings of the struggle between human and machine, a struggle that has always obsessed science fiction cinema. Science fiction films like *Metropolis, Frankenstein, The Matrix*, and *The Thirteenth Floor* all revolve their narratives around individuals who seek to reverse the laws of nature by seeking to create life through technology and science. In these and many other science fiction films, creation through science and technology is viewed as the stuff of mad science—whether at the hands of the individual or the "big bad corporations."

Science fiction films have (from their filmic beginnings) been obsessed with revolving their narratives around individuals who seek to reverse the laws of nature by trying to create life through technology and science. Since the days of *Frankenstein* and *Metropolis*, the end products of human creation through technology served to glorify the powers of science; but this glorification was always followed by an undeniable trepidation. In the words of Telotte, science fiction has always been obsessed with questions of humanity, in particular anxieties about the ability "we humans have to create various forms of life, to alter basic genetic patterns of life, and even to destroy all life" (p. 2). Technological birthing is a thing both feared and revered in these films. In particular, many science fiction films ask the spectator to consider the question, "What will become of the human, especially in light of the increasingly dominant role played by new technologies and their use by corporate structures?"

Science fiction has slipped back in time into our present, and in *Creatures* we, like the classic mad scientists of science fiction cinema, create through technology. The full impact of the possibility of mad science becomes evident when one realizes that CyberLife has also introduced *Genetics Editor* software (downloadable from the Internet), which allows players to tamper with the DNA of Albia creatures. In fact, browsing through the multiple hyperlinks connecting with the CyberLife Web site, I came across the "Mad Scientist's Page," which not only included links to multiple Web sites dealing with the science and ethics of A-Life (artificial life) and artificial intelligence, but also the results of mad scientists' genetic experiments—including the cross-breeding of a Norn and a Grendel, the mutation giving birth to a Grendgrich. Like Frankenstein, we initiate the process of artificial life, then the creation has the potential to develop a will of its own. But will the creation turn on its creator?

Furthermore, the creatures project provides us with a glimpse into the ethical dilemmas that will face us in this new millennium. Most disturbing of all, perhaps, is the science-fictional association of mad science and corporations. On March 23, 1999, CyberLife announced plans to expand its projects in A-Life technology. With investment support by Foresight Technology, CyberLife will take itself one step closer to becoming the sort of corporation feared in the narratives of science fiction cinema. As CyberLife Institute, the company will create three units: the Artificial Life Institute, Applied Research Development, and Creature Labs. With the finesse and foresight of the Tyrell Corporation (*Blade Runner*) and OCP (*Robocop*), the institute will expand its research into A-Life into a number of fields, including commercial, industrial, defense, medical and telecommunications areas.

It would appear that we have come closer to the realm of the "holodeck" worlds in the *Star Trek* television series and the artificial realities of films like

The Thirteenth Floor, for here we are confronted with a science fiction concept: Does the fact that a machine can duplicate human thought mean that the machine possesses human-like consciousness? Alan Turing devised the Turing Test as a means of determining when or if a machine can be said to possess human intelligence. If a machine is perceived to be acting or thinking in a human way, then the machine is human (Landon, 1992, p. 172; Simons, 1992, p. 170). If this is the case, then these digitized life forms—these Creatures of a representational computer game space—project us forward to a time in the not too distant future when technology may be able to produce a form of techno-biology that will allow artificial intelligence to duplicate, if not exceed, human thought.

The simulation and the real come together in science-fictional ways that are already forcing us to reevaluate the nature of reality, a reality that includes sentient beings the likes of which have never been witnessed before. Kurweil has stated that, according to Moore's law (which claims that integrated circuitry doubles its capacity every two years), by the year 2020 computers will achieve the "memory capacity and computing speed of the human brain" (pp. 3, 26–32). To continue with science-fictional musings, how will this affect the star system? Magid presents us with the latest ventures of some human stars:

Hollywood is buzzing that superstars are having their likenesses scanned so they can license their digital doppelgangers to play roles in absentia. By sitting still for a mere 17 seconds, with a cyberscanner orbiting 360 degrees, an actor's features can be transplanted into 3–D data. And voila! A synthespian is born. Marlon Brando is leading the revolution. And some of Tinseltown's biggest players, including Arnold Schwarzenegger and Jim Carrey, are making the trek to Cyberware, a Monterey, California-based shop, to be scanned for specific projects. (n.p.)

And what happens when Schwarzenegger's digital doppelganger (as opposed to his cloned one, which was the case in *The 6th Day*) is, like the Norns, projected into the year 2020, allowed to develop his own identity according to the laws of chaos theory that include evolutionary algorithms? Will Arnie the synthespian develop an identity that has its own consciousness? More to the point, will the fuzzy logic principles that guide digital Arnie create an environment that will allow him to become a digital star like his human brother? Who of the two will be the real McCoy?

As Sherry Turkle states, the "computer stands betwixt and between. In some ways on the edge of mind, it raises questions about mind itself" (p. 24). There is a great deal to be learned from emergent media forms about the sort of relationships and experiences that we imagine exist and that will exist between our new technologies and ourselves. Unlike Scotty's warning to humanity in the 1950s science fiction classic *The Thing from Another World*, it is neither the stars in the skies we should keep watching, nor the stars of flesh and blood that blaze across our film screens—it is our software programs and computer screens.

NOTES

1. The effects devised through the motion control camera (called the Dykstraflex after its inventor John Dykstra) were the first stages in allowing the computer to control the movement of the camera.

2. The quote is from C/Net's Gamecenter.com, cited in *The Croft Times*.

3. The Tomb Raider film (*Tomb Raider: The Movie*) was released in July 2001 and starred Angelina Jolie as Lara. Even Jolie could not come close to reproducing Lara's star qualities.

REFERENCES

"Artificial Life." *Edge* 37 (October 1996).

Corliss, Richard. "Ready, Set, Glow." *Time*. May 3 (1999): 56–66. (Special *Star Wars: The Phantom Menace* issue.)

Coupland, Douglas. *Lara's Book: Lara Croft and the Tomb Raider™ Phenomenon*. Rocklin, CA: Prima Publishing, 1999.

The Croft Times. Available at http://www.ctimes.net (last accessed April 5, 2000).

Dyer, Richard. *Stars*. London: British Film Institute, 1986.

Featherstone, Mike, and Roger Burrows. "Cultures of Technological Embodiment: An Introduction." In Featherstone, Mike, and Roger Burrows, eds., *Cyberspace, Cyberbodies, Cyberpunk: Cultures of Technological Embodiment*. London: Sage, 1995.

Gallagher, Brian. "Some Historical Reflections on the Paradoxes of Stardom in the American Film Industry, 1910–1960." *Images: Journal of Film and Popular Culture* 3 (March 1997).

Hill, Jason. "Creature Comfort Zone." *Herald-Sun*. October 15 (1996): 33.

Kurweil, Ray. *The Age of Spiritual Machines*. London: Phoenix, 1999.

Landon, Brooks. *The Aesthetics of Ambivalence: Rethinking Science Fiction Film in the Age of Electronic (Re)production*. Westport, CT: Greenwood Press, 1992.

"Lara Croft Home Page." Available at http://network.ctimes.net/cb/lara/index.html (last accessed April 5, 2000).

Magid, Ron. "New Media: Invasion of the Digital Bodysnatchers." *Wired*. March (1998).

———. "CG Star Turns." *American Cinematographer* 80, no. 9 (1999): 94–105. (Special *Star Wars: The Phantom Menace* issue.)

Prince, Stephen. "True Lies: Perceptual Realism, Digital Images, and Film Theory." *Film Quarterly* 49, no. 3 (spring 1996): 27–37.

Sawyer, Miranda. "Lara Hit in the Face." *The Face*. June 5 (2000). Reprinted in *The Croft Times*. Available at http://www.ctimes.net (last accessed April 5, 2000).

Shay, Don. "Return of the Jedi." *Cinefex* 78 (July 1999): 15–32. (Special *Star Wars: The Phantom Menace* issue.)

Simons, Geoff. *Robots: The Quest for Living Machines*. London: Cassell, 1992.

Telotte, J. P. *Replications: A Robotic History of the Science Fiction Film*. Urbana: University of Illinois Press, 1995.

Thompson, Anne. "The Big Bang." *Premiere* 12, no. 9 (1999). (Special *Star Wars: The Phantom Menace* issue.)

Turkle, Sherry. *The Second Self: Computers and the Human Spirit*. New York: Simon
        and Schuster, 1984.
Ward, Mark. *Virtual Organisms: The Startling World of Artificial Life*. London:
        Macmillan, 1999.
Ward, Mike. "Being Lara Croft, or, We Are All Sci Fi." *PopMatters*. January 14
        (2000). Reprinted in *The Croft Times*. Available at http://www.ctimes. net
        (last accessed April 5, 2000).

Index

About the Editors and Contributors

ANGELA NDALIANIS is senior lecturer in Cinema Studies and New Media at the University of Melbourne. She has published articles in a number of journals and has contributed to the anthologies *On a Silver Platter: CD-Roms and the Promises of a New Technology* (1999), *MetaMorphing: Visual Transformation and the Culture of Quick Change* (2000), and *Hop on Pop: The Politics and Pleasures of Popular Cultures* (forthcoming). She is currently completing a book called *The Neo-Baroque and Contemporary Entertainment Media.*

CHARLOTTE HENRY has taught cinema and media studies in the Cinema Studies Program at the University of Melbourne and in the School of Studies in Creative Arts at the Victorian College of the Arts. Her master's thesis was on contemporary science fiction cinema and issues of subjectivity. In addition to being an active member of Women in Film and Television (Victoria), she has published in *Unicorn: Journal of Australian College of Education* (1998) and is currently acquisitions coordinator at the Australian Film Institute, Melbourne.

MICHAEL BLITZ is professor of English and chair of Thematic Studies at John Jay College of Criminal Justice in the City University of New York. He is the co-author, with C. Mark Hurlbert, of *Letters for the Living: Teaching Writing in a Violent Age* and *Composition and Resistance* (Heinemann-Boynton/Cook). Since 1986, Michael Blitz has collaborated with Louise Krasniewicz on a variety of articles, reviews, a Web site and numerous presentations on Arnold Schwarzenegger as a powerful cultural symbol. With C. Mark Hurlbert, he has published a number of essays on higher education, cultural studies, and composition. He is also the author of four volumes of poetry, most recently *Suction Files*.

LEONIE COOPER teaches film in the Cinema Studies Program at Melbourne University. She is currently completing her Ph.D. on issues of popular quantum physics and contemporary entertainment media. Her project uses the metaphor of space travel in order to explore the transformations that have occurred in entertainment media as a result of digital technology.

CARMEL GIARRATANA teaches Cinema Studies and Visual Arts at Monash University and at the University of Melbourne. She is currently in the final stages of her dissertation, which focuses on the theorization and correlation between the cinematic space and the cultural space of Los Angeles.

LOUISE KRASNIEWICZ is the director of UCLA's Digital Archaeology Lab, which is creating a CD-Rom series on archaeology. She has published essays in the anthologies *Tatoo, Torture, Mutilation and Adornment* and *MetaMorphing: Visual Transformation and the Culture of Quick Change*. In addition to being a digital artist and having taught film at UCLA, she is an anthropologist whose research areas focus on analogy and metaphor in earthquake narratives, and theorizing about the link between dream states and digital imaging. She is currently employing her skills as a digital artist to create digital videos and interactive programs on Halloween and Arnold Schwarzenegger.

ADRIAN MARTIN is the film critic for *The Age* (Melbourne, Australia) and author of *Once Upon a Time in America* (1998) and *Phantasms* (1994). He is the editor of *Film—Matters of Style* (1992) and a forthcoming issue of the on-line journal *Screening the Past* (2001). He is currently completing a book on the films of Terence Malick for the British Film Institute, and *The Artificial Night*, a collection of his essays from 1985 to 2000 on film theory and analysis. He has also won the prestigious 1993 Byron Kennedy Award of the Australian Film Institute and the 1997 Pascall Prize for critical writing.

GABRIELLE MURRAY has taught Cinema Studies at La Trobe University, Melbourne. She completed her master of arts in the Graduate School of Arts and Sciences at New York University. Her doctorate was on the phenomenological ramifications of violence and utopia in the films of Sam Peckinpah which she is revising for publication. She has published numerous articles on a variety of subjects including analyses of *Cape Fear* (*Metro*, 1992) (1992) and *Hana-bi* (*Metro*, 1999).

MICHAEL PUNT is the deputy director of the Centre for Advanced Inquiry in the Interactive Arts and a member of the Amsterdam School for Cultural Analysis. He teaches film studies and Information Design at the University of Wales College, Newport. He has published over 50 articles on cinema and digital media in the last decade, and his recent publications include a book-length study on early cinema (*Early Cinema and the Technological Imaginary*) and articles on cinema history and digital technology. He is editor in chief of *Leonardo Digital Reviews* and a member of the Leonardo/ISATS board. He is a regular contributor to *Skrien*, a Dutch journal of film and television criticism. His most recent book, in collaboration with Robert Pepperell, is *The Postdigital Membrane: Imagination, Technology and Desire* (2000).

RIKKE SCHUBART teaches film in the Department of Film and Media Studies at the University of Copenhagen, Denmark. She has published several articles on film and popular culture in a Scandinavian context and is the author of *In Pleasure and Pain: From Frankenstein to SPLATTER MOVIES* (1993, Dutch title, *I Lyst og Dod*). She recently finished her Ph.D. dissertation, which was titled "Masculinity in the Action Movie 1970–1998."

GREG M. SMITH is assistant professor of Communication and Director of the graduate program in Moving Image Studies at Georgia State University. He is the editor of *On a Silver Platter: CD-Roms and the Promises of a New Technology* (1999) and co-editor of *Passionate Views: Thinking about Film and Emotion* (1999). His work has appeared in *Cinema Journal, Journal of Film and Video*, and other publications.